The Small Business Start-Up Workbook

A step-by-step guide to starting the business you've dreamed of

Cheryl D. Rickman

Published by How To Books Ltd,
Spring Hill House, Spring Hill Road, Begbroke
Oxford OX5 1RX, United Kingdom.
Tel: (01865) 375794. Fax: (01865) 379162.
info@howtobooks.co.uk
www.howtobooks.co.uk

First published 2005
Reprinted with amendments 2006
Reprinted 2006
Reprinted 2007
Reprinted 2008
Reprinted 2009 (twice)
Reprinted in 2010 (twice)
Reprinted 2011
Reprinted 2013

British Library Cataloguing in Publication Data.
A catalogue record for this book is available from
the British Library.

ISBN 978-1-84528-038-3

Produced for How To Books by Deer Park Productions, Tavistock
Edited by Diana Brueton
Cover design by Baseline Arts Ltd, Oxford
Typeset by Pantek Arts Ltd, Maidstone, Kent
Printed and bound by Bell & Bain Ltd, Glasgow

NOTE: The material contained in this book is set out in good
faith for general guidance and no liability can be accepted
for loss or expense incurred as a result of relying in particular
circumstances on statements made in the book. Laws and
regulations are complex and liable to change, and readers should
check the current position with the relevant authorities before
making personal arrangements.

Contents

About the Author

Cheryl D Rickman runs her own group of businesses – CherryJam – with her partner James in Hampshire. Her first company, WebCopywriter – a web copywriting consultancy, helps other businesses to improve their online presence and Cheryl provides workshops to local businesses on writing and marketing for the web.

Her clients include AnitaRoddick.com, PeterJones.tv, Business Link Wessex, Motorola and Microsoft. Cheryl also co-founded I Like Music – ilikemusic.com – with her partner, James.

Cheryl has been a freelance writer for the past 11 years, writing on business issues for *Better Business* and *Internet Works* magazine, and interviewing business leaders and music celebrities. Cheryl is author of booklets, *111 winning ways to promote your website successfully* and *127 insider ideas on creating a winning website* and has been a Judge at Hampshire's Awards of Web Excellence for the past three years. In 2007 Cheryl helped Peter Jones, multi-millionaire and star of BBC's Dragons' Den, to write his own book – *Tycoon*. And, in 2009, wrote *Born Global* for Neal Gandhi. She now works as a ghostwriter and author at www.writer.uk.com

Acknowledgements

First, a huge thank you to *Better Business* magazine and the team at Active Information: Sophie Chalmers, Richard Reed, Andrew James. Thanks for your support and for enabling my learning journey. I hope you will continue to keep up the great work to create one of the best small business magazines around.

Thanks to Dame Anita Roddick, Julie Meyer, Sir Richard Branson, Madonna (and my mum) for inspiring me, and How To Books for publishing me.

Thanks to everyone who's contributed to this book. You've helped me fulfil a dream in doing so.

Respect is also due to James and Louie, for all your love and support.

Foreword

As the Founder of The Body Shop, I often get asked to talk about entrepreneurship – even by hallowed institutions like Harvard and Stanford. It makes me smile that the Ivy League is so keen to 'learn' how to be an entrepreneur, because I'm not at all convinced it is a subject you can teach. How do you teach obsession, because more often than not it's obsession that drives an entrepreneur's vision? How do you learn to be an outsider, if you are not one already? Why would you march to a different drumbeat if you are instinctively part of the crowd?

One of the great challenges for entrepreneurs is to sit down, reflect and wait to collect information. We all suffer from hurry sickness. We have an abundance of energy and commitments. We can create something out of nothing, but we're not very good at organization and follow through. We are essentially outsiders and that is the best definition of an entrepreneur I have ever come across.

So here's my advice to all you budding entrepreneurs. Be optimistic. Successful entrepreneurs don't work within systems, they hate hierarchies and structures and try to destroy them. They have an inherent creativity and wildness that is very difficult to capture.

Finally, be passionate about ideas. Entrepreneurs want to create a livelihood from an idea that has obsessed them. Not necessarily a business, but a livelihood. Money will grease the wheels, but becoming a millionaire is not the aim of a true entrepreneur. In fact, most entrepreneurs I know don't give a damn about the accumulation of money. They are totally indifferent to it – they don't know what they earn and they don't care. They don't care about the nameplate culture. What gets their Juices going is seeing how far an idea can go.

So read this book, learn from other people's experiences, take note of all the helpful hints and tips to help you successfully launch your ideas. This book is to guide you through the transition of starting out on your own and you can use it as a handbook through every process.

Dame Anita Roddick

This book is dedicated to:

The memory of my courageous and amazing mother,
Denise Rickman (née O'Farrell)
who taught me how to dream, believed in me and gave unquestioned support.

Thank you mum.
Forever in my thoughts.

My dearest James
For putting up with my workaholic side and crazy moments and for being
a creative genius. 'Big up!'

My daughter Brooke Denise
You are my inspiration.

The late great Dame Anita Roddick – an incredible inspirational
and courageous woman who spoke out, empowered others
and made changes happen.

Introduction

The road you live in, the bakery you stop at to get your morning coffee and pastry, the pub you frequent; none of it would be there if someone hadn't dreamed about it first. This workbook aims to help you shape your dreams of running your own business into rock-solid reality, acting as a guide for each step of the way.

So, what are your circumstances right now?

Because it is that – circumstance - which creates entrepreneurs.

Some extroverted entrepreneurs concocted money-making schemes in the playground and were 'born to do business', others come from a long line of entrepreneurs, but the majority of self-made types are ordinary people doing extraordinary things. You don't have to be an exceptional high-achieving superhuman to be an entrepreneur (although the superhuman bit can help in times of deadline mania and crisis-management). As long as you've a great idea, product, team, belief, passion and the crucial ability to listen, learn and work very hard, you can become a successful entrepreneur.

Why a Business of Your Own?

Maybe you're just fed up with the daily grind. Maybe you've just decided that, because you spend most of your life at work, you want to enjoy your work more?

And you're not alone. Today, it is small business that is driving the economy.

Indeed our very own 'Enterprise Minister' says that "Small and medium-sized businesses are the engine room of the UK economy." Certainly, British entrepreneurship is on the rise. According to the Small Business Service, there were an estimated 4.7 million SMEs in the UK at the start of 2007, up by 400,000 since the start of 2004, employing 59.2% of the total private sector workforce.

Barclays Bank reports a 28 per cent rise in the number of women deciding to become their own boss since 2000 too. One million UK businesses are now owned and operated by women. 'We've become an important part of the community contributing over £115 billion to the UK economy,' says Karen Gill, co-founder of everywoman, an online network and resource provider for women business owners.

Furthermore, there are now more sole proprietorships than medium-sized businesses, with 2.9 million sole traders in the UK.

These figures aren't surprising, with the technological advances of recent years resulting in an increase in working from home and much wider access to the information you need to go it alone. If you speak to a handful of friends, you'll no doubt find that some of them would like to pack in their jobs and start up on their own. Nearly a quarter of us think about it, according to a Jacks of London survey, but a small percentage of us actually go on and do it.

We all have ideas in the shower or during moments of inspiration, but few will act on those ideas. Those who do take action are the entrepreneurs – the go-getters. So are you a sitter or a do-er? A what-if-er or a go-getter?

This book will help you to uncover the answer to that, and many other questions you'll face as you enter the world of entrepreneurship.

With independence the biggest motivation for going it alone, financial concerns and perceived lack of business experience often stand in the way of taking the jump towards solo sustainability. Many entrepreneurs only get the push they need when they are made redundant and forced to make the choice between finding a new job or starting up on their own. That's what happened to me.

I had all the concerns that small business start-ups face. I was worried about running out of cash, didn't enjoy the prospect of failing miserably and wasn't convinced about my selling skills, despite my strong belief in my business ideas. Years later I do not fear failure anymore and know I can do it, simply because I've proved it to myself, just as you will prove to yourself that you can do it too. I've now set up and run two of my own businesses and have consulted many others on theirs, as well as interviewing a great many successful entrepreneurs as a writer. And all this time I've been storing up knowledge which I'll be sharing in this book to help you improve your own chances of succeeding in business. I've made heaps of mistakes, but learnt from them all, and that's what it's all about – arming yourself with knowledge and stepping onto the learning curve. Just like me, you can overcome your fears with knowledge, skills and a large dose of belief.

Now, despite *always* being harder than you think it will be – starting up in business on your own needn't be a complete nightmare.

Your worries about money or lack of expertise are healthy, as they are your warning signals; your reality check. But, you can set those worries to rest, by getting informed about the choices available to you.

This workbook has been written to help you prepare for the opportunities that will present themselves as you embark on the business of starting up. You'll get an understanding of the potential journey, be able to weigh up the 'pluses and minuses' of the idea and the circumstances you find yourself in, resulting in an informed decision about taking the right step.

Sadly, by the end of year three in business (according to research by Barclays), half of all new firms will be no more, with a fifth ceasing to trade within the first 12 months. Of course if you have a good idea that you believe in, you mustn't let statistics like these stop you. Let this book improve your chances of being in the percentage that does succeed. (It's great to be able to extend the proverbial middle digit to the banks reporting the high business failure rate when you get to year four, having managed to keep your head above water!)

Indeed, if you are considering adding a new vertebra to the backbone of the nation's economy by starting your own small business, this handy workbook has been written with you in mind and will provide you with a modern approach to self-employment.

How The Guide Can Help You

I won't be alone in guiding you through the steps to start-up. You'll find insider tips and entrepreneurial secrets from leading business people who've been interviewed especially for this book, including Dame Anita Roddick and Julie Meyer, Stelios Haji-Ioannou and Simon Woodroffe.

Plus, there's a toolkit of tips, templates, practical exercises (yes, you'll be getting your hands dirty), checklists, worksheets and case studies, to really whet your entrepreneurial appetite. You'll discover how to research and formulate your business idea; how to stay motivated and manage your time-starved life, and how to use competitive intelligence to your advantage.

Rather than plain old business plan know-how and the traditional acumen churned out by the business school curriculum, you'll uncover the mechanics of success by learning from successful business leaders, who spill the beans on their worst decisions and mistakes.

In essence, this is the nuts and bolts of *real* business start-up, as experienced by real people, who've run real businesses.

Herein lies my first warning: be aware of the array of advisors who haven't run their own businesses, such as some government agency advisors and banks, who can give out-dated, impractical advice that may not always work in practice – one of the key reasons this book has been written in the first place.

This book aims to prepare you so you know what to expect *before* you pensively jot that letter of resignation. It will help you to identify how to take forward an initial idea, while also going some way to helping you to improve your self-belief and sort areas of your life that you want to fine-tune. You'll learn how to research, plan, market and sell effectively, and will be able to clearly identify your goals, vision, targets and skills required to achieve these. So you'll be ready to launch forth having analysed your financial requirements, set clear goals and planned exactly how you will achieve them.

The guide examines:

- how to weigh up the pros and cons of going it alone;
- how to select the right business opportunity and achieve focus;
- how to define customer profiles and target audiences;
- how to create a message and brand that customers will want to know about;
- how to get that message heard by the right people at the right time.

The first chapter reviews the pleasures and pains of starting and running a small business. You will have considered many of these and have no clue about others until you 'get your feet wet'. The aim is to help raise your awareness about the implications of being self-employed, before adding a sprinkle of inspiration and a dash of motivation.

CHAPTER ONE

Where to Begin –
What's The Big Idea?

'What man can conceive and believe, he can achieve.' Napoleon Hill

If you want to start a business but don't know where to start, read this chapter, complete the exercises and you'll either be ready for the challenge and rewards of being an entrepreneur, or dropping the book on the floor and running very fast back to the comfort and security of your job. Either way, you'll have the conviction to take the right path for you – self-employed or employed (if you decide it's not worth the bother).

By the end of this chapter you should be able to answer the following questions:

◆ How will balance be created between work life, personal life, and your satisfaction and expectations?
◆ What are the qualities and motivation factors affecting the proposed business?
◆ What are the advantages and disadvantages of going it alone?
◆ Why do you want to start up your own business and is it for you?

STEP 1: HAVING A DESIGN FOR LIFE

Before we get down to the business of business, I want to take you on a journey that will uncover what you fear most, and reveal what you want most from your life and work.

Once you have visualised and focused on what you *really* want to achieve from starting your own business, you'll be better prepared to launch forth and get to grips with the nitty-gritty.

It's not Rocket Science

Unless you intend to start up as a competitor to NASA, running a business isn't rocket science. Anyone can have an idea for a new business. The entrepreneurs are those who put that idea into wheel-spinning, cash-registering action, and brilliant ideas require some brilliance in terms of planning and moving forward.

An idea is just that – an idea – and one that is in limbo until something is done with it, until it is seized and actioned. That is where goals play an important role.

1

Having no written goals and no list of aspirations is very much like embarking on a very long journey without having a final destination and without taking a map – not the most common-sensical approach.

◆ TOP TIP ◆

Creating a plan from your idea, with a set of *written* goals and then *visualising* having achieved them, will make you far more likely to be successful in your endeavours.

The power of pen plus paper

I tell my clients, '*Create the link to what you think – mark it in ink.*' You may think that sounds a bit cheesy (ok it does) and you may also think that writing lists of goals is a futile exercise, but you'd be wrong. Here's the proof:

In 1953, a group of graduates from Yale University were asked one question: '*Which of you has written specific goals?*'

Just three per cent of the students answered affirmative. That three per cent had clear, written goals.

Fast-forward some 20 years to 1973. The same group of graduates were surveyed once more. That three per cent who had written clear goals had accumulated more wealth between them than the remaining 97 per cent combined!

More proof?

Until I set up my first business, I had dreams and ambitions in my head but I didn't commit them to paper or, if I did, I certainly didn't do this enough. I saw them as possibly unattainable, and didn't spend much time thinking about them. I only actioned ambitions I saw as achievable. What chance did I really have of getting to swim with dolphins, interview celebrities, write a book or meet my 'idols'? The funny thing is, as soon as I wrote my goals down and began to focus on them, they started to take shape.

I went to Gibraltar to swim with dolphins, I got a publishing deal (the result of which you're reading right now), and through one of my businesses – ilikemusic.com – I began to interview celebrities, from Alicia Keys and Katie Melua to Gary Numan and Gabrielle. My wishes were coming true.

Furthermore, not only did I meet one of my idols – Anita Roddick – but I also started to work for her, promoting her websites www.anitaroddick.com and www.takeitpersonally.org.uk. This goal-writing really does work! By writing down my goals and taking tiny steps to bring them to fruition, I had energised my aspirations and tuned in to my targets.

So make sure you commit your goals to paper. Mark your intentions, hopes and ambitions and, in doing so, you've taken the first step to fulfilling them.

You need a clear vision of what success means to you in order to achieve it.

Bill Gates dreamed of a time when there was 'a computer on every desk' and Henry Ford wanted to create 'a car for the masses'. Dame Anita Roddick wanted to 'expose the lies of the beauty industry and make a difference in the world'. They all achieved those big dreams. What's your vision? Write it here:

◆ **EXERCISE** ◆

◆ I dream that one day:

_____

_____

◆ Not only that. I also dream that I will:

_____

_____

Wishing on a ... business

We make wishes as we blow out candles on a birthday cake, or find a wishbone in a chicken. Making wishes is part of every culture around the world. But wishes can only come true if they are focused upon, thought about, and if the wish-maker has enough motivation, encouragement and reminders to help them turn their wish into reality.

Most people think wishes won't come true because they've wished for things in the past that haven't materialised. The reason many people believe that wishes don't happen is because they wish for events and experiences as happening in the future. And if it's happening in the future, it isn't really possible for someone to experience it or change it.

This is the reason why many experts on the subject of 'making your dreams a reality' suggest that you make **affirmations** in the present tense. For example: *I am healthy, happy and successful.* In her book *The Circle: How the Power of a Single Wish Can Change Your Life*, Laura Day says:

'There is not 'I want', but rather 'I have'. Phrase your wish as if it has already happened. If you focus on 'I want', you direct your inner resources to reinforce wanting rather than having. If you focus on 'I have', 'I am', 'I feel', or 'I embrace', your inner resources will find opportunities for this to be true... Remember always to phrase your wish as if it were already fulfilled.'

This creates what Louise Hay, author of *You Can Heal Your Life*, calls a 'cosmic shopping list' something ex-Spice Girl Geri Halliwell used to great effect. In her 1996 diary, she wrote that her single, video and band were hugely successful and that 'George Michael is my husband.'

As well as a few more present tense wishes. These all came true, and rather than marrying George Michael, she became his friend and escaped to his home after leaving the Spice Girls.

So… What are you waiting for? It's time to get those goals down onto paper.

◆ EXERCISE ◆

Write down your goals, big and small, below.

MOVE THE GOALPOSTS

Start with the big ones and break your goals down into long-term and immediate goals. Your immediate goals will have an effect on the long-term ones and, by taking actions to reach your immediate goals, you're climbing the hill towards your long-term vision – your own personal summit of success, your own treasure chest on your treasure map.

Plus, the sense of achievement you get from meeting immediate targets will ensure you enjoy the hill climb. You are equipping yourself with the right tools and experiences to climb the summit, challenge yourself, achieve your goals, live the dream.

Long-term Goals, Ambitions and Dreams

◆ The Big Vision
Where do you see yourself/your business in five years' time?

_____

_____

Where do you see yourself/your business in 15 years' time?

_____

_____

◆ Annual Goals/Targets
Where do you see yourself/your business in one year from now?

_____

_____

◆ **EXERCISE** *(cont)* ◆

Where do you see yourself/your business in two years from now?

_____

_____

Immediate Goals

◆ Daily goals/targets – say these while brushing your teeth and/or in the shower as you start your day and post them on a pinboard above your desk or keep them in your wallet. (Eg: I have three new customers, I've completed my tax return with minimal pain, etc.)
◆ Weekly goals/targets – what do you want to achieve by the end of the week?
◆ Monthly goals/targets – what do you want to achieve by the end of the month?

Complete this sentence. By the end of this month I have:

_____

_____

Now write down why you think you deserve to achieve these goals.

I deserve to:

_____

Because:

_____

Yes, you do deserve to. And in order to do that you need to focus.

Try out resources that help you focus on your goals, such as www.goalpro.com, a website that helps you to define your goals and track your progress, and www.wish2getha.com – a website where you can store your own wishlists and find motivation to help them come true.

When you write your business plan, marketing plan and overall life plan, always come back to your list of goals to check that you are moving in the direction of achieving them and aren't holding the metaphorical map of your destiny upside down.

The grass isn't always greener

Now I've got you feeling the passion of your ideas, goals and dream, I'm going to put a bit of a downer on things and make like a roller-coaster – a metaphor for your journey of running your own business. It's time to reveal some of the negative sides of starting up. No pain no gain, as they say.

Remember, the grass often looks greener on the other side and those who have never run their own business (particularly those who would never consider doing such a thing) will see you working for yourself as a golden opportunity strewn only with gold and glory.

'It's alright for you,' said a friend of mine soon after I'd started up. 'You're your own boss and can start and stop when you like, and make loads of money…' I smiled, letting him rant. But at that time, close to initial start up, I could have replied with 'it's alright for you! You get paid to go on holiday or paid when you're off sick; you get paid every pay day on time. I work 12 hour days, earn the same or less than you, but have much larger overheads and much less disposable income. I can't afford to take time off to go on holiday, let alone pay myself to do so and when I invoice I might not see that money for months!'

So expect the 'it's alright for you' comments and realise exactly what you are likely to be letting yourself in for before you become properly self-employed.

Pleasure and pain

There are huge risks and pressures involved in starting and running a successful business. Everybody who runs their own business will tell you over and over that it's so much harder than you could have possibly ever imagined, and you are sure they are right, but know you'll be able to handle it. After all, you're not afraid of a bit of hard work. Right? But there are so many variables that come together to make a business work. You have to consider everything before taking the proverbial plunge into the big-and-sometimes-bad world of running your own business.

The pressures of being self-employed are huge and you can't get away from them as easily as quitting a job. It's like a job is 'renting' and starting your own business is 'getting a mortgage'. You take on a responsibility that is harder to get out of, but are investing more in your future. Of course, running your own successful business is harder than getting a mortgage (although some first time buyers may disagree).

From dealing with no human interaction or 'cabin fever' when working from home, to working long and unsociable hours, getting into debt and dealing with non-polite customers politely, I've yet to meet a small business owner who hasn't experienced the 'tearing their hair out' feeling many times.

♦ TOP TIP ♦

Consider the possible stresses and strains of setting up and running your own business, and weigh up all the pros and cons before spending any time on your business idea.

The runner-up in the Women Entrepreneurs of the World Lifetime Achievement awards, Debbie Burke of ROC recruitment, says:

'Be realistic! Never underestimate how hard it's going to be. You are your sales, your admin, your company secretary – wearing 15 hats and accomplishing them all is very difficult. It's easier to be an employee than employer, but if you're driven and honest with yourself, and evaluate what you really want, it is worth it.'

Similarly, Julie Meyer, Founder of First Tuesday and Ariadne Capital, who was once named as one of the top 30 most powerful women in Europe by *The Wall Street Journal* and Young Entrepreneur of the Year, frankly advises:

'If you're considering being an entrepreneur, remember it's easier to work in a corporate situation. If your whole being is not telling you that you've got to launch your own business, don't do it. Because it will totally consume you and you're not going to be a good daughter, or have lots of time for your friends, and you're probably going to have to put your boyfriend on the back burner. If there's any other way that you can make your livelihood and be a happy person, go do it.

Because as an entrepreneur you're not going to have work-life balance, you may have more flexibility, but you're going to be working almost every moment of your life. And why do that unless you feel so compelled to do it that you'll probably max out all your credit cards and forget your dad's birthday? People need to know that it really is as hard as they think – even harder than that. But once people reach a certain level of success they won't tell you how hard it was at the beginning.

Lastminute.com aren't going to tell you that they almost went bust. People have a glamourised view of success, given the profile that the successful entrepreneurs have. But nobody can take you through how difficult it is, until you go through it and you survive. Most businesses go bust, and if you have anything else going on in your life, like stress or financial instability or health issues going into the business, you probably shouldn't do it. It's an all-consuming thing.'

If that hasn't got you scrambling back to the safety net of a nine to five job, let's examine those difficulties right now.

Pros and Cons of Starting a Business

Although starting a business offers many advantages, it is a good idea to be aware of the drawbacks and take steps to minimise their effects on your business. Easy money isn't easy. You must earn it. Facing unfathomable challenges and entering unchartered territory are part and parcel of entrepreneurship. Think hard before you take the plunge.

Disadvantages: the downside

Running your own business means that you will:

- ◆ Face being lonely and isolated, especially as a sole trader working from home. Cabin fever can be hard to deal with, especially if you're used to swapping stories over the water cooler in your open plan office. Be warned and use the radio, Internet Relay Chat or MSN Messenger and other technologies, such as Facebook and Twitter, to interact on a daily basis in real-time.
- ◆ Be unable to blame others, instead having to carry responsibility for your own mistakes. The buck stops with you.

◆ Be under pressure of the financial risk that comes with no regular income or security. A monthly or weekly wage is a safety net and that will be removed.

◆ Need to be heavily committed, which could put a strain on relationships with family and friends.

◆ Rely on yourself, your skills, your staff, your suppliers and many others who could let you down.

◆ Probably work very long hours (certainly longer hours than you would in your job). I've yet to meet a business person who doesn't take their work home with them even if it's only thinking about work, having left tasked work at the office. It's not a half-hearted thing, you live and breathe it; you have to.

◆ Have no colleagues or managers to ask for advice (although these can be replaced by mentors, advisors and 'network' colleagues).

◆ Have to forfeit holidays for a while as there may be little opportunity or available funds.

◆ Have no sick pay, so will either need to soldier on regardless or not get paid while you're recuperating.

◆ Have your family/social life disrupted.

◆ Probably suffer from higher stress levels which could affect your health.

◆ Have to constantly multi-task and meet customer deadlines, satisfy others and still rely on others (suppliers, partners) to deliver.

◆ EXERCISE ◆

Are there any more drawbacks to running your own business you can see in addition to these? List them here:

_____

_____

The main factors that drive a lot of individuals to self-employment are the opportunity to be more in control of their own lives, the independence and the much higher level of personal job satisfaction that self-employment brings.

Many people willingly put in long hours and work very hard at starting and running a business, because they are doing it for themselves and their own future, rather than lining someone else's pockets and funding someone else's dream. As someone interested in running your own business you will also feel it gives you a better chance of being able to fulfil your own personal life goals. And you'd be right.

Yes, we're back on that roller-coaster again, because being your own boss and in control of your own destiny can also be fabulous. Here's why.

Advantages: pros

Running your own business means that you will:

◆ Be your own boss! Make your own decisions and work at your own pace. Nobody will be telling you what to do or expecting you to be in at a certain time. There's no reporting to someone else (except for your clients, who will be relying on you, and for this reason, slackers still need not apply).

◆ Take credit for each success and be proud of your achievements.

◆ Develop a particular skill you've always been keen to improve.

◆ Be rid of petty office politics and related nonsense forever.

◆ Potentially remove your earnings 'ceiling'. In your job there may only be a certain limit to what you can earn, depending on promotions through the ranks. Despite the risk, your potential earning power can be greater with no fixed earnings 'ceiling'. If your business is successful, you will take the credit and the profit and could make a good deal of money (eg more than your current MD).

◆ No more commuting or traffic jams (if you set up from home).

◆ Improve your self–fulfilment through greater job satisfaction and improved confidence in your abilities.

◆ Be free to choose your own hours to achieve greater flexibility in your life. Yes, you will be able to swap Wednesday for Saturday if you want to go to the beach, and if you've a wireless laptop you could even take your work with you. Being your own boss allows an incredible amount of flexibility and freedom (depending of course on work load!) and you'll be able to plan your own working day and take time off without asking the boss. If you want to lie in and work later or have an extended lunch break and catch up with an early start, that's your call. Everything is your call.

◆ Have the opportunity to become an employer.

◆ Improve your confidence. If you can run your own business, you can set your mind to achieve anything.

◆ EXERCISE ◆

Are there any more personal benefits you can see in addition to these?
List them here:

_____

_____

It's an uphill struggle but it can be worth it. Whether you have vast experience in something or not, you must enjoy it to feel energised by it. So here is a **quickie do and don't:**

◆ Do something you genuinely enjoy. Things do not happen overnight in business. So do something you enjoy and are passionate about – having money as your only motivation will not bode well in difficult months.

◆ Don't rush into it. Answer this question: could you survive for five years on minimal income, 70 hours a week of work and no holidays? Would job satisfaction and the passion for building your dream be enough to keep you going? Be honest!

The Inspiration Game

The world can be a harsh and unforgiving place, and the business world is no different. It is ultimately your ability to stoke your engine with passion and belief that will act as the trigger to help you work, commit, make choices, overcome obstacles and persist.

As you start working for yourself you will find that inspiration will be interrupted by the daily grind and denied by the demands of your business, so take daily doses. Get your inspiration fix often and keep that engine burning.

Consider passion and inspiration as your own self-made entrepreneurial elixir.

◆ EXERCISE ◆

Get Inspired... by others

- What inspires you? (e.g. music, kindness, strong women, driven people, ancient cultures, children).
- Where (places) inspires you? (e.g. home, the countryside, the sea, abroad).
- Who inspires you? (e.g. Anita Roddick, Madonna, my daughter Brooke, my boyfriend James, best friend Jennie and godson Oliver).
- What's motivating you to start up in the first place? (e.g. flexibility, belief in my idea, belief I can help and employ others, to provide more choice, give myself a chance to achieve my life ambitions).

Your turn:

- What inspires you?

  _____

  _____

- What places inspire you?

  _____

  _____

- Who inspires you?

  _____

  _____

- What's motivating you to start up in the first place?

  _____

  _____

Write these here, but also get yourself an **inspiration and ideas** book.

Don't write your plans and schedules in this book, only fill it with quotes from those who inspire you, pictures, colours, something your best friend said, images of beauty, keepsakes from treasured places and achievements.

Flick through this whenever you're feeling run down or lacking in inspiration and need some morsels of motivation to get you back on track.

◆ TOP TIP ◆

It will become essential for you to focus on what inspired you to start your business in the first place, especially when times are hard.

Stay true to your initial inspiration. Even the most highly respected entrepreneurs need to constantly add fuel to their fires.

I asked Dame Anita Roddick what inspires her daily to continue when things are tough or working against her.

She told me that, apart from the true luminaries and activists of the world like Vandana Shiva, it is 'people who stand up and challenge and protect'. She is inspired by employing people and giving people more choice within their own lives:

'Activists inspire me, but within the Body Shop it's the direct-sales business, The Body Shop at Home. Every conference I go to, whether there are 1,000 women there or more, it's exactly the inspiration I had for The Body Shop – employing thousands of people. This new part of the business is about women choosing to earn money when they want, and being free to juggle kids and their business or decide on a career path and earn the rewards they choose to.'

Body Shop At Home employees effectively run their own mini-businesses, hosting parties where they can sell the company's wares, and they can climb the ladder from Consultant to Area Manager or Senior Executive Manager, it's up to them.

Anita continues:

'For me, it was never about money, it was about employing people. So within The Body Shop itself, that gives me huge inspiration and motivation.

Language, literature and art can also inspire creative ideas. I can go into a market place in Ghana and see how they display things and that'll give me a trigger. I can go into art galleries and see things that would look great as a poster. So I get ideas from a lot of visual imaging and a lot of other products, but not from the beauty business. For example, paint – I look at the language of the painting or language of different disciplines and see where I could use it within my own company. We've got some new products which are really good for wrinkles, like a little Polyfilla. The cosmetic industry wouldn't be so honest. So using different languages, lexicons of words can be great to inspire. I use poetry constantly, and visit great photographic exhibitions to really inspire me. The arts world, literature and poetry, I use all of these as a quick fix of inspiration.'

Try to do the same:

◆ Dedicate some time to reading or watching biography videos, visiting an art gallery or simply 'people watching' – get inspired by a film, a life story, by someone overcoming the odds to achieve their goals. Consider what people, places and situations inspire you and take some time to visit those people and places. Take your notebook or dictaphone with you to record your thoughts and ideas and note down inspirational quotes.
◆ Look for small moments that offer joy. Weave these feel good factors into your day. If you adore the smell of bread as you walk past the bakery, put that in your day and appreciate it. Value what is good about the regular bits 'n' pieces of your daily life and stay inspired.

We all lead busy lives, but you need to take time out and get into the right mindset before taking the plunge. Getting inspired puts you into the right frame of mind to take the action you want to take, rather than the action you think you need to take.

For example, the story of Australia's blind athlete and ultralight pilot, Gerrard Gosens, and his motto that *success is a journey, not a destination*' has inspired me to appreciate what I have and go get what I haven't got, while realising that I should enjoy the journey and not get overly caught up in the destination. Destination is important (it's your ultimate goal) but so is the journey that takes you there.

As a small business owner, it's very easy to get so caught up in what you're aiming for that you forget to enjoy the process and 'smell the roses'.

Thirty-four-year-old Gerrard, who has recently flown a fundraising flight through rural Queensland to raise funds for the blind says:

'People are often bemused by a totally blind person's dreams. I may not be able to enjoy the views, but I think that is where I am different. It is not about the conquest, it is about the journey in conquering such a challenge. We often have to lose sight of the land if we are to discover new oceans.

When we are born we only have two fears: that of falling and of loud noise. Every other fear is learnt during our lifetime from failure, heartbreak or tragedy. But you need to believe in yourself, recognise your fears and always have goals. Every single one of us can be successful and make a difference in life.'

Do you have a winning attitude like Gerrard? If not, go out there and find it. Remember, you won't find success by a) sitting in watching TV every night or b) telling yourself you can't succeed.

Uncover inspiration within yourself, from other people, within your product and in your purpose to succeed and thoroughly enjoy getting there.

◆ Visit the library and get a book out that has inspired you in the past, or that people tell you is an 'inspirational' book. Make time to read it.
◆ Create an **inspiration and ideas** (I&I) book to file cuttings, quotes, ideas.
◆ Transfer your notes from this workbook into your I&I book and refer back to it regularly.

Get inspired... by yourself

A lot has been written about the notion that entrepreneurship cannot be taught – some say success in business and life is to do with personality and psyche, rather than business school savvy. True, there are common characteristics among the elite entrepreneurs, but there are also many variables that go toward making a business actually work; from personalities and people to the viability of an idea, state of the market and, often, circumstances outside a business owner's control. Certainly there is no entrepreneurial elixir you can swiftly drink to make you automatically successful (except your own home-made passion-fuelled one). But you can prepare yourself to seize opportunities and make it happen for you.

All you can do is make sure you develop the skills and characteristics you need to make the best decisions throughout your life in business. As Dame Roddick says, there are certain skills that are critical in helping entrepreneurs on the road to success:

'Energy has to be the major one. Communication too has to be a major skill, because if you can't communicate you're just not there on any level. Networking too. These are the skills that you need to succeed. Having antennae for what's out there and what's about to come, that's a real skill too, as are design, language, marketing.

To get these skills you just have to ask questions, read books, get information. The last thing you need to do is go to business school. But you must have this energy and drive.'

You may have no experience of management and zero business acumen (neither did I, neither did Dame Roddick), but you may have good instincts, a strong desire to achieve your goals, determination, energy and bounds of enthusiasm. If this sounds like you, then you would make a fantastic entrepreneur.

Harness your raw passion because this is your key strength.

◆ Customers buy from people who are passionate about what they are selling or doing.
◆ Suppliers choose to supply to people who are passionate about their business.
◆ Investors invest in businesses that have passionate people at the helm.

Use it, work it. Let your undiluted, undisputed passion flow and shape your purpose and actions. Use your passion as fuel, as your own energy drink, and guide your passion for growth. Consciously direct it by referring to your 'Inspiration and Ideas' book as you schedule your weekly goals and tasks. And record every milestone, as these can be overlooked when peering out from a paper pile the size of a Peruvian mountain.

STEP 2: PRACTISE SELF-BELIEF

Believe and You Will Achieve

1. Do you believe in yourself?
2. Do you believe in your business idea?

All of us have some element of self-doubt or self-depreciation and sometimes think we simply couldn't do something, especially if it's something we've never done before. But when you do have self-belief and belief in your idea, keep it strong, because in business you absolutely must believe in both to succeed.

◆ **TOP TIP** ◆

You're going to need confidence and belief to get you through the hard times. Self-belief comes in most handy when you're just about to jack it all in and give up. It's what sees you through, so you must have it. Work on improving your confidence and self-esteem if these are things you struggle with.

Doing well in business will certainly give you a confidence boost, because running your own business is in itself a big pat on the back. The fact that you've bought this book means that you already believe in yourself and have some kind of business idea, or know, at the very least, that you'd quite like to be your own boss and work for yourself. That alone takes an element of self-assuredness, so believe in your chances of succeeding and you are more likely to. Conversely, thinking you won't succeed will ultimately become a self-fulfilling prophecy.

Think I can't and you won't. Think I can, I will and fly!

The Idea and You

Taking the plunge and starting a business of your own can be a nerve-racking and downright scary time of your life, so the more prepared you can be, the better.

You – your characteristics and skills

Of course it isn't just about the idea you've had, the market you intend to jump into or the quality of the product or service you are planning to sell. A business can only succeed if the person behind it trusts and believes in it. There is no right or wrong person to enter into business, and no such thing as a typical entrepreneur, but there are certain characteristics that can be helpful when going it alone.

Assess your own strengths and weaknesses. Be honest.

◆ Do you have the necessary organisational skills required to get your idea off the ground?
◆ Do you have the right temperament? Are you strong-willed and dedicated?
◆ Do you enjoy working alone?
◆ Do you have the money or potential finance? Are you willing to risk assets or large funds?
◆ Do you seize opportunities – always?
◆ Who do you know who could help you?
◆ Do you believe in yourself and in your idea? Why? (You should, but it's good to list why you are confident that you can make your business idea work.)

- Do you know about the market?
- Are you an expert in any area?
- Are you reliable and honest?
- Are you a good communicator?
- Are you flexible and thick-skinned?
- Are you creative?

Remember if you are not any (or some) of these things it doesn't mean you shouldn't go into business. You should simply look to improve the areas where your skills are lacking, or partner with/find staff who have those abilities to complement your own.

◆ EXERCISE ◆

Why are you proud to be you?

Create a list of achievements you've accomplished that you are proud of and pleased about, going right back to your school days.

If you start to think about yourself as already successful, having achieved quite a bit, you can encourage your own regard for yourself and trust in your abilities. How you think about your business idea and your own abilities is of crucial importance, both when starting your business and when you are right in the thick of managing and growing it. Belief is one of the main reasons why some businesses succeed and others don't.

Got the record at school for 400m relay? Write it down. Helped out that friend or family member when you didn't have to? Got your letter read out on the radio or TV? Write it down. List what you've already done that you're proud of.

My achievements

_____

_____

You are literally your greatest ally, but only if you believe in yourself, your business, the idea and concept, your products, services, team and collective abilities – only then will you have the edge in business and life.

Who else has faith in you and/or your idea? If this list is minimal that's ok, as you've got plenty of time to convince others. The most important person to believe in you and your ideas is *you*!

Now write down any skills you'd like to learn that you feel would make your launch into business more comfortable, from basic book-keeping and marketing to PR or networking. Anything that you think will help you strengthen your faith in your idea.

_____

_____

Your own skills and knowledge will not only come in handy for running your business, but can be used to trade and barter for services, products, skills or advice that you don't have. For example, I was able to persuade a well-known successful entrepreneur to mentor me by trading some of my expertise on website usability and marketing, and I've received discounts in exchange for services, services in exchange for advice, and so on. The ability to trade and barter as a small business owner is highly useful, and something you realise the value of soon into the journey.

Challenging your belief in your capabilities

Roger Bannister was the first man to break the four-minute mile barrier. Until the day he did that, nobody thought running a mile in four minutes was medically possible. But after Roger ran, 52 additional people ran the four minute mile too. Once they accepted it was possible, others did it – they achieved a goal that had previously been considered impossible.

◆ FACT ◆

Roger Bannister forced the world to change its limiting belief that the four-minute mile was impossible.

Everything seems impossible until you try it. So think about what beliefs you have that limit you, and, when you have your own staff, find out what beliefs limit them. Start to challenge those assumptions. You can do anything you set your mind to.

Before you start testing, researching and digging to see if your idea really is viable, try this 'no limits' exercise.

◆ EXERCISE ◆

Consider what's stopped you starting your own business in the past. Why is it that you're not already running your own business? List your reasons and fears here.

_____

_____

Complete the following sentence in your own words:

If I wasn't afraid I would:

_____

_____

Think big, reach for the stars. Consider absolutely no limits. Just imagine it.

If I wasn't afraid I would: travel the world, write to Sir Richard Branson, start my own retail business, remortgage my house, write a song, etc.

_____

_____

◆ EXERCISE *(cont)* **◆**

Now write down and complete the following sentence in your own words:

If I knew I could not fail and success was guaranteed I would:

_____

_____

And again.

If I knew I could not fail and success was guaranteed I would:

_____

_____

Get excited about your idea; imagine if success were guaranteed, what would your business look like? Stretch your creativity and imagination.

Of course, you're not superman or superwoman, nobody is. Powerful images of genius entrepreneurs can faze us as well as inspire us. Nobody is brilliant at everything, because nobody's perfect. But you can do whatever you set your mind to by focusing on your strengths, improving weaknesses and hiring the right staff to complete your dream team.

Don't give yourself a hard time when you make mistakes (as these are great learning tools in themselves, and you'll see at the end of the book how even the most successful entrepreneurs have made some real 'clangers'). Think positive, believe and you *will* achieve.

'Leap and the net will appear'. Julia Cameron

Now it's time for some real exercise. I suggest you go for a walk, and take a dictaphone or notebook and pencil with you. It's time to clear your head and focus, so that you can really visualise on what you could achieve, on what the possibilities are.

Stretch!

While you get your half an hour's exercise, getting some fresh air and clearing your head, try to visualise and picture your success. Where are you? Who are you with? What are doing? What have you achieved? Picture the business as you want it to look. Visualise it. Create a picture of it in your mind's eye. Make it real in your mind. Then imagine telling someone the story of how you got to your successful position. Record or write down your thoughts.

This will help you to stretch your ideas about where you might take your business idea, by thinking big, taking some risks and going for it. It gives you something to work towards, and now that you have visualised it and/or written it down – your big dream – it is already more likely to happen than had you not.

'You constantly have to visualise the possible. I think if you have this passion for what you want to do it creates a vision in your head which becomes the present. It's never something you aspire to, it is the present, and therefore you never see any problems. No entrepreneur that I've ever met has ever seen a problem with their idea.' Dame Anita Roddick

Dreams are the seedlings of reality. If Bill Gates hadn't dreamt of a computer on every desk at home and work, I wouldn't be sitting here now typing these words.

'I started my business in 1989. I was 19 years old. When I started I worked from a spare room in my mother's house, I had no mortgage, no commitments and it was an ideal time to give it a go. I remember my excitement when I bought my first fax machine and my first mobile phone (the size of a house brick). Now I employ around 30 people and have a 5,000 square foot building. If the young entrepreneur had seen it he would have been beside himself with excitement. Turnover this year is £1.2 million.'
James Coakes, founder of TeamBuilding.co.uk.

Don't Fear Failure

Success is available, but most people don't grab it because the risk of failure is too much to bear. That's what makes the difference. The majority of successful entrepreneurs don't see failure like that. They see failure as an opportunity to learn.

'Success is going from failure to failure without loss of enthusiasm.' Winston Churchill

'I'm an optimist. I see all failures as an ability to shape things. I never see them as failures, they are just opportunities.' Dame Anita Roddick

Keith Milsom of Anything Left-Handed agrees that it's the trait of an entrepreneur to be a repeat failure:

'But you don't see them as failures, only as lessons. I get things wrong sometimes, learn from it and do better next time.'

Worry can be the enemy, as whatever you worry about can become a self-fulfilling prophecy.

Relinquish the fear factor. Resolve your demons ... and relax!

Be prepared to fail, because **it's better to try and fail than not even try.** Overcoming any fear of failure you might have is the key to success, both in business and in life.

Not fearing failure was certainly part of the secret to Julie Meyer's incredible success. As a 23 year old American in Paris with little money and knowing few people, Julie realised she had a bit of caché and set up her first business, a communications consultancy, calling it, with typical self-belief, the Meyer Group. Since then, nothing has fazed her.

'That helped me later on when I came to the UK after business school not knowing anyone. It didn't faze me to set myself up in business, because I'd been used to taking risks at an earlier age. So I figured, whatever will happen I'll figure out how to get through it. And I've definitely come close to the wall, but you find a way, and find a plan B if necessary.'

It is certainly a common personality trait that entrepreneurs care little for what others think of them, and this helps them reduce or entirely diminish that fear.

'Maybe if I had been a Kennedy or a Rothschild I'd have more to lose, but I've always considered myself smart and hard-working, and I don't buy into any of these distinctions nor do I come from some major dynasty, so the idea of failing just means that I didn't try hard. I don't have that self-imposed concept of failure and my parents would be happy with whatever I did, so long as I'm happy, and I don't care much for society's views, otherwise I wouldn't have done so many unconventional things, so I've been lucky that I don't have the concept of success or failure that others have.'

The question here is why? It's because she's not trying to impress anyone other than herself, and knows that all she can do is try her very best regardless of others' views or perceptions. So if you believe that you can do your best and try your hardest, then there is no need to fear failure.

'It is better to try and fail, than not try at all and always wonder what if I'd done that. If it all went wrong tomorrow, I could earn a living just talking about how it all went wrong.'
Simon Woodroffe of Yo Sushi.

His peer, Sir Richard Branson agrees.

'You fail if you don't try. If you try and you fail, yes, you'll have a few articles saying you've failed at something. But if you look at the history of American entrepreneurs, one thing I do know about them: an awful lot of them have tried things and failed in the past and gone on to great things.'

Red Letter Days founder Rachel Elnaugh is also of the opinion that '*if you aren't regularly failing as a business, you're probably playing it too safe*'.

Rachel made the headlines recently when Red Letter Days went into administration. However, before the business failed, Rachel had grown the business from her bedroom into a 18m turnover company. As such, she has learned a huge amount from both the success and failure of the business (read her story on page 227).

'It's a very fine line between success and failure,' says Rachel. *'The average successful business person has 3.2 failed businesses behind them (statistically). So you should never stop learning from your successes and your mistakes.'*

Now Rachel is set to take the new business opportunity she has invested in, EasyArt.com, to AIM and grow the business. Having learned from her mistakes, she's still achieving.

***'Only those who dare to fail greatly can achieve greatly.'* Robert Kennedy**

◆ EXERCISE ◆

Now write down your answers to the following questions:

- ◆ How will I create balance between work, life, personal satisfaction and expectations?
- ◆ What are the qualities and motivation factors affecting my business?
- ◆ What are the advantages and disadvantages of going it alone?
- ◆ Why do I want to start up my own business? Is it definitely for me?
- ◆ Is there anything standing in my way? (real or imagined)
- ◆ Will I be willing to make sacrifices, such as working harder for less financial reward, or not being able to switch off from work mode?

_____

_____

_____

_____

_____

_____

Remember, success starts with a clear cut decision to make it happen, to go after it. As Tenessee Williams once said, 'Luck is believing you are lucky.'

So make your choices, make your own luck, and make it happen. Choose your purpose and choose success.

Now the dreaming part is dealt with for now (it should be continuous – regular visualising walks are very beneficial) it's time to focus on the practical issues.

Is the idea viable? How will you make it work? What obstacles might you face? Now it's time to focus. Read on to find out how to take your idea to fruition, figure out finance and get guidance from gurus who've been there and done that more than once.

Believe!

CHAPTER TWO

What to Do and Sell – Opportunities, Products and Services

By the end of this Chapter you should be able to answer the following questions:

- Do you have a unique idea or new invention?
- Are you keen to go into manufacturing a product, distributing a product, or both?
- Are you thinking of buying an existing successful franchise or starting from scratch?
- Do you want to go into consulting, design, (service) retail or wholesale?
- What are your strengths?
- What do you enjoy doing?
- Are your hobbies marketable?
- What do you know a lot about?
- Do you want a complete change from your previous career, or to harness what you've learnt to create your own business doing something similar?
- Do you want to write, sell, tutor or teach?
- Are you looking to build an empire or build a lifestyle and merely want to earn a decent living from working from your own home, but have no plans for huge growth?

You'll need to consider all of these questions when deciding on your business idea and subsequently testing its viability.

Whatever choices you make and opportunities you seize, there are many variables that work together to create a successful business. The core of business is to sell things to people for more than they cost you, but to really succeed you need to believe in yourself, be a credit to the business, have a good product or service, and have a sizeable market and the ability to achieve a decent market share by striving for difference. Plus you'll need access to resources, and be able to create and implement good plans, processes and controls. So getting the initial idea right is half the battle.

'You start with the product. You can't have this energy for change or doing something worthwhile without a product or a service. You've got to give birth to your product or service first. And you've got to have something within you that makes you dance to a different drum beat to make you stand out from the rest and create your own thumb print.' Dame Anita Roddick

This chapter introduces you to the various business possibilities and opportunities available to you and includes case studies revealing how entrepreneurs have made the most of opportunities presented to them with details of their 'light-bulb' moments. Internet only opportunities are also briefly reviewed, for those entrepreneurs keen to take advantage of the low overheads of the online option.

By the end of this chapter you should have a clear understanding of:

◆ The preparation and planning required prior to launching forth with your own business.
◆ Identifying how you will take your business idea through to fruition and how to identify your own personal business aspirations.
◆ The skills you'll need to meet these goals.

STEP 3: DECISION-MAKING – STICK TO WHAT YOU KNOW OR EXPLORE NEW AVENUES?

Skills Pay the Bills

'If I was starting out today, I'd be thinking about what are my strengths that will earn me a great livelihood and the freedom to do what I want. I wouldn't be shackled in the corporate world to save my bloody life.'

Yep, straight to the point, that's Dame Roddick, but she speaks the truth.

The first thing to do is to look at what you enjoy doing and then evaluate your skillset and strengths. Good successful businesses tend to be run by people who enjoy doing what they do. Would it be worth the pain if you didn't?

◆ EXERCISE ◆

Use this worksheet to asses your qualities, skills, interests, creative ideas, strengths, weaknesses and the opportunities that come to mind as a result of doing this exercise.

What hobbies and activities make you feel the most content and the most energised? Could any of these be turned into a business of your own? Or maybe you have enough contacts and skills within the industry you already work in to create a small client base? What rocked your world at school? Do you have knowledge of one side of an industry, but are keen to explore another side of the same industry? What do you spend your time thinking about? What skills do you want or need? What are you good at? What jobs don't you like or find you're weaker in? Are you good at making ideas happen or better at coming up with ideas?

Use this space to write some notes and answer these questions. Once you've completed the chapter you may find other ideas come to mind. So add these to your list as you think of them. Create some light bulb moments of your own.

◆ **EXERCISE** *(cont)* ◆

_____

_____

_____

_____

_____

Do a 'data dump' in your 'Inspiration and Ideas' notebook, jotting down your business idea so far: why you think it will work, what is involved, who might be useful to know and who might be your customers? Do you know anyone who could advise you or supply you? Do you have anything to trade for advice? Have you seen any adverts, colours, brands, or messages that share the same focus as your idea? Gather ideas to add to your own. Take just 15 minutes to do this, just empty your brain.

Write a short sentence describing your business idea as it stands now. This could change as you dig more into specific opportunities and targets, but you should register each stage of the creative ideas process in any case. Keep it clear and simple.

_____

_____

The case for sticking

The majority of successful business owners run businesses that involve something they are passionate about and have a lot of knowledge, skills and expertise in. Many people I've spoken to who've contributed to this book have done so. For example, Rob Tavendale worked as a consultant and had a hobby that involved talking about and doing up old houses. He set up his online business to pursue his passion for period homes with www.periodproperty.co.uk.

The three Feel Good Drinks Company co-founders worked together for Coca-Cola™ before leaving to set up on their own. The competitive, brand-led environment of the big soft drinks players demands creativity, sound commercial thinking, strong project management, budget control and influencing skills. So when they left this environment to create their own business and brand, these skills came in very handy.

Dave, who worked at Britvic™ for five years and Coke™ for six years, brought commercial acumen to the table, while Steve had a successful track-record in marketing soft drinks, having been Head of New Product Development at Coca-Cola™. '*Steve is a real consumer expert and understands what people want, what's missing in the marketplace, and how to speak to people*,' explains co-founder Dave Wallwork.

Chris has a sales and operational management background, so he has been responsible for creating the network of quality third party suppliers.

'We have a range of skills and a good degree of experience, but we recognise the gaps and we fill them by having the right suppliers in place.'

Amanda Strowbridge set up her home-pampering business, Heaven @ Home, after 20 years experience in the beauty industry. She advises:

'I've been doing this for 20 years. It always puzzles me when people start in business knowing nothing about the industry they intend to work in. Know your industry and your customer needs.'

And when Sally Preston, a 39 year old mother of two, left her job to have children, she used her 11 years' experience, working as a food scientist in the ready-meals area at Marks & Spencer, to set up her frozen baby food company, Babylicious. Her brand is now stocked in Sainsburys, Tesco, Asda and Iceland and boasts the most famous fan of all - Victoria Beckham - who fed Babylicious to her son Romeo. Sally explains:

'I lamented the absence of a product in the market that I felt would fill a gap. Then I did some very low-key market research in the consumer groups and found out this was a really good opportunity.'

Having worked as a tyre-fitter since leaving school, Shell LiveWIRE Young Entrepreneur of the Year, Michael Welch, aged 26, set up Black Circles, a company that sells tyres over the internet and through orders taken at its Peebles call centre. While working as a tyre-fitter, Mike realised that the industry was rather 'tired' (excuse the pun) and needed a fresh stock of ideas, so off he went to launch Black Circles. Sticking to the trade he knew has certainly paid off. Two years in the company already had a turnover of £700,000 and boasted corporate clients such as Sainsburys, McDonalds, Scottish Courage and Marks & Spencer.

Now nearly four, Black Circles is successfully challenging the traditional tyre industry and has become the largest of its kind in the world. The growth is being sustained thanks to a good management team and systems that are sustaining the company's growth. *'Stick to what you know,'* advises Mike. *'Understand your industry.'*

◆ TOP TIP ◆

It is these examples of harnessing existing skills, knowledge and expertise that cause many small business owners to offer 'Stick to what you know best and enjoy most,' as their top piece of good business advice.

This is a good business mantra and can ring true in many cases. But this isn't necessarily a must-have. After all ... *What if you know nothing about the industry?*

The case for exploring

You might have an 'idea with legs' that you strongly believe will work, but prior to researching the idea you've had absolutely no experience of that market, of that product, or of running your own business. Should you give up on the idea before you begin, just because it doesn't fit with the suggestion to 'stick to what you know'?

Not necessarily!

A passion for exploring a new avenue or market can drive a business to success as much as passion for a hobby or well-honed skill. Many successful business owners not only had zero experience of running a business, but also had minimal or non-existent experience of the market they were entering in to.

We knew nothing!

Simon Woodroffe, founder of Yo Sushi, had spent his career as a bus conductor, roadie, stage designer, TV rights distributor, ski bum, sports filmmaker, in that order. *'I knew absolutely nothing about the restaurant business,'* admits Simon who set up the unique sushi restaurant and takeaway brand in 1997. But he knew enough about international business in general and plenty about design, and he got the right people in to do the food and run the company. He also had passion for his idea, and the drive necessary to take it to fruition.

Now, with a recent £10million management buy-out, Yo Sushi has 14 UK restaurants and has expanded to Athens and Dubai. Simon still owns 22 per cent of the business and continues to focus on developing other YO! brand businesses, including YOTEL and YO! Japan, the clothing and accessories range.

Dame Anita Roddick also had no experience of the retail trade or running a business prior to establishing The Body Shop, but was able to put what she'd learnt on her travels to good use.

'It was never meant to be serious, it was just to pay the bills and mortgage. The reason I chose cosmetics is because of my travels – I learnt right from the grass roots as to what you should put on your body, it was just taking that knowledge into the business. I shouldn't have survived, there were only 20 products in a tiny shop, but it had amazing creativity, because we had no money.'

By having no money or business experience, Anita Roddick was forced to get really creative with marketing and product ideas. This led to her innovative marketing campaigns, which made The Body Shop one of the business success stories of our time - £700 million at its peak. Yet, if she'd had big budgets she'd probably not have gone the same route.

Rather than 'sticking with what you know,' Sir Richard Branson says that once you know how to run one business you can run any business.

'If you can run a record company, you can run an airline. If you can run an airline, you can run a bank. If you can run a bank, you can run a soft drink company.'

Certainly, the core elements are the same, and with belief, passion and all the other variables working together – great staff, products, customer service – you could run any business you choose to.

Inspiration + perspiration = success

Bobby and Sahar Hashemi built their £30 million Coffee Republic business from their kitchen table, having no previous business or retail experience, and no experience of the coffee industry whatsoever.

Sahar, a mini-skirted London lawyer, came up with the idea for Coffee Nation from a customer's perspective. She saw a gap in the market from a customer's point of view. Her brother Bobby, a New York investment banker, however, saw the business possibilities. She was the ideas person and he was the implementer, a perfect partnership for success. Coffee Republic now has over 100 outlets.

♦ TOP TIP ♦

The key is finding the right combination of inspiration and ideas, and creating enough perspiration from implementing those ideas. If you're a creative ideas person and you know an implementer of ideas, hook up.

Anita Roddick's husband Gordon takes the role of the organiser and implementer, while Dame Roddick is the creative ideas and energy of the partnership, a marriage made in heaven.

We'll examine how to create effective partnerships in Chapter 4, when you look at creating your dream team. But you can see, many successful business people chose to ignore the 'stick to what you know' rule, and still achieved massive success.

No experience necessary
The internet revolution and subsequent rush to start up pure dotcom companies led to the downturn in the 'e-conomy', partly because of the consistent lack of good management teams, and partly because they overspent. However, many successful online businesses have been created, despite the founders' lack of experience in their market.

Will Walsh, for example, had no experience of the internet or greeting card industry when he set up his greeting card website - Sharpcards.com. Now it's very successful and has even licensed its offering to Royal Mail and WH Smith. Will explains:

'The brother of a friend of mine is Purple Ronnie. He has made quite a lot of money and has become a national name, so through him I became aware of the money in the industry. A few hours of research later and I discovered the greeting card industry is worth over £1 billion a year.'

For Will it was about spotting a viable opportunity. After all, the greeting card industry is a far cry from Will's previous profession of law. He had studied law at Newcastle University, but soon realised it wasn't for him. Instead he turned his attention to business.

'I didn't know much about cards. I was a lawyer but I always wanted to run my own business, and the internet came along and seemed like a good opportunity. At the time Amazon was the big thing in the press, so I asked myself why books sold so well on the internet. Cards seemed like an obvious thing to sell that would work – they're not touchy feely, you look at the image and then you buy.'

So Will did some research and it all pointed towards cards potentially selling well over the internet.

'In fact Forrester Research had a table that had eight key points you had to fulfil in order to sell anything effectively on the web, and cards came higher than books on it. So I saw a gap and I went for it.'

Will then used the services of a friend who knew a lot about the internet, and was introduced to someone who knew a lot about cards. The three of them set up Sharpcards together and weathered the dotcom storm. After three years they achieved profitability on a large investment.

◆ TOP TIP◆

Just because your knowledge of retail or other industries is minimal does not mean credibility and success in that market are unattainable.

As famous direct marketer Ted Nicholas says, '*If you read each day for one hour on one topic for one year, you can become the world's leading expert on that topic.*' Can you spare one hour per day, or even half an hour? Try it. Pick a subject you want or need to be an expert on and get reading.

Find topics that interest you that complement your business idea or form your business idea – if you're going to read a lot on a topic you need to find it interesting, but also see the commercial viability of the knowledge you'll gain. As an expert you can bring in additional revenue streams and/or improve your credibility and visibility by writing articles for industry magazines on the topic you've learnt about, writing a book and/or speaking in public, giving seminars and workshops – a fantastic method of marketing you and your skills, your expertise and your business.

Remember, nobody makes it big from sitting in every night watching TV.

If that's something you like to do, starting a business may not be for you. For starters you're unlikely to have time to do so.

But don't worry if you have zero business acumen or are unqualified in your prospective area of business. This simply means you will be more open-minded and more likely to think creatively and proactively – outside the box – which could result in solutions an MBA graduate just wouldn't have seen.

Whether you know the industry and have the skills or not, you should love what you do – if only because it is that passion and belief for what you are doing that will carry you through the hard times. Enjoy your business. It's going to be hard work and a lot of effort, but, if it fills you with energy and passion, you're likely to succeed. And if you don't, you'll have far more fun trying.

Opportunity Knocks

♦ EXERCISE ♦

Reflecting on opportunities

Draw a line down the centre of an A4 piece of paper. On one side of the line, list the opportunities in your life so far that you clearly remember seizing, pursuing and making the most of, and on the other side, list those opportunities you can remember not taking up and missing out on – times when you've regretted not volunteering at school or speaking to that celebrity when they passed you on the street, or things you wish you'd said or done when you'd had the chance, but let the opportunity slip by.

Opportunities

Seized   Missed

------------------------------------   ---

------------------------------------   ---

------------------------------------   ---

------------------------------------   ---

Get yourself into the opportunistic frame of mind. Consider why you didn't seize the opportunities on the 'missed' column – what did you think you had to lose? What lesson have you learnt from not grabbing that opportunity and, if the same opportunity arose now, how would you react? Then consider why you did make the most of those on the 'seized' column. Did they seem safer options? What did you gain from seizing the opportunities? What, if anything, did you lose?

Do you feel ready to embrace opportunities with both hands yet? If not, what are you afraid of? Revisit Chapter 1, and see if you can find out.

You'll feel a lot more ready and able to run a successful business once you've researched your idea. But before you invest your time on that, you need to get focus.

The ideas traffic jam

As an entrepreneurial person, you may be a veritable grab bag of ideas set to burst, but might be unsure which one to pursue first. The key is to not attempt to develop all your ideas (or more than one or two of them) at once, even if you are confident you could pull it off. One of the biggest bug bears of small business owners across the land is that 'there's just not enough time in the day', and that's to set up, run and manage just *one* idea.

By setting up more than one idea at a time, you could fall short and dilute the success of each.

'Be focused, incredibly focused on what you're trying to achieve. Bring the goalposts in. You can't do everything well, because you spread your attention, talents and money thinly, but you can do things you focus on well, if you really focus properly.' Coffee Nation's Martyn Dawes

So focus on one idea at a time. This chapter will help you get your creative juices flowing and could generate a dozen great business ideas, but you need to tune in and focus on the one you believe in the most, have the best gut-feeling about, the one that has the most promising market outlook and is the most timely.

Easy tiger!

Michael Parker, of successful online retro sweet retailer, AQuarterOf.co.uk says: *'Don't try to run before you can walk. You'll start off with a million ideas, and if you try to get all of the ideas going to start with, you won't do anything properly. So don't try to do everything at once.'*

Unfinished Business

'Entrepreneurs can't complete things,' says Mike Southon and Chris West, authors of *The Beermat Entrepreneur*.

'They're forever coming up with new ideas. They love brainstorming sessions, they blaze with excitement at new projects. 'Why don't we…', 'Suppose we…', 'And then we can,'… If you are an entrepreneur, please make yourself focus on detail. More importantly, listen to your closest colleagues when they focus on detail.'

When I first went into business I made this very mistake, and tried to juggle establishing and running my own website review business with a freelance editorial role and the set-up of additional websites that I thought would 'practically run themselves'. Of course, that was before I knew the well known mantra of entrepreneurs, that 'everything *always* takes longer and costs more than you envisage'.

The stress of trying to juggle everything meant that the quality of work for the primary business was suffering and I had no time to find new business for it. Something had to give. Fortunately I was able to restructure before moving on to the next idea, and I've learnt from this mistake that focus is crucial to a business's success.

◆ TOP TIP ◆

Lack of focus can dilute your efforts and damage relationships. Don't let that happen to you and focus on one idea at a time.

Soak it up

Each idea you have is precious. Inconsiderately, your brain will decide to pop one into your head at the most inconvenient of moments – as you're about to drop off to sleep, as you're driving in the fast lane. Keep a notepad and/or dictaphone to record your ideas as that brain of yours pops them out, or record them into your phone.

'Take a notepad with you everywhere: in the car, by the bed, everywhere. Stuff comes to me all the time. My trick is to carry a notebook and I write things down immediately, right away, otherwise you forget the ideas.' Simon Woodroffe

If you find it hard initially to come up with ideas, this doesn't mean you'll make a poor entrepreneur. It may mean you hire in a creative type, because you're better at the implementation of ideas.

One thing is certain, as soon as you make the decision to start up on your own, you will notice more and more opportunities that you'd probably not noticed previously. You'll automatically read the sign-writing on vans, because therein may lie a potential customer or contact. Your 'business radar' – a kind of 'potential customer awareness', heightens. Soak it up and harness your new-found antennae. Write down business names and locations, contacts and ideas. When you're next in a creative frame of mind, bring these notes out and brainstorm for new possibilities or ways of getting more business, targeting new markets, creating new product ranges and so on.

STEP 4: ANALYSE YOURSELF AND YOUR IDEAS

Your Personal ACE Analysis

Whatever your proposed business will be, you need to consider carefully the role you intend to play. The purpose of this exercise is for you to identify your own personal strengths and weaknesses and become aware of the opportunities and threats that may affect your proposed business idea.

On the worksheet below (ACE – my own version of SWOT analysis, where you review strengths, weaknesses, opportunities and threats only), write down your strengths. What are you good at? What skills do you have? What experience do you have? Get your CV out. What qualifications do you have – are you using them? Do you want to use them? Write this in column 1 under Abilities-Skills/Qualities/Strengths.

Write down business possibilities in your mind so far. Record your feelings about the creative strengths of that idea in column 2, Creative Ideas. The 'science' bit will come later. (Don't worry if you haven't crystalised your idea yet, as you'll revisit this page near the end of the book.)

Also list what you enjoy doing, what you like to talk about, what your interests and hobbies are. Put these in column 3: Enjoy-Interests.

Now note down your weaknesses. What are you not so good at? Which areas of your skillset could be improved? Do you have a lack of experience, no credibility, little personal confidence, or does your product face seasonal demand and strong competition? Write all this in the Weaknesses/Improvements column 4.

Might your business idea be subject to external influences, such as the weather? Maybe you are going to need large capital expenditure to get the idea off the ground, or perhaps there is not much scope for expansion and resources available to you are limited. You'll be able to add to this section once you've completed Chapter 4, where you'll collect more information on opportunities and threats in the marketplace.

◆ **EXERCISE** ◆

Complete the ACE (Abilities, Creative Ideas, Experience) Assessment Worksheet

1. Abilities – Skills, Qualities Strengths	2. Creative Ideas	3. Enjoy – Interests

Skills/Qualities:
    Computer-literate
    Good communicator
    Good telephone manner
    Writing abilities
    Implementer of ideas
	Playgroup/nursery/creche
	Bespoke travel services
	Travel Tours
	Teach writing/childcare/yoga
		Yoga
		Travelling
		Writing
		Reading

Qualifications in:
    Childcare
    Yoga
    Business studies
	Write column on yoga
	Set up new age parenting mag
		Music

Experience in:
    Childcare
    Recruitment
    Secretarial
    Travel rep
    Yoga and pilates		

4. Weaknesses/Improvement/ Threats	5. Plan of Action	Cost	Timescale
Lack of marketing knowledge	Buy *Dummies Guide* and spend half an hour reading each night	£25 + webtime	1 month
Lack of accounting/ book-keeping knowledge	Go to night school and do book-keeping course	£75	6 weeks
Not up to date with latest childcare legislation	Speak to Childcare Recruitment Association		1 month

Your turn:
Do your own ACE Assessment here

Abilities – Skills, Qualities	Creative Ideas	Enjoy – Interests
Skills/Qualities:		
Qualifications in:		
Experience in:		

Weaknesses/Improvement/ Threats	Plan of Action	Cost	Timescale

Remember, weaknesses are simply obstacles, and they can be overcome. Brick walls can be knocked down or walked around. For example, you may need large capital expenditure (like Yo Sushi did), but you may be able to raise this on the back of your great idea and your own passion and energy.

Now consider the opportunities you have and the ideas that spring to mind as you look at the page. Also list these in the Creative Ideas column (2). Is there a gap in the market? Is there a market in that gap? Does the product or service have good potential for rapid growth? Have you recently discovered you are good at something you hadn't realised previously? Is there a trend towards products such as the ones you intend to sell? Have there been changes in legislation to allow you to pursue an idea previously not viable? List opportunities here (in column 2) and revisit this page as you pick up further possibilities with your antennae. Once you've completed the research, you'll be able to add weaknesses and strengths as you uncover them.

Finally, write down any main threats you know of so far in the Weaknesses column (4). What are the areas of concern? Who is the competition? Does the future look economically sound for the industry you intend to enter into? Could changes in legislation affect your idea negatively? How will new technologies affect your idea? Write these in the Threats column (4).

Next, think honestly about the answers to the following questions:

◆ What skills do you already have that you've enjoyed using in business/life?
◆ What skills do you really wish you had?
◆ How might you apply/translate your existing skills to your own business?
◆ How will you gain the additional skills you desire or require?

Put your answers in the relevant columns (Skills (1), Weaknesses (4) and Actions (5)) and figure out how much time you will spend on these tasks and what actions are required to enhance your strengths and reduce your weaknesses.

Now see how all this fits in with the opportunities out there. You might have a business idea 'with legs' that nobody has done in the way you plan to, or you might want to start an accountancy, aerobics or acupuncture business. Maybe you've been a tree surgeon for a firm, and want to start up on your own in the same trade? Maybe you want to design clothes, sell clothes or manufacture them? You might hire boats, set up boarding kennels or a bridal shop, set up an events agency, florist or café. Maybe you're keen to become a freelance writer, photographer or designer. Think about how you can apply what you've written in your ACE Worksheet to a potential new business of your own.

◆ EXERCISE ◆

Write down the opportunities and ideas you've created or spotted in the past few months, even those you consider entirely 'pie in the sky'. Have you noticed an empty shop for rent in an area that's crying out for a stylish salon? Or has a franchise opportunity caught your eye recently? Get it all down. Also write summaries of your own businesses ideas.

What business ideas have you already had for a while, and which new possibilities spring to mind from your ACE record? This is the first step towards creating your Business Idea Profile. It's time to dump that data.

_____

_____

_____

Now that you are in the right mindset, it's time to get serious, get out there and find the right opportunity to dedicate your life to. You may already know exactly what you intend to do, but you still need to uncover all the opportunities available.

STEP 5: FIND THE RIGHT IDEA FOR YOU

The good news is that you don't have to come up with a ground-breaking, earth-shattering idea, or even one that is completely unique and original. Modification of successful ideas is the best way, but it should still have some unique factors to differentiate from the rest.

This doesn't mean you should jump on the bandwagon. Running and maintaining a successful business is much more difficult if you don't believe in it, and if you're just jumping on the bandwagon you won't have as much belief, because it's not your idea.

So how can you find or create the perfect product or service for you to sell? Here are a few ideas.

Examine your skills

When I started my first business, I thought, what do I know? What am I good at? What isn't being offered right now? I'd been gaining expert knowledge through writing booklets and learning how to market them via the web, and realised many small business owners had limited time to learn how to fine tune or promote their websites, something I could offer. My first business WebCritique was born, reviewing websites and creating reports and online marketing plans. Only a few people were doing the same (mainly in the States). So off I went, harnessing my own skills and knowledge, to create a solution. As I honed my skills and focused on writing, WebCritique became Web Copywriter: writing user and search-engine friendly text (copy) for websites.

- What services do people need that you could provide them with?
- How can you offer something better, faster, safer, than the rest?

There are also services that will always be required. Unless technology creates a fool-proof way for people to cut their own hair, there will always be a need for hairdressers. Similarly we'll need builders, plumbers, electricians and engineers for some time to come. Starting a trade business can be a good opportunity, but is equally high risk because of the intense competition. Consider how you might be an edgier salon or the local genuinely reliable plumber, or jargon-less lawyer. Seek out the unique if your competition level looks high.

Look for growth markets

Technology, communications, the mobile industry and teleconferencing, SMS messaging – all of these changes in our society and how we communicate have created growth markets. People made pots of cash selling fax machines during the 1980s. Look for areas of growth within your chosen market and work out how you can take advantage of this rise in sales.

The sport compact performance market, music therapy and foot care markets are currently growing in the US, along with data storage.

Globally needs and demands are being created by the information age that you might be able to fill. Back in Blighty, alternative therapies and healing have seen recent high growth. The 'work from home' population is also growing. Do you have a product or service that could provide a solution to those who work from home?

The market for organic produce is growing too, on both sides of the pond.

You may already know what your product or service will be, but those questions could reveal additional markets you'd not previously considered and give you food for thought.

Owen Weekes of IT consultancy, SSS Ltd says that spotting a growth area and expanding sector is important.

'That's the secret of success really. If you look at other companies in these lists that have done very well from a growth perspective, they've all spotted a growth sector. For example Carphone Warehouse have done very well out of the mobile phone sector, which is explosive growth, we've done very well out of the explosive growth in the IT outsourcing space, and we're moving into the business process outsourcing space which has ten years of significant growth which we can piggyback off.

I think being in a growth area overrides any other 'secret of success' as you could have the best people at their jobs working efficiently in the coal industry, or another industry that's fading, and it would be much harder to make it work.'

Seek out industries where there has been year on year growth

◆ Contact trade and professional associations and, if you're thinking of turning your hobby into a business, contact your local hobby association to see if they have statistics on the growth or decline of the market in your area.

◆ Get an insight into which markets are the most prosperous. Look at the *Financial Times* or financial pages in your daily newspaper to see which markets appear frequently. Checking out the *Sunday Times'* Rich List is another way of finding out which markets have seen growth or have created many successful entrepreneurs. Naturally, markets that have experienced long-term growth already and have many established and successful businesses with plenty of competition can be risky to enter into. This is why finding a niche and differentiator to avoid the risk of going up against established companies can be a good strategy. In these instances you need a clearly defined target market and/or something that makes you stand head and shoulders above the rest.

◆ Buy today's local business paper or magazine. If one doesn't exist, that's a gap in the market right there. Are there any markets that you can see a growing interest in by reading the paper from cover to cover? Look out for issues that reappear frequently in the news. Monitor interest: can you take advantage of a growing public interest in a market you intend to enter into?

◆ Ring suppliers of the kinds of products or services you are thinking of selling. What are their best sellers and what can they tell you about the market in terms of demand? Is it rising or falling?

Go online

◆ These days, you have access to answers to every question you could ask. Need to know about commercial mortages? Go online and type 'Commercial Mortgages FAQ' into Google or Yahoo. Need market figures on childcare? Type 'uk childcare market' or visit the National Statistics website. You'll uncover other resources, such as listings of competitors who have websites. And you can also visit the Companies House website to see if anyone else has registered a company name that's similar or the same as your intended one, and how competing limited companies are doing in terms of annual returns filings.

◆ Research popularity of an idea. Search for a term that describes your business idea topic (say 'fashion') and then type 'discussion' or 'message board' and see how many appear. If there are a lot of message boards, you may be on to a good thing. If there aren't you may have found a niche area, with less competition. Whatever the case, have a look and see what kind of subjects people are discussing. Find out what people need and want. What questions do they want answered? What problems do they want solved? By posting messages on these discussion boards, asking if these people (your target market) might be interested in a solution to that problem, you will discover if you have market potential pretty quickly.

◆ Look for entrepreneurs of the year and winners of recent Business Start Up awards, or e-commerce and internet awards if your business idea focuses on the web. Learn what works well in your given market and what kinds of ideas inspire confidence.

Go overseas

Think laterally. Some companies attribute their success to being in the right place at the right time with the right product, having spotted a sizeable gap by looking overseas. Some of the best business ideas have come from abroad and have been refined to suit the UK market.

◆ Martyn Dawes of Coffee Nation went on a reconnaissance trip to New York to find his idea for a network of 24 hour, self-serve, gourmet coffee-to-go stations.

◆ Simon Woodroffe took the Japanese conveyor belt sushi bar concept and revolutionised it after speaking to a Japanese friend. In Japan, a conveyor belt sushi bar is like a greasy spoon café. Simon wanted to take the concept up market and modernise it. He not only did that; he revolutionised it. 'It's all about perception,' says Simon.

◆ Dominic McVey, scooter entrepreneur, imported products we didn't have on these shores when he was just 13 years old. He spotted collapsible scooters available from the USA on the internet and ordered one. He then sold it and bought two more. The public caught on to his idea and made young Dom a teenage millionaire.

Scooters, Cabbage Patch Kids, coffee-to-go – all these ideas are imported. So if you can spare the time and cash, go on an adventure and find your Cabbage Patch Doll.

The Lightbulb Moment

◆ Sahar Hashemi of Coffee Republic wondered why you couldn't order a slim cinnamon latté coffee in London, like you could in the stylish New York coffee bars. Her brother Bobby remembered a prospectus his boss had put on his table about growth in the luxury coffee industry, and bingo – they had their idea for a business – to open up US style coffee bars in the UK. Bobby saw the gap, Sahar went out to find a market in that gap, and they were off.

◆ The founder of The Gadget Shop left his Christmas shopping to the last minute and couldn't find the gifts he wanted, which resulted in the seed being sewn for The Gadget Shop.

◆ During her travels after leaving the teaching profession, Dame Anita Roddick spent a year living with pre-industrial fishing groups around the Indian Ocean and Pacific Islands. There she noticed women rubbing cocoa butter on their silk-like skin. 'That was education through experience, and it was where I got the ideas for The Body Shop.' On her return, Anita ventured into her local chemist and found it impossible to buy small bottles of shampoo. 'I used to think to myself, "Why can't I have a small bottle? Why can't I refill it?" And the entrepreneur in me would say, "Why not, why can't you?".' That dissatisfaction gave me the energy to set it up.'

◆ The founder of Vision Express took the plunge after his wife cried when her optician told her she'd have to wait seven days for new glasses.

◆ The idea for YO! Sushi came from a remark by a Japanese acquaintance that told Simon Woodroffe that he should open a conveyor belt sushi bar with girls in black

PVC miniskirts. After two years' development and the investment of his life savings of £150,000, he opened the first restaurant in Poland Street (without PVC miniskirts!), which rapidly became successful and quickly led to further openings.

Have you had your lightbulb moment?

Read on to find out what makes a good product or service in today's business landscape.

What Makes a Good Product or Service?

Sir Richard Branson has a theory on this from Virgin's perspective. He has managed to incorporate five criteria into every business he has started and every joint venture he has entered. A product or service can only be associated with Virgin if it:

- has high quality
- is innovative
- provides good value for money
- is challenging existing alternatives
- has a sense of fun.

You could strive for these qualities for any product, service, partnership or joint venture that you enter into.

Think resourcefully

Is the demand for your potential product high but seasonal? If so think resourcefully. How might you keep revenue coming in during quieter months?

If you are likely to see seasonal demand, try to see the bigger picture and create ways to subsidise your earnings during low periods, like Jo Browne has done with her fashion and bridal business Jo Browne Centre:

'The financial side is still a bit tricky because, with the bridal business there is such a long lead time and it's really seasonal. So I have a market stall to top up my income and a new clothing range: Sheva.

The range uses Indian saris made into a clothing range, using raw silk. I do a lot of bridesmaid dresses in raw silk, so I'm able to use leftover material for the new range. I'm also starting to do parties, where I demonstrate the new range. And I'm acting as an agent for a girl who does beautiful Moroccan crystal jewellery, as her products complement the range.'

Making the most of your resources and materials, and partnering with others who can complement your offer, are great methods of turning seasonal demand into custom all-year-round.

Look to society

Another way to find a good product or service is to consider how you can solve society-wide dilemmas. This is how Dame Roddick has tuned into her customers' needs. By thinking outside of the box and creating innovative products and services that provide more than traditional benefits of saving time and money, or items that focus on a relevant age group or societal problem, you can profit from having a purpose.

When quizzed about her thoughts on what makes a good product or service, Dame Roddick echoed this purposeful ethos:

'Now is so different from 30 years ago. We have the oldest population in Western Europe. So any product or service that is focused on the 70s and 80s age group I think would go on and last forever. Because one of the biggest dilemmas that I'm seeing is loneliness, so if you have anything that can take away loneliness, whether it's going into people's homes and teaching them to do web stuff, or something within the service industry – these are business ideas that can really work and make a difference.

Also at the moment, anything to do with healthier eating or lifestyles would be fantastic, although we're still a fast food culture. So I think anything that disposes of the diluted coffee culture and moves towards traditional tea would be great. Just go in the opposite direction to everybody else and don't copy.'

Look at what the Government is doing. Opportunities can be created via Government intervention, or the lack of it. For example, in the UK childcare has seen a boost, thanks to additional funding. Whereas cuts to funding for music programmes in schools across the States led to exponential growth in the number of music therapists and the music education market. Business is about providing a choice – in what markets are new choices being created? What is hot today? What's going to be hot tomorrow?

Tap into the gap

If there is a significant gap in the market, an unmet demand, this creates many great opportunities for a successful profitable business.

Uniqueness of an idea, product or service is the best characteristic your business can have to set it apart.

'The thing that makes Coffee Nation fundamentally successful is, in terms of concept – it is uniquely differentiated. It's pioneering, so you've got to sell a lot harder to customers, suppliers and investors, but the potential is far greater. If you set up a company selling widgets like the bloke down the road, but your widgets are cheaper than his, you'll make a living, but that's all you'll achieve. If you can be truly differentiated and unique, and protect that in some way – then you've really got something.'
Martyn Dawes, founder of Coffee Nation.

Similarly a market that is currently not being served well by the industry can create a gap for a business that does serve them well.

> ◆ TOP TIP ◆
>
> Seek out markets where companies are consistently not satisfying their customers. There might be a high amount of competition, but if you can satisfy customers where others can't, you can take advantage by creating change in an industry that needs it.

Be the change

Instead of reacting to changes in society, why not *be* that change, instigate it, push it. As Ghandi once said: *'Be the change you want to see in the world.'*

In her twenties there were many times when Julie Meyer felt people were trying to control and constrain her.

'When I got to First Tuesday, I thought, 'If I truly believe that there is an opportunity for a new kind of investment firm in Europe that will be hugely successful, that's just talk unless you're willing to get out there, put your money where your mouth is and do it.' If I believed that investment firms should operate in a different way, I had to be that change. That requires an enormous amount of hard work and energy.'

Sir Richard Branson also uses the 'be the change' philosophy and says his measure of success is creating a business whose practices are completely different from the way others do things, whose staff can be proud and whose product or service makes a positive impact on consumers. In essence, being that change. Branson says:

'There's no point in going into a business unless you shake up the whole industry. Then, you are not just making a difference for yourself. You find the whole industry has to react to your being there and change the way it does business.'

Virgin Direct has won customers from competitors by charging lower fees for financial services, and created luxury service for low-cost fares with Virgin Airlines. Every other financial services company and air travel company in Britain has had to reduce its rates to compete, which is just the kind of reaction Sir Richard Branson revels in.

Natwest Young Entrepreneur Of The Year, 22 year old James Murray Wells, has broken the mould of the traditional optician and threatens to turn a mature and established industry on its head. Eighteen months in, GlassesDirect.co.uk is turning over 1.1m because James discovered he could supply glasses from 15.

'And we don't want to stop there either,' smiles James. 'I also want to bring the direct proposition to other industries as well. Wherever I feel I can save the public money by bringing good services direct from the wholesaler to provide direct to the public.'

◆ TOP TIP ◆

Be revolutionary. Think about how your product or service might force big changes within the industry you're entering into, or at the very least will win you custom from those disgruntled with the industry at large. Are you a web designer who can offer transparency, quick turnaround, indexable sites and free search engine registration on the top ten search engines and directories, without using confusing jargon? You'd certainly benefit from happy clients, referred business and great testimonials as you'll be way ahead of much of the competition.

STEP 6: VIEW THE BIGGER PICTURE

'*Think big - it's as easy to take the first steps towards a big vision as it is a small vision,*' advises Alan Clayton of CHOCaid. And he's right. At planning stage it's worth looking at the bigger picture so you can take the right steps and paint your picture by numbers, bit by bit.

Look for Opportunities

Repeat custom

Look at the bigger picture. Look for opportunities that will enable you to upsell and cross-sell to customers. For example, you might set up a business selling musical instruments, and could then go on to sell music tuition courses and instrument insurance to the same customers. I started off selling website appraisal reports, but have since expanded to website copywriting and promotion services, consultancy, and also outsource web design. I'll also be launching a range of low-cost information booklets to support my services. Look for the upsell and consider opportunities such as franchising or licensing, as well as repeat business opportunities.

> '*The best business decision I ever made was to go franchising.*' Dame Anita Roddick

License, franchise, growth

Consider licensing your product or building a franchise from your business idea. Would that be a possibility? If you are developing products or software, licensing is plausible. For example, Paulette Ensign of Tips Products International has made her fortune selling and licensing information. Her booklet *110 Ideas for Organizing Your Business Life* has sold almost 1 million copies in various languages and formats, without spending a penny on advertising. She expanded her booklets to seminars and sold videos and audiotapes of those workshops, teaching others how to profit from publishing their own booklets. Now she licenses her information products to other companies, and offers a rebranded version of her booklet for companies which want their logo printed on multiple copies. An empire from one 16-page booklet.

Licensing – where someone buys from you the right to use your material for their own purposes, including repackaging for resale, can be a great profit-making method, particularly if you've created the product already and simply need to hand over a copy of the original and a licensing agreement.

Franchising is another way to grow profits. It is how Dame Roddick expanded The Body Shop.

'I think the best decision I ever made was to go franchising without knowing about franchising. With friends saying, 'Oh if you can open up this for £3,000 and you can't even read a balance sheet, then we can do it.' Because we were so much into relationships, it gave us the groundwork of some of the greatest people who are the guardians and the gateposts of the ethics of The Body Shop – the franchisees – in Canada, Australia, New Zealand, wherever they were – they championed what we stood for.'

Initially friends of Anita's opened up small Body Shop units locally, in Brighton, Hove and Chichester, and she knocked the products together in her garage and packed them in urine sample bottles, then supplied her franchisees with the products.

'We only had 20 different products, but we made it look like more as we sold them in five different sizes!'

◆ Consider how you might be able to offer white label solutions whereby you license your product, software, service to another company.
◆ Consider how you might be able to franchise your idea, once you've got the business model working. Setting up a franchise involves selling other people the license to set up versions of the first. Processes and user manuals become even more crucial if you decide to franchise the business, as they will need duplicating for franchisees who also need to be supplied with materials, products, resources and processes to run their own franchise effectively in line with the vision of the first.

The Internet Option

Some businesses start up as pure dotcoms without an offline operation. Sharpcards.com, PeriodProperty.co.uk, ilikemusic.com and AQuarterOf.co.uk are all examples of such businesses. Others have a website purely as an extension of their existing business. We will cover setting up and launching a website in Chapters 10 and 11. However, it's worth knowing what products tend to sell well online and what the benefits are.

Hobby-related goods, easy to package goods, items that are already selling well via mailorder, such as clothes, books, CDs, cards, gifts and gadgets sell very well online.

However, it's not a case of building it and they will come. Websites must be usable and easy to navigate; professional in appearance; indexable by the search engines; and webmasters must be able to dedicate time to promoting the site, fulfilling orders, dealing with plenty of e-mails and a plethora of accompanying administration. Updating the website to keep it fresh also takes time and/or money, depending on whether you keep this in-house. And credit card merchant account providers can take months to pay.

Sometimes hosting companies can let you down (servers can crash) or changes might not be made by your design firm in the timescale you expect.

Despite the pitfalls, the web can provide a great platform for business and an extension of an existing traditional business, but it can prove costlier than you may envisage and may not be the all-singing-all-dancing sales platform you think it will be, so be aware that it takes work to make a website profitable.

Whatever the case, small businesses are faced with the dilemma that, if they don't offer their customers the extra choice of visiting a website, their competition surely will. For this reason, always be thinking: 'how will this fit on my website, or relate to my website?' If you don't have one when you launch, you will probably have one soon, or you'll find yourself left behind.

◆ Do you have any knowledge of the internet or know anyone who does?
◆ Can you uncover proof or statistics that your product or service could sell well online?

◆ TOP TIP ◆

> As an expert matcher of investors and businesses seeking investors, Julie Meyer knows what to look for when assessing whether an idea has legs or not. She helped Lastminute.com secure some of their funding. So what does she look for? It's all about people.

'The number one thing I look for is the quality of the leadership – breakthrough leadership rather than breakthrough technology. People who are able to persist when a mere mortal would simply pack up and go home. People who won't take no for an answer and don't give up or go away. They push things out of their way and simply make it happen. You know when you meet these people that they are going to take your investment and do something with it. And you feel it'll be fun watching them making this happen. It could be in any market or area, because a great idea and great leadership can be in any sector. So it's really about the people.'

We'll look at creating the dream team of people in Chapter 4. In the meantime, you'll have a much better idea of how viable your business idea is once you've looked into it further, through digging, researching, networking, asking questions, and generally going out there and foraging.

Once you've had the lightbulb moment you need to act immediately. Don't let your idea go cold and off the boil. Back your idea up with real facts and figures. It's time to research and devour knowledge. Time to find out the information to back up your ideas, seek the answers to your questions, find information to help you estimate sales and find out who your customers will be, where they will go and why they will buy.

So book yourself on that networking event or evening class, phone your friend in marketing, surf the web… it's time to research, assess and plan.

Explore! Equip!

CHAPTER THREE

Who and Where?

Researching Your Market, Target Audience and Opportunity

Identifying Customer and Market Potential

Knowledge is power, and you want some power in your business rocket when you launch it. You'll be tempted to rush ahead, but should focus your attention on researching.

This chapter discusses in detail how to find out who your customers are likely to be and where they are likely to go, both online and offline, to find relevant products, services or information. Various practical exercises will help you to better understand your potential customers and define your target audience to create customer profiles. You'll also get the chance to find proof that you can make your business work and study your competitors. It's time to go on your fact-finding mission, so consider this your study period. We'll explore your idea thoroughly and test its viability.

By the end of this chapter, you should be able to answer the following questions:

- ◆ How viable is my business?
- ◆ What can my business achieve long-term and short-term?
- ◆ Who is succeeding in the market I intend to enter and why?
- ◆ Where will I find customers?
- ◆ Who are my customers likely to be and why will they buy from me, rather than my competitors?

No customers, no business

Whatever business you start up, it will only be successful if you have enough custom. Once you *have* a customer, you're no longer spending money on attracting or securing that customer, they are yours, so long as you take good care of them. So your costs can be kept down by getting the right customers (those who'll remain loyal). We'll look in more detail at the basics of good customer service in Chapter 8. In the meantime, it's time to roll up your sleeves and do your homework.

Why research?

Throughout this chapter we'll piece all the parts of the research jigsaw together. Prior to launching your service or product to the world (or local community) you must:

◆ Define your product/service and understand its core benefits. What advantages or perks does it have over other products/services in the market? What makes it stand out from the rest? Is it quicker, cheaper, better quality? Will it save people time or money? Improve their hair or make their life easier? (We'll focus more on the uniqueness and benefits of your offering in Chapters 4 and 7.)

◆ Uncover customer characteristics and the level of demand for what you are offering so that you can work out the potential size of the market and your potential share of it. Ascertain your own market place position and market share. How large and accessible is the market? How much of a chunk of the market pie will you be able to establish? How much good competition is out there?

◆ Determine what customer preferences are and uncover their spending and buying habits.

◆ Source and identify prospective customers and learn other core needs and wants. What problems can your business ultimately solve for them? And what level of service, quality and price are they likely to expect?

◆ Work out how much those customers are likely to pay and buy – how often and why so?

◆ Figure out how long it will take you to market and sell your products and how many you are likely to sell by when. This can only be an estimate when starting out and will need tweaking as sales and results come in.

◆ Understand how you'll communicate to these people and through what means you will reach them.

◆ Discover opportunities and threats. Is the market growing, declining or static? What are the recent and forecasted trends for the market?

◆ Choose the right location for your business if footfall is a factor.

◆ Find out prices, whether men, women, adults or children need your product and what you might need to include with your product when distributing. Will instructions be required?

◆ Figure out what expenditure you are likely to need and whether you'll require outside funding.

STEP 7: GIVE YOURSELF THE BEST CHANCE – INVESTIGATE AND RESEARCH

By doing market research you are arming yourself with crucial information so that you can make informed business decisions. You will be able to find out about your competition, how successful they are, what they do and don't offer, how you might be able to fill a gap in their offering, all to give your own business competitive advantage.

And if there's little competition around now, there probably soon will be. Unique ideas don't stay unique for long in business.

Furthermore, based on your research, you'll be able to forecast your approximate sales and expenditure more accurately, rather than stabbing in the dark with guesswork about what you'll make. You'll discover your target audience's core wants and needs, and the reasons they buy, so that you can satisfy those needs and keep doing so as they change. If you aren't aware of those needs and desires, you'll have a very difficult time selling to them.

How can you get someone to part with their hard-earned cash if you don't know what they want?

Similarly, if you can't persuade people that your idea will work, you'll find it difficult to get outside business financing, so it's even more crucial to get the proof you need if you are likely to require outside funding.

As Martyn Dawes, founder of highly successful Coffee Nation says:

'Research the marketplace and prove your concept works before attempting to get funding.'

CASE STUDIES Market research: A tale of two coffees

Coffee Nation
Seeing New York as somewhat of a hot bed of innovation, Martyn Dawes went there to seek out innovative retail ideas. *'I saw a frozen yoghurt company and loads of things. And I came back with the idea that coffee in convenience stores would be really good. If I could bring good coffee-to-go to local shops in the UK it'd be great. After all, Britain used to be a nation of shopkeepers.'*

Martyn knew nothing about coffee so set about researching the convenience retail sector and coffee. He looked into the vending market, talked to Nestlé™ and lots of machine companies and set about writing his business plan. He had £50,000 equity to plough into Coffee Nation having sold his previous consultancy business, but discovered some of his plans were flawed.

He had employed an operations manager and began selling Nestlé coffee via instant coffee machines, but it wasn't spinning the wheels. *'I was selling cups of coffee, but nobody was really getting excited about it, I wasn't selling enough of it, and all this while I was trying to raise money.'*

'And therein is the first lesson – you've got to prove the concept before you can raise money. You need to prove the thing works first.'

Be Flexible
'There was a time, sitting in my London bedsit eating a tin of cold spaghetti and contemplating an eye watering overdraft, that I realised I'd made a mistake. It wasn't the concept, I still believed in that passionately, it was the product. I had been trying to sell instant coffee to a customer who was now looking for the real thing. So I had to change my whole business plan.'

Had Martyn spent more time understanding the customers' core needs, he could have avoided this. So with hindsight, what would he do differently?

'I would have spent more time researching my idea. Although I couldn't afford it at the time, it would have saved me a lot of effort if I had recognised that consumers wanted top quality gourmet coffee through machines, rather than the instant product that was part of my original business plan.'

Fortunately it wasn't too late, and Martyn made the jump to using real expresso coffee – bean to cup. *'That was the first time I tried putting the name Coffee Nation there, so I took more space, had a real expresso machine, Coffee Nation branded cups, put the price up – and hey presto the sales went up. I then replaced some of the instant coffee machines and sales leapt up. And I thought ok, I'm onto something.'*

And he certainly was. Now there are over 450 Coffee Nation stations in shops and garages and the company is profitable, with turnover at over £10 million a year. *'We've just signed a big contract with Tesco, which means that Coffee Nation has really arrived.'*

The lesson here is to do enough research to get it right first time, and if you don't get it right first time, think creatively about changes you can implement to push things in the right direction and go for it.

Be flexible. If you discover customers want something different, change tack. If you find they want something outside your core area of business, and would rather buy from you than elsewhere, be flexible and go outside your core area.

Coffee Republic

The brand of US style coffee bars, Coffee Republic, also had to be flexible when numbers were down after an initial sales spurt. The Hashemi siblings who'd founded the business realised this when their high class designer interiors were putting off the regular London punter.

They saw that their stark white walls were off-putting so, despite initially spending a lot on the interior design and hiring a famous designer, the pair repainted the walls a warm caramel-beige and immediately saw this pay off. By making this simple change, they were able to meet their original objectives, of enabling regular people to enjoy luxury coffee. They were flexible enough to rethink elements of their original plan and it worked.

The two proved they were a dab hand at uncovering market issues as they set about researching the market. With neither of them having any experience of retail, catering or the coffee industry, Sahar and Bobby set about learning everything they could about coffee, devouring oodles of information. They widened their opportunity with knowledge. They searched for stories and hunted the headlines. They found out who the main players were and what issues faced the coffee industry. They looked into who was supplying the industry, their prices, the competitors' pricing models, delivery information and payment terms.

Sahar and Bobby took one of the most important steps to successful business start-up – *preparation*. They understood the market, despite knowing nothing about it a year before. They spotted the gap and armed themselves with all the knowledge they could gather.

Sahar Hashemi pretended to be opening a normal sandwich bar to get information from ten coffee suppliers in terms of cost and gross margin on cappuccino. She found out how many cups of coffee they would be likely to sell per day by asking suppliers and calculating footfall. She invested in a counter from a stationery store and clicked each time someone walked past their prospective location during rush hour to get foot traffic figures.

She requested figures from London Transport to see how many people walked out of the local tube station. She rang business divisions of utility companies who provided her with an estimate of utility costs based on similar operations. She phoned Customs and Excise to find out about import duty and found chartered surveyors to help them source the first site for their first coffee bar. She was also able to uncover potential problems, including the fact that landlords are reluctant to let to start-up businesses with no track record.

When Sahar and Bobby visited their suppliers they found that one of them had an introductory coffee-making course that they were able to attend free of charge. *'There we learned many of the tricks of the trade, and we met others who were opening coffee shops. The trading of information that took place between us was invaluable,'* says Sahar in *Anyone Can Do It: Building Coffee Republic from our Kitchen Table – 57 Real-life Laws on Entrepreneurship.*

You need to probe for information in two key areas:

♦ The market and industry overall, including the competition.
♦ The customers.

So let's deal with these one at a time.

STEP 8: UNDERSTAND THE MARKET AND WHAT'S ALREADY OUT THERE

Your task now is to find out as much as you can about the market you will operate in, who already exists in the marketplace and where you might position your business amongst them.

Studying the Competition

What is being offered at the moment and by whom? What actually sells at the moment? How are these products being sold? Where and from whom do customers buy? What do customers think of their existing suppliers and products/services? What would encourage them to switch? Is this something you can provide? Where is the pulse of the industry? Are large corporations planning similar ideas in your area?

Source competition

- Look through your *Yellow Pages* in the sections you would advertise your own business in. Note down any direct competition, words that appeal and what people are offering.
- Get of a copy of your local Chamber of Commerce business directory, listing businesses in the local area – and a copy of any Trade Association literature with similar listing information.
- Make notes and see which of those have websites (you may find there are lots of competitors locally, but few of them may sell online, so having an e-commerce website accepting credit cards could give you the competitive advantage). Type in terms you'd use to search for your own product or service to find global competitors.
- Note down all the web addresses for your online research.
- Visit each of your competitors' websites or request a brochure and list exactly what they offer and don't offer.
- Download free company information from Companies House: www.companies house.gov.uk but remember, a company with a deficit in accounts may have heavily invested in something which is about to take off.
- Become a customer and request more information via e-mail, phone and in person. Visit their websites and/or stores.
- Evaluate. Once you've collected all the data you will need to evaluate it.

Your competitors' weaknesses are your stepping stones. By offering something that differs from your competitors, highlighting a strength you have where they have a weakness, you'll have something unique. By understanding your competitors you'll also be able to see what benefits your customers and their customers (the same market) will be looking for.

You may find you have a competitor or a whole bunch of other businesses vying for your customers' business. Don't let that put you off.

If Sir Richard Branson had let huge competition from the likes of British Airways put him off, he wouldn't be consistently voted the most popular entrepreneur in Britain. Branson sees a 'bigger, softer underbelly' that he can use to his competitive advantage – what he refers to as the 'Big Bad Wolf' theory. 'We look for the big bad wolves who are dramatically overcharging and underdelivering,' he explains.

This is also the theory that Stelios, founder of easyGroup, has harnessed to build his brand. Stelios told me:

'At easyGroup we are always looking for large industries that have grown inefficient, where we can re-engineer the business process in order to lower prices to consumers. Having now created a powerful brand, we are also looking to extend the brand into further industries in cooperation with reputable and established entities.'

♦ EXERCISE ♦

So it's a case of either beating them, joining them or a bit of both. How can you use your findings to give you a competitive advantage?

List ways here:

_____

_____

CASE STUDY

As part of your research try asking straight out or posing as a customer '*My research included quite a few sneaky things,*' Elena Soutto of lingerie company, Ooh La Laa smiles.

'*My friend's dad knows someone who owns a lingerie company, so I got quite a lot of inside information that way. I placed quite a lot of orders and asked a lot of questions, such as 'do you get a lot of returns?' or 'is that in stock?' 'how many do you keep of that item?' and you'd be amazed at how much people will tell you,*' explains Elena.

Elena soon noticed that if she put a suit and a bit of make-up on and marched into lingerie stores with a bit of paper she could glean a lot more information.

'*I popped into a popular London store with a pen and paper, doing my research, counting how many they had of each different style. And they must have thought that I was someone from head office because they were so nice to me. They didn't ask me who I was, but they must have thought I was important or maybe a mystery shopper, because they answered all my questions about packaging, stock and so on, and even took me to the changing rooms for a look around and bra-fitting.*'

Sensibly, Elena's research included visiting plenty of online forums to ask questions and advice in preparation, before setting up on her own, and she got competitors' accounts from Companies House and bought/returned items to look at packaging.

Do the same as Elena did. Visit retail stores or outlets selling products that you are considering selling – is more floor space being dedicated to certain products recently? Can the manager tell you how the market is changing from their viewpoint or how often people buy a certain product? Does the store provide free delivery, or must the customer collect or pay for that service? Ask questions constantly.

◆ **EXERCISE** ◆

- ◆ Phone shopfitters, suppliers, surveyors if you will need to lease premises.
- ◆ Visit possible locations and take photographs of competitors' stores (discreetly).
- ◆ Visit suppliers, ask questions about best-selling items, available credit terms, minimum orders.
- ◆ Revisit the source of your idea.
- ◆ Become your competitors' customer.
- ◆ Gather retail prices and supply prices.
- ◆ Source property prices and utility estimates.

Action

While conducting your research create a Document called **Media and Publications**. Every time you are browsing the web and see a relevant targeted news website or magazine, copy and paste the web address and contact information into your file. Useful if you opt for article writing or PR when it comes to selecting strategies to market your business.

Remember that the market tomorrow may have changed; you are only as good as your current knowledge of the market place.

So make calls, visit suppliers, go on the web, do what you can to answer the questions in the worksheet below.

MARKET RESEARCH: PHASE 1 – THE MARKET WORKSHEET

- ◆ Are there any new marketplace entrants? What impact might they have? Who are their clientele?

  _____

  _____

- ◆ List your main rival businesses and alternative products/services. Who are the main players? Are there any news stories about them? What are the competitors' strengths and weakneses, are there any gaps in their offering? Any windows of opportunity?

  _____

  _____

- ◆ What are their prices? How much or how many are they selling? What are your initial thoughts on your own pricing? What do they charge? What methods and equipment do they use? Do they sell their products from their website? Do they have a catalogue?

  _____

  _____

▶▶

◆ List the main local and national suppliers.

_____

_____

◆ What are their minimum orders and delivery/payment terms? What are their best-selling products?

_____

_____

◆ Is the bargaining power of suppliers and customers low or high? (Suppliers who have few competitors may be rigid and not so flexible. Also, with more competition within your market your customers will have more bargaining power as they can shop around.)

_____

_____

◆ Are there any waves of change taking place? Is the market headed in a certain direction (move into technology, etc?). Is local or national Government forcing the market to go in a certain direction? Will rising climate or recycling affect your market? Are environmental issues a concern or opportunity? Does technology affect your market place? Is there a move towards learning and teaching, creating and designing or delivering solutions that change with consumer needs and technological advances? How can you use this to your advantage? Look for 'waves of change' within your chosen market industry in other countries too, as those changes could happen here a few years later and you can catch the wave before it hits UK shores.

_____

_____

_____

_____

◆ Is the market growing or static? (Review spending figures or statistical data for a given market. You can see if it is growing or declining by comparing figures with past years. Once you've figured out the size of the market, you can figure out if there is sufficient demand in the marketplace and what share you might be able to achieve.)

_____

_____

◆ What equipment will you need? What level of funding will you need? What additional skills will you need to learn or outsource?

_____

_____

Identify opportunities and avoid threats. Stay aware and informed. Use your research to uncover customers' future needs.

CASE STUDY

When taking his Anything Left Handed business online, Keith Milsom worked out his potential market share by finding out that 10–15 per cent of the population are left-handed worldwide across all cultures and countries (except China and Muslim countries, where left-handedness is suppressed), then finding out the number of people with web connections in developed countries who have credit cards. Based on the previous percentage he worked out how many of those are left-handed. *'This reveals that we've got a fairly easy target of 46 million left-handers who are already online with web connections in developed countries.'* Based on this, Keith has set his own target for 50 orders from his site a day. *'That's 0.4% of our immediate tarket market, so we haven't even scratched the surface,'* says Keith.

Finding the information

So where should you go to find this plethora of information?

◆ Dig around. Talk to people. Find local experts.
◆ Look on the internet if starting a wine business, type 'demographics of wine buyers' into Google, or 'total wine expenditure UK' or more appropriate search terms for your market and gather results.
◆ Examine the trade press.
◆ Read competitors' literature, order their products.
◆ Uncover published statistics, read white papers and reports.
◆ Sign up to newsletters and subscribe to magazines.
◆ Speak to former colleagues and contacts who inspire you.
◆ Conduct surveys.
◆ Study the electoral register.
◆ Book an appointment with your local Enterprise Agency once you have chosen your business idea. They may be able to provide you with some case studies of businesses similar to yours, including useful contacts and resources.
◆ Order media kits from magazines and other media.
◆ Visit your local Business Link website and download information sheets for reading material.
◆ Visit a local trade association (eg local parents' association, builders' association, IT networking group or home business association, whatever is applicable to your chosen target market(s).
◆ Visit a trade show or conference to see what new products and services are coming to market or are on the market that you weren't aware of. Introduce yourself to potential suppliers and ask questions.
◆ Read daily and weekly newspapers as sources for contact information and leads to potential customers. Watch for names of people who have been promoted, have won awards, have opened new businesses, or who may be potential customers.

◆ Use your personal network. Ask your friends if they know of people who can use your services, or people who may know others who could use your services. And ask your customers if they can refer business to you.
◆ Visit your local library.

Dig deep.

Seek out:

◆ Government reports and statistics.
◆ Technical press.
◆ Business directories (local and national).
◆ Press articles.
◆ Telephone directories.
◆ Specialist detailed market research reports from Mintel, ICC Keynotes, Jordans Surveys, Euromonitor, Frost and Sullivan, *The Economist* Intelligence Unit, *Kompass Register, Kelly's Manufacturers and Merchant's Directory*, Business Monitors, or IQuest.

'One good source for market research without paying for it is www.freepint.com. It's a portal for those in the marketing/research sector. You'll have to join (it's a free membership) and then post your question into the bar area. If anyone using the site over the next few days has the info, they'll gladly share it with you. It's a great community site where everyone helps everyone if they can.' Adrienne Cohen, Hothouse Communications.

Or try www.texperts.com – where you can text questions to be answered within minutes.

◆ TOP TIP ◆

Use Google Newsalerts to send you an e-mail with a link to any website they find that has a news story relating to your chosen keywords. So if you set up a news alert for 'acupuncture industry', you'll receive alerts each time that is mentioned on a variety of news sources. You can also use these for your company name, to track when you're mentioned on the web. www.google.com/alerts

When searching the internet, use quote marks to refine your search, so type "fashion market growth" instead of fashion market growth.

Go with your Gut Instinct

Some entrepreneurs avoid analysing market potential and take risks instead. Simon Woodroffe didn't research the gap in the market he was entering into, but has still built a successful business:

'I did this because I thought it was absolutely fascinating and I wanted to do it. If I'd gone out and done 'gap in the market' and researched conveyor-belt sushi in those days, with robots serving the drinks, it would've come back negative, and everyone would have said, 'you've got to be joking'. But I did it because I had an instinct that it would work.'

It certainly has, with 14 restaurants and a global brand in the making.

Karan Bilimoria, founder of Cobra Beer™, also took a risk entering an uncertain market.

'*If we had done a management consultancy analysis, "should I have started Cobra Beer, in the position I was in 12 years ago, at the beginning of a recession, in the most competitive beer market in the world" – the answer would have been a definite "No!" It was against all odds,*' says Karan, who has built Cobra Beer to a £60m turnover company by targeting an untapped niche – selling beer specifically to Indian restaurants across the UK.

Evidently, business can frequently be about following your gut instinct. If you believe in your product, team and business and the market isn't looking great, it could be better to weather the storm and come out the other side stronger, than to put the idea on hold altogether.

◆ **TOP TIP** ◆

Research early on can save time and money spent going down the wrong track and can make the journey much smoother, but it is your intuitive belief that will drive its success. Belief and *targeting* what you sell at the right audience.

Every single case study and contributor to this book has targeted a specific audience, even if they haven't researched the market in detail.

Coffee Republic targeted office workers, shoppers, commuters, students and tourists. Coffee Nation targeted service stations and supermarkets. Simon Woodroffe targeted upwardly mobile sushi-lovers in London. Period-Property.co.uk has a niche audience of people interested in buying or restoring period homes. Anything Left-Handed predictably targets left-handers, while Cobra Beer is a niche audience success story.

But without such a clearly defined market as 'web-users with credit cards who are left-handed' or 'Indian Restaurants in the UK', how do you identify who your customers are?

STEP 9: UNDERSTAND YOUR CUSTOMERS

Your job is to uncover your product's value, and therefore your company's value, in your customer's life.

Demographics/Psychographics

You need to figure out who your customers are/will be to create accurate customer profiles and make the marketing and sales process much easier, with a better chance of getting a positive return on your investment.

Consider **demographics** (statistical info, such as geographical location, age, gender, ethnic background, occupation and family status) and **psychographics** (psychological characteristics, such as personal behaviour/values, buying style, lifestyle and how they see themselves/hope to be seen).

For example, demographically my customers for WebCopywriter are mainly based locally, with 25 per cent based in Hampshire and surrounding areas, 15 per cent based in London, 55 per cent based elsewhere in England, and five per cent from the USA. The majority are aged between 35–60 with an approximate 50 per cent split between male and female customers.

Psychographically, my customers are confident buying online, but prefer to browse websites and phone or e-mail their enquiry through. They are happy to pay extra for quality and quick turnaround. Thirty per cent of customers order related services between six months and a year after their first order. Sixty-five per cent of the websites owned by my customers are business-to-business, the rest are business-to-consumer.

This means I can focus my marketing on the percentage of those who are my best customers (those I enjoy working for the most and who provide me with repeat custom).

As a start-up you won't yet have customers, but you can find out what kind of people do business or shop with your competitors, and uncover target audience information during your fact-finding mission.

Demographics

♦ Are your customers affluent city dwellers or penny-pinching locals?
♦ How old are your best customers and where do they live and work?
♦ Are they graduates or trades people? Single or married with children? Predominantly male or female?

Psychographics

♦ How often does your market buy (weekly, annually, on impulse, on birthdays, once-only)?
♦ How do they spend their leisure time?
♦ Do they act on impulse or compare prices and shop around?
♦ Are they sceptics, cautious when shopping, or are they ambitious and status-driven?
♦ It's important to look at both demographics and psychographics, because one customer might fit a demographic that might be most likely to buy your lower cost items when, because of their own self-concept and how they imagine others see them, they opt for the higher priced items. In essence your white van man demographic might be a Ferrari buyer.

Why Do Customers Buy?

It's important to understand what buying factors come into play with your different customer sets so you can price, position and promote yourself accordingly. Those who compare prices and make buying decisions based on the cheapest available will need a competitively priced offer to entice them. Those to whom quality and clear benefits are most important can be sold items at a higher price, if the product and service quality are top notch.

Those who buy on price, buy twice.

Quality is long remembered after price has been forgotten.

Why do people buy products like yours and why would they buy from you specifically?

Cotswold Aromatherapy (www.aromatherapy.uk.com), for example, has achieved £100,000 online turnover by offering competitive prices to achieve high volume sales.

'Our prices are the lowest online, and I regularly check them to keep them so. I have a guarantee refunding double the difference if the same product is found elsewhere cheaper which has never been taken up. We charge £2.30 for products that others charge £7.30 for.'

This way Ian Alcock gets volume but not as much profit per sale. It's working for him with sales of £15,000+ per month.

Conversely, you may target customers who don't mind paying extra for superb quality and extras. If that fits your customer type you'd be better off pricing at the top end of the market so the perception of your product is high. For example, floor cleaning machine manufacturers, Cleanfix UK Ltd, are Swiss manufacturers of highest quality machines with prices to reflect that. Their customers don't mind paying a premium price for quality as it saves them in the long run. The benefits their customers are seeking are improved reliability, less frequent breakdown/call-outs, and longer lasting products. They also want added value, which Cleanfix provides through its customer service and innovative online asset management system.

How to find out what your customers want

Discover your customers' key 'wants'. You can then focus your efforts on satisfying the wants you've identified.

◆ EXERCISE ◆

Develop a profile of your customers

Review your market analysis and identify your target market. You need to write a profile of your customer, their needs and problems, wants and desires.

Be Objective. Trying to think like your customer and really getting into their mindset is the most important tip when it comes to researching the market. Think of him or her as an individual.

Be as descriptive as possible, right down to the clothes they wear and political views. Magazines do good customer profiling of their own. Phone up a target publication and ask for their media kit, which should include a customer profile. Study this and include matching details in your own profile.

◆ EXERCISE *(cont)* ◆

Customer Profile

◆ What type of person or business will buy your products? Who are they? Think of him or her as an *individual*. (For example. He is a marketing director for a wine wholesaler. He is 35 years old, has a good salary, has a team of 20 under him. He is looking for... The main frustrations he faces are... The things that motivate him are...

_____

_____

◆ What do they do? How old are they? Where are they based? (For example: are they professional males who work in the City, single mums with children under 5, nurses, academic professionals under 30, women with high disposable incomes living in Hampshire, teenage girls who wear braces, sole traders with internet connections, small medical practices, e-commerce websites with over 500 daily visitors, parents within a 30 mile radius of the M25, Italian restauranteurs, local doctors' surgeries, London commuters, local students?)

_____

_____

◆ How much spending power do they have? And who, if the targets are other businesses, makes the buying decisions?

_____

_____

◆ What concerns keep them up at night? (For example how will they juggle and fit everything in today: childcare issues, environmental issues, not having enough money or time?)

_____

_____

◆ What do they value most? (For example luxury, bargains, feel-good products, saving time, saving money, friendships, relationships, success?)

_____

_____

◆ How do they approach shopping for products/services? (For example, they might use the *Yellow Pages* or the internet to source products. They might ask friends for recommendations or read certain magazines to get information. They might shop locally or virtually. It's your job to uncover this information, which you can do by tailoring the customer survey, on page 62.)

_____

_____

Now complete the following sentences:

◆ My target audience is…

_____

◆ Their age group is and they are located at and they do.

_____

◆ EXERCISE *(cont)* ◆

◆ What they need is

_____

◆ To find out more about them. I can

_____

◆ To give them what they need I will

_____

Profile your customers throughout the life of your business. Add notes and make changes as you increase your customer base. You may find your target audience diversifies as your product range does. Keep track of all this.

STEP 10: FIND YOUR NICHE – NARROW THE SEARCH

The Importance of Targeting: Define your Audience Segments

With limited resources you cannot hope to compete in all available markets. For a small business this either means finding a highly specialised niche in a national or international market, or tailoring a product or service to compete in local markets.

Look for a niche group of customers within your customer base or intended market – this is essentially a group of customers within your target market who have common tastes, needs, characteristics and are likely to be your best customers. You will then be able to tailor your product to suit your niche target market's needs; market specifically to them and be better prepared to reach them.

CASE STUDIES

As a professional photographer with pet ferrets, Karen Parker spotted the potential for a company providing ferret-themed gifts in December 2001 and established Ferretsuk. By creating unique images and combining them with unique products, online trading and a memorable name, she has since created a very successful business that was exporting to the largest ferret company in the USA within a month of trading. The gifts include calendars, Chateau Le Ferret wine, ferret mouse-mats, cufflinks, cross-stitch, welcome mats and mugs, and her niche audience is... people with pet ferrets.

Founder of Cobra Beer, Karan Bilimoria, decided to enter the beer market in 1989. Just over a decade later Cobra Beer is selling more than £60 million worth of beer per annum, half of which is consumed in 5,600 Indian restaurants throughout the UK. Despite sharing just 0.02 per cent of the total UK beer market, Cobra beer is *the* beer you'll find at your local curry house – now a well-known brand. This is all down to finding a targetable niche within an overall target audience and aiming marketing and sales to that section of the market.

'*By targeting a niche, they managed to survive – it was a niche that [none of the big brewers] had thought of,*' says John Band, a drinks analyst at Datamonitor.

Find your niche. Consider location, frequency of purchase, the significance of your price, age, gender, socio-economic group, lifestyle factors and how they are likely to buy. Are they newly-weds or single, or older couples with an empty nest?

◆ **EXERCISE** ◆

Complete this sentence:

My potential niche markets within the overall market include:

_____

_____

It's all very well to target and uncover a group of people with similar tastes, but this group must:

◆ be large enough to give you enough custom
◆ be easy to reach
◆ have common characteristics that lead to similar buying decisions and behaviours.

So what better time to uncover whether your target audience fits these criteria and introduce yourself.

It's time to speak to your potential customers firsthand.

Find out how your product or service is likely to solve a problem or fill a need for them, and if they tell you they'd rather by online than at your store, or prefer one logo or colour of packaging, write it down. Remember, all anyone cares about when shopping for products or services as a business or as a consumer is **what's in it for them.**

When you bought this book, you probably considered a few factors – would you really read it, did you have the time, would it be worth your time or money, would it have the information you were after, what would you get out of your purchase, what would it do for you? Thanks, you chose to make the purchase and I hope that you get what you expected from it (and more) and that you become a satisfied customer using this as a guide to set up on your own. Because that makes me feel good, and means you might buy other books or even recommend this one to your friends – helping my dream of helping thousands of people to start up their own enterprises. So... what will *your* product or service do for your customer and what will they get from it? What's in it for them?

Desire: what are your customers hungry for?

You might need a laptop with top of the range features but the desires and benefits sought would include spending more time with the family by being able to sort your e-mails while on the train home, or being able to surf the web from the bottom of the garden. It is ultimately those benefits that make you buy, rather than the fact that the laptop has got 3.0 GHz and 512MB RAM. So anyone trying to sell a laptop would be best advised to focus on those benefits rather than product features.

Your customers might want to be in control, be successful or popular, be part of a crowd, be secure or feel more glamourous. They might need a new way to vacuum rugs, a new dress for the office party, or a faster delivery service when they order wine. Unearth their wants but also appeal to their needs too.

Will it make their life easier or give them peace of mind and how? Will you be able to back up your benefit-rich promises and find out which is most important to them – having peace of mind or an easier life? Which of these benefits holds the most importance to them? Once you've spoken to or surveyed your intended customers you need to prioritise their wants and needs in order of importance from their point of view.

List benefits in your survey and have potential customers number them in order of importance to them.

This means you can craft your marketing messages around the benefits they list as top priority.

Types of Survey

To get a snapshot of consumer attitudes, opinions and behaviour in terms of percentages, you should survey a large number of people via the phone, mail or in person. This is known as **quantitative** research.

To get a more detailed picture you should use **qualitative** techniques instead, and use focus group discussions and one to one in-depth interviews.

Adapt the customer profile survey on page 62 for your own uses and, once you know who you are targeting, survey your potential customers.

Survey tips

◆ Build a question round your objectives. What do you want to know? Your objective to find out where to market your product could be uncovered by asking where people look to find services such as yours.

◆ Ask market research students at your local college or university to carry out a local study on your behalf as part of their own project.

◆ Monitor feedback, as well as the language used by those filling in the survey or members of a focus group if you have one. What do they say when they discuss your products?

◆ Write down verbs and descriptive words they use and explanations of the problems they see your product or service solving. How do they describe your product and the solutions it offers?

Explanatory note: I'm going to be providing a new kind of florist service and would like to ensure that I meet the needs of those I'll be providing the service for. Many thanks for your time.

CUSTOMER RESEARCH SURVEY

Tracking Reference: M04

Date

Name _____

E-mail _____

Contact No _____

Address _____

Q: When you're looking for a Florist* do you look in:

◆ *Yellow Pages*?
◆ Regional newspaper?
◆ Free paper?
◆ On the web?
◆ Ask friends for recommendations?
◆ Other?

Q: When do you find yourself buying flowers? For what reasons and occasions?

_____

_____

Q: How many bunches of flowers do you buy each year? eg (0–5) (10–30) (30+)

_____

_____

Q: Which outlets/brands have you used and bought from most often?

_____

_____

Q: What magazines do you subscribe to? Which newspapers do you read?

_____

_____

Q: Of the following, which holds the most importance to you? Please list in order of importance?

◆ Saving time?
◆ Saving money?
◆ Only buying highest quality (price not an issue?).
◆ Please list other benefits you seek when buying flowers.

_____

_____

Thank you

* replace with your own business type

How much are your customers going to buy?

This can be very difficult to work out as a start-up. Sahar Hashemi spoke to suppliers and similar businesses to ask how much they were selling to local sandwich bars and managed to discover how many cups of coffee those sandwich bars sold per day and per week. Can you figure out a way to estimate quantity of sales?

CASE STUDY Focused Research

When setting up RE5ULT.com in 2003 (which became 82ask.com before re-branding to Texperts in 2007) – the first-ever pay-as-you 'know' text message service, Sarah McVittie and Thomas Roberts spent a lot of time and money on research.

'We commissioned NOP to do a survey," explains Sarah. *"They spoke to 2166 people, a cross-section of society and that provided us with some positive feedback. We then went to speak to people we'd both worked for previously, who both had experience in the venture capital start up business. They both said it was a good idea and that we should go for it.'*

Tom and Sarah used one closed question in their NOP research, asking how much people would be prepared to pay (from nothing to £3) to receive information straight away, such as a share price, football result or who won Big Brother. Results showed that all participants were prepared to pay for quick and direct information.

'We saw that as a good market and a lot of scope to proceed,' comments Sarah.

Through other criteria, including demographics and age, Sarah and Tom were able to check which regions of the UK would be most responsive. South East England and Central Scotland proved to be, so the pair selected 40 friends and family from those regions to take part in a free trial of the service.

'We took a massive cross-section, including bankers, secretaries, and farmers, and a variety of age groups, and we asked them to use the service only when they really thought it would help, so we could get a real feel for demand,' Sarah explains.

'Due to the nature of questions people asked us, we decided to pursue the corporate/business market.'

After re-branding to become Texperts in 2007, the company was acquirecd by the operator of the 118 118 services, Knowledge Generation Bureau. The company now employs 250 people in 12 countries and sees average monthly growth of 20%.

You may have limited funds and be unable to fork out initially on commissioning professional research and may have to do it yourself. Just like Sally Preston of Babylicious. She grabbed an influx of mums with babies who congregated outside her children's primary school and gave them bags of her cauliflower cheese and Lancashire hot pot, requesting their feedback. Once she'd done this, she was ready to modify what was necessary and roll out with the manufacture of her frozen baby food brand, Babylicious, which is now stocked in four of the major supermarkets.

A What do you already know about the marketplace?

1 Identify the age, gender, and occupation of some people who might buy the product based on the customer profile you've researched and created.
2 Adapt the simple questionnaire to discover potential customers' attitudes to the product and where they go to find products/services like yours.
3 Carry out market research using the questionnaire – by phone, in person, via mail or the web.
4 Tabulate the results of the questionnaire.
5 Write a description of the results of the questionnaire.
6 Make five recommendations concerning the marketing of the product, based upon the results of the questionnaire.

B Work out your market size and share

Write your market segment here (eg women aged 35-55 who live/work in Birmingham).

My market consists of the following segments:

_____

_____

Find out and write here the total local, national or global market (depending where you are targeting) for what you are offering (eg women's clothing, takeaway sandwiches, childcare places, DIY products). (For example the market for women's clothing in small independent shops in Birmingham is 22,800 customers who spend approximately £9m per annum.)

The market for _____ is approximately _____

customers who spend approximately _____ per annum on _____

Estimate how much each customer spends per week/month and/or year, and find out how many shops or outlets or websites cater to that custom. For example each customer visiting independent clothes shops in Birmingam spends an average of £394 per annum.

_____

_____

From this figure work out how many customers each shop might get (based on them being fairly distributed) and then what the average turnover of those shops/outlets/websites might be. (For example there are 125 independent clothes shops in Birmingham, so each one has around 182 customer visits (where sales are made), making each shop have an approximate annual turnover of £72,000, 0.8% share of the total (£9m) market).

C So What's The Big Idea?

Create a business profile.

◆ What's your idea? Flesh it out a little. Find out who else is doing what you're planning, and think about how you could improve on that. Also focus on the uniqueness of your own idea.
◆ What is the business and what will it do?

◆ **EXERCISE** *(cont)* ◆

- ◆ Who will it sell to (primary and secondary markets, any niche markets within those – see Chapter 4).
- ◆ Describe your experience and skillset.
- ◆ What are the initial aims and objectives of the business?
- ◆ What are the longer term goals?
- ◆ Where do you see the business in one year, five years, ten years and beyond?
- ◆ What skills are required for setting up such a business?
- ◆ What skills are required for managing such a business? (Eg if setting up a nursery, you would need good hygiene, knowledge of the curriculum, have skills in childcare, first aid, plus a good dose of characteristics such as patience, motivation, understanding and so on.)
- ◆ Would you buy your product or service?
- ◆ List five people who you think would buy it.
- ◆ Why would they buy?

_____

_____

_____

_____

STEP 11: ASSESS VIABILITY

So Will it Work?

So how do you know if your business idea is going to work? There is no selection or interview process, you are the only person who can say whether or not an idea will work. Don't rely on your bank manager to assess its viability (find out why in Chapter 6).

You need to be able to analyse your idea yourself and get additional insight from family, friends, business advisors. Remember though, the only person who really knows if you've got what it takes is you. And of course, plans, goals and estimated returns when starting a business are just that – estimations, so it is a gamble. But you can see for yourself if your idea is viable by trying the following tests.

How feasible is the idea? First try the very quick three Ms test:

- ◆ **Money** – can you find enough to start up and keep the business afloat and yourself clothed, fed and watered with a roof over your head? (See Chapter 6.)
- ◆ **Management** – can you manage the business effectively? Do you have the time, skills and inclination?
- ◆ **Motivation** – can you be bothered?

The viability flowchart

Management

Who will be in charge? List strengths, weaknesses and gaps in any skillsets. Ponder on these for a moment. Will you be able to harness strengths and strengthen weaknesses?

Motivation

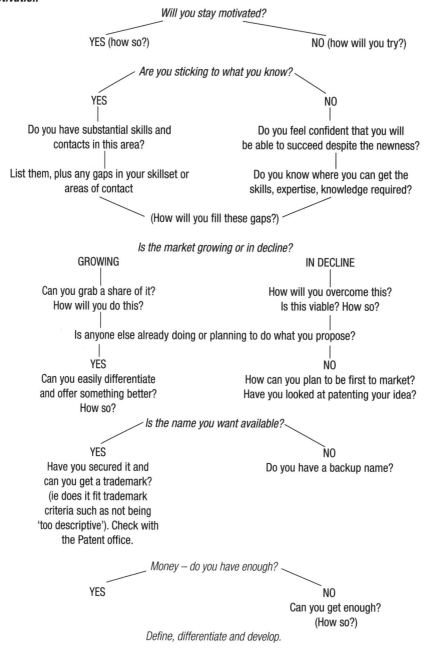

Will you stay motivated?

YES (how so?)　　　　　　　　　　　　　NO (how will you try?)

Are you sticking to what you know?

YES　　　　　　　　　　　　　　　　NO

Do you have substantial skills and contacts in this area?　　　　Do you feel confident that you will be able to succeed despite the newness?

List them, plus any gaps in your skillset or areas of contact　　　　Do you know where you can get the skills, expertise, knowledge required?

(How will you fill these gaps?)

Is the market growing or in decline?

GROWING　　　　　　　　　　　　IN DECLINE

Can you grab a share of it? How will you do this?　　　　How will you overcome this? Is this viable? How so?

Is anyone else already doing or planning to do what you propose?

YES　　　　　　　　　　　　　　　　NO

Can you easily differentiate and offer something better? How so?　　　　How can you plan to be first to market? Have you looked at patenting your idea?

Is the name you want available?

YES　　　　　　　　　　　　　　　　NO

Have you secured it and can you get a trademark? (ie does it fit trademark criteria such as not being 'too descriptive'). Check with the Patent office.　　　　Do you have a backup name?

Money – do you have enough?

YES　　　　　　　　　　　　　　　　NO
Can you get enough? (How so?)

Define, differentiate and develop.

CHAPTER FOUR
Who Are You?
Defining Your Brand

This chapter looks at the importance of brand image, how to create a good brand and evoke your business's personality through that brand.

By the end of this chapter you should be able to answer the following questions:

♦ How does your brand distinguish your business from the competition?
♦ Who are you and your business?
♦ Who do you want your business to be?

Just about every good brand is well-targeted, clear and consistent, meaningful and actionable. This chapter will help you to create a good brand that meets all of these criteria.

'*Brands are dying, because consumers are tired of being lied to and manipulated,*' said Dame Anita Roddick in a speech she gave at the Global Brand Forum in Singapore (as she sat next to the 'Just Do It' man from Nike™ and 'It's The Real Thing' Coca-Cola™ brand managers):

'People are immune to brands. They want something real. They want brands that are honest, moral and local. They are irritated with the way the big brands are taking over public space, not just on billboards but in their heads. They don't like the bigness, the mental clutter, the sense that somebody is selling to them the entire time. And most of all they don't like their sameness, their mediocrity, their reassuring blandness.

Those companies that succeed in getting their message across are the ones that are daring and breathless and brilliant and subtle, but – above all – honest about themselves.

They are the ones that don't need batteries of marketing consultants and over-sophisticated research to tell them what they need to be, because they know what they are.'

◆ **EXERCISE** ◆

List words that describe your personality first, then words that describe the personality of your proposed business. What animal does your brand make you think of? For example, independent online music magazine, ilikemusic.com might relate to the cheekiness of a monkey or the independence of a cat. Which celebrity would you associate with your brand? Ilikemusic.com might opt for an independent artist or bands who pack lots of good content into their music, such as Franz Ferdinand, The Streets, or UK Hip Hop's Mark B.

_____

_____

_____

What Do You Stand For?

'When you need to bring people with you, it's all about inspiring them. When circumstances aren't good or you're entering a downturned market how do you inspire people then? By being transparent, being accountable, being responsible. The values of the organisation, what you stand for in the market, all of that becomes really critical.' Julie Meyer

So you need to have a point.

What's your point and personality?

The Body Shop famously turned their shops into action stations for human rights.

'We lobbied our customers to speak out on issues that affected them. It meant that we used spaces to create an atmosphere, deliver a message and make a point.' Dame Anita Roddick

◆ What point do you want to make?
◆ What message do you want to deliver?
◆ What personality do you want to put out there?

STEP 12: DEFINE AND DEVELOP YOUR CHARACTER

To really compel people to sit up and take notice of your brand and in doing so create brand longevity, you need a cause, purpose and objective that people, including your staff, will buy into and stay loyal to.

Furthermore, you need to make sure everything reflects the desired personality, from marketing literature and other collateral to letterheads and staff, so that all elements of your brand are working together. Contradictions can blur the identity and create confusion, so keep your brand consistent across all areas.

Have a cause

CASE STUDIES

'Skype.net has 15 million clients right now, and they've done that all on the back of viral market-ing,' says Julie Meyer of her Ariadne Capital clients, Skype™, the global peer-to-peer telephony company that is changing the telecommunications world by offering consumers free, high-qual-ity calling worldwide.

'When you get that viral marketing effect, it's great! First Tuesday had it, this buzz, and became a phenomenon. That's what most companies who are taking off are hoping to achieve. So you can try to engineer it by having a cause and objective.'

'Apple Computer wanted to create insanely great computers, First Tuesday wanted to help smart people win and spread entrepreneurship throughout the world, and Skype™ wants to take on the telcos and provide low cost cheap calls over the internet, and it's having that cause or mis-sion that everyone signs up for. Because, if you don't have that, it's hard to get people's hearts and souls,' says Julie. And she should know, having grown First Tuesday into a global brand and helped Skype™ to grow their brand geographically.

'You have to be honest with yourself about what do you do better than anyone else in the world. Don't try to be something you're not, but play to your strengths and keep on doing what you're really good at – then people will seek you out. Build a brand around that, around something that people recognise. You're not selling your brand, that's the reason people come to you, you're just packaging it up, articulating it and communicating it.'

Feel Good Drinks

Good branding with a clear purpose can make life a lot easier. One example of this is Feel Good Drinks, which has exceeded all the founder's expectations growing into a £3m-turnover com-pany in just a couple of years, achieving their dreams of creating *'a product that puts a smile on people's faces'*. Co-founder, Dave Wallwork, puts it down to:

◆ creating a simple concept
◆ giving consumers what they want
◆ creating a strong brand identity
◆ having a great team.

'The business is growing very fast because it's meeting everyone's needs and we're not trying to overcomplicate things,' explains Dave. *'It isn't a complicated thing that we do – we make fantastic tasting healthy natural drinks, put them in groovy bottles and sell them to people,'* he smiles.

Furthermore, this clear purpose is displayed on the back of every single bottle:

'Three reasons to Feel Good:

1 We're a little company who love making delicious drinks just for you.
2 We use the finest juices and other gorgeous goodies from mother nature and add lovely healthy vitamins.
3 This refreshing Cranberry & Orange Juice drink combines the Naturally Cleaning essences of Aloe Vera & Jasmine.'

That's having a clarity of vision and purpose: a clear brand. It's building a relationship with the consumer, presenting a clear message to a clearly defined audience.

So every new business should focus their brand on what the business is contributing, what their purpose is. Street sweepers are making the locality a nicer and cleaner place to live and work; car hire companies and taxi firms are helping to make people's daily lives less stressful. What contribution will you make to people's lives? Therein lies the core of your branding. And if you can zoom in on a market or story that people are keen to talk about and create a buzz, even better.

As Dave Wallwork says:

'The reason we've had such great publicity (around 180 consumer press stories written about us since we started) is because we have a brand that people want to talk about. If you pick up any women's monthly magazine, there's a wealth of stories about how to live your life more positively. And when you present those journalists with a soft drink which is playing to that, it's a no-brainer for them to just write about it. So we produced most of the publicity through developing the brand the way we did in the first place, and our PR agency have done a terrific job for us in maintaining that momentum.'

Just a couple of years after starting up, The Feel Good Drinks Company now has its drinks stocked in 6,500 outlets in Superdrug, Safeway, Sainsburys and Total garages.

Google wanted to organise the world's information. Coffee Republic wanted to give regular people luxury coffee. The Body Shop even had its human rights purpose written into its 'Articles and Memorandum of Association'. Their clever use of consistent graphics makes it clear that they are against animal testing, support community trade, activate self-esteem, defend human rights and protect the planet. The majority of Body Shop customers and employees are people who relate to and/or share those values with the company they buy from/work for.

Relate To Your Audience

In this information age, people need to relate to your brand quickly.

So what does your business want to do? What is its core purpose? What are your values? Revisit Chapter 1 and read your notes. Combine them with what you've discovered from your fact-finding mission. Write your purpose below.

◆ **EXERCISE** ◆

With my business, I want to:

_____

_____

_____

Before you go ahead and write your business plan, which you'll start to do in the next chapter, try to achieve clarity.

◆ **EXERCISE** ◆

Write down the ten things you value most as a customer or generally in life, such as quality, friendly service, fairness, honesty… Now pick three of those values to help you **shape** your business objectives.

Write them here.

The three values I value most in business and life are:

1. _____

2. _____

3. _____

STEP 13: PERSONIFYING YOUR BRAND

The You Factor

Now you need to focus a little on *you*! When you walk into a room you want to be noticed for all the right reasons. You want to appear confident and interesting, charismatic and interested.

Remember, you are unique. Regardless of whether or not you've located differentiating factors within your product or service offering, you will have many unique selling points of your own, there's *nobody like you*! You are unique and therefore brilliant. So what's your handprint? What's the hallmark of your character?

◆ **EXERCISE** ◆

What is there about you that is the essence of your business brand? Find it because you'll need to amplify that when you walk into a room to tell people about your services or product.

- ◆ What are *your* core values?
- ◆ What are you passionate about?
- ◆ What do you/will you teach your children?
- ◆ What do you preach about to your friends?

_____

_____

_____

_____

Review your Personal Assessment in Chapter 2 and uncover the strengths in your character.

For example, I know someone who is incredibly proactive, constantly thinking creatively to bring about new ways of doing business, coming up with ideas for new products and services and generating the most brilliant ideas.

Another person I know is reliable and organised, logical and good at spotting problems and troubleshooting. This person plays 'devil's advocate' when necessary.

Another person is a real grafter, commited to working hard, to human rights and achieving regular goals.

Another is fantastic at introducing like-minded people and businesses, building relationships, networking and being sociable.

How would people describe you? Are you a creative thinker? Are you an opportunity-spotter? Are you logical and reliable or sociable and witty? What do you want to be known for? Do these contrast? If so, tell people when you've spotted an opportunity or had a creative idea. Walk the talk and people will remember you as that 'young guy with the creative energy' or 'the fast-working girl who always delivers before deadline'. Walk the talk and make more of *you* and how you brand *yourself*!

◆ **EXERCISE** ◆

Choose two ways that you can encourage people to see you as you wish to be seen and raise your profile. Include them in your business and marketing plans as actions with specific deadlines. Take the opportunity to shine like you did as a child.

_____

_____

What Elements Make Up Your Brand?

Here are ten key elements that contribute to and reinforce brand personality:

1 Name
2 Slogan
3 Logo
4 Style
5 Character
6 Packaging
7 Advertising
8 Promotions
9 Promotional materials
10 Publicity.

As well as having your business personality at its core, the second strand of your brand is a clear and consistent message about why your company is valuable.

We shall look in more detail at brand elements 7–10 in Chapter 7, but the first parts to focus on are the name and message.

STEP 14: DECIDING ON A NAME

If you haven't already found the perfect name for your business, it's time. Bear in mind the brand personality of your business, what you offer, your unique selling proposition (USP) and consider implications of being listed alphabetically.

Playing the Name Game

Choosing a name you later change your mind about is a costly exercise. Spend time on the name. And consider issues you may have. For example, WebCopywriter has served my business well in many ways, but I hadn't considered the implications of being listed near the bottom of alphabetical directory listings on the web, or that it might be misheard or misspelled. But I've since learnt that lesson.

A good name is short and memorable, with less than nine letters and three or less syllables. A good name will also feel good, so go with your gut feeling.

Some company names that meet these criteria include Habitat, Asda, Comet, Yo Sushi, Kwikfit, Pepsi, HUG.

◆ EXERCISE ◆

The Name Game

I suggest you do this exercise when you are at your most creative. I find my most creative period is late at night and again around 10am. You can do this alone, with friends, or both (it can be useful to get fresh ideas from friends who will look at the possibilities from a different perspective).

1. Invite your friends round or stick the kettle on and prepare for a brainstorming session.
2. Describe your customer's experience. Refer back to the benefits they'll attain from buying your product or service, from walking into your establishment, or visiting your website. Think of words that describe that experience.
3. Flick through US and UK phone directories. Remember, you can use US company names as your own legally, but cannot use an existing UK name. It's great to generate ideas of what makes a good and bad name.
4. Browse magazines, get your scrapbook out, list names that you like.

The great names you come up with may already be taken, so search the Companies House website and, once you are sure it's the name for you, protect it.

Do this by:

◆ Registering it as a domain name. Places you can register a domain name include: www.just-the-name.co.uk and www.easyspace.com. Your domain name is www.yourdomainname.com – the bit that goes after www.
◆ Applying for the trademark of the name. Before you do this, use the Patent Office website to search for your name and make sure it's not already trademarked, or being trademarked. Visit www.patent.gov.uk to search and find out all you need to know about applying for a trademark. It costs £250 per name to apply for a trademark which has to be paid even if your trademark is refused, so read up on the subject. For example, WebCritique was refused on the grounds of being 'too descriptive'.
◆ Register your name with the National Business Register www.anewbusiness.co.uk and Companies House www.companieshouse.gov.uk. As a sole trader, this is not compulsory however.

Secure Your Website Address: Domain Name

Registering your business name online is crucial, so register your own domain name. This will cost anything from £9.99 to £35, depending on whether you opt for a .co.uk extension or a .com extension (.com's are the higher priced).

As soon as you have a domain name, you'll also have e-mail. Anythingwhatsoever@yourdomainname.com.

You are only buying or renting the name. You still need to have the website designed (graphically) and developed (coded and programmed) and pay a host to use their web space. We'll look at all of that in Chapter 10. In the meantime, even if you're not planning to launch a website yet, you may do soon, so secure that name before someone else does.

Hitting the Target

You must consider your target audience when creating your brand. So review your customer profile. Do it now. Go and stick the kettle on and read through.

You should always create a brand that communicates who its audience is: McDonalds' use of primary colours and Ronald McDonald suggest that the audience is kids and time-starved people living fast-paced lives; Apple targets non-conformists and elitists, with the apple symbolic of the apple falling on Isaac Newton's head while Toys R Us clearly targets children.

But don't get too carried away. Stick to your core values and customer identification when branding and not what you want to be seen as, unless that desire fits the values and target audience appropriately. You might want to be seen as fresh, hip and funky, but if you are a business-to-business supplier of electronic equipment or engineering products, you aren't funky or hip. So you would be better off focusing your branding on being quick and efficient or reliable and sleek. Uncover who you are and how your customers will realistically be able to perceive you.

People will pay for items from a brand that oozes quality, style and kudos; as long as it lasts and keeps its promises. This is why BMW, Bang & Olufsen, Cleanfix and other quality manufacturers (of cars, audio/video items, floor cleaning machines) get such good custom despite higher than average prices. Quality branding works for affluent customers and budget branding works for those who are more financially stretched.

Seek the unique in your message

In the previous chapter you researched your main competition to see if you could uncover products, services or extras that our competition doesn't offer; something to make you stand out from the crowd; differentiating factors also known as your **USP** (**unique selling point**).

◆ TOP TIP ◆

Find at least one USP and do everything possible to make sure that USPs are recognised and understood by your customers.

Offer your solution in your message

At your message core should be your USP, so it can be presented to customers at every opportunity. In fact, most great businesses create their strapline from those factors that make them unique.

For example, '*gourmet chocolate gifts with a conscience,*' is CHOCAid's. They've summarised what they provide in one snappy sentence, because what they do is unique. '*Making life taste better,*' – Sainsbury's or '*Every little helps,*' for Tesco, and '*All you need for all you want*' Yellow Pages are other examples. Tesco is targeting consumers who are seeking bargains and low-cost shopping so speaks in the customers' language and focuses on saving money. Sainsbury's aims for the top end of the market, therefore focusing its strapline on providing special quality goods.

According to branding expert Rob Frankel:

'Branding is not about getting your prospects to choose you over your competition; it's about getting your prospects to see you as the only solution to their problem.'

Saga are making over-50s think they are the best solution to a host of problems. Originally experts in holidays for over 50s, when Sidney De Haan bought his first seaside hotel in Folkestone, Saga has since branched out to holidays and cruises on their own ships, a magazine, insurance and financial products, along with radio stations. They know that their target market trusts them more than new entrants to their market.

The Saga Group has it origins in the 1950s, when the late Sidney De Haan OBE identified three critical factors for the company's future success – concentrating exclusively on older customers, marketing to them 'direct' and offering value for money. Today the £19m turnover Saga Group continues to focus on these principles and serves what is the fastest growing demographic group in the UK. Their strapline makes it clear what they offer: '*providing high quality services for people 50 and over*'.

STEP 15: WRITE YOUR STRAPLINE

Define your expertise, your cause and your USP in just one phrase for your strapline and it will enable prospects to make a much stronger connection with what you do.

So what is your USP?

How can you help your customer and improve their lives in a meaningful way? Refer back to your survey results and see what benefits were most sought after.

- Will you be able to make their life easier and simplify things?
- Can you help them be more effective? Make something happen faster for them?
- Can you help them to make more money? Save more money? Learn a new skill? Progress in their career?
- Can you help your customer to be more successful, or successful quicker?
- Can you help them to save time, optimise their time, make tasks easier, quicker or more enjoyable?
- Can you help them be more organised? Better prepared? More informed? More productive?

How can you boost their ego?

◆ Can you help increase their standing in society?
◆ Can you help them to improve their self-esteem or feel better about their appearance?
◆ Can you make them healthier and fitter?

Drill down and achieve clarity. Make the message instantly comprehensible. Your customers should be able to see your unique selling point and exactly what you offer from looking at your logo and strapline.

The final ingredient of your core message should drive action. You want recognition, but you also want people to act, register, buy or enquire. To do this you need to communicate the benefits they'll get from choosing you.

Offer a single, powerful, simple benefit in one sentence.

The Dyson cleaner's features are that it has no bag which results in more suction. The resulting benefits are saved time (no need to change bag as there isn't one), making life easier and providing peace of mind for quality cleaning.

The strapline is simply: the cleaner that doesn't lose suction.

◆ EXERCISE ◆

What Benefits Will Your Business Offer Your Customers?

Brainstorm some straplines here:

_____

_____

_____

Customers have choices – and many distractions. With goldfish-like attention spans when browsing for goods at retail or web stores, your product or service must grab their attention over thousands of others vying for their eyes and wallets. Whether your message is competing with others in the *Yellow Pages*, on the web or on your packaging, it is *crucial*, so stick to one clear and compelling point. This is the précis of the **elevator pitch** – an American entrepreneurial term that helps you convey what you do quickly and clearly, even under pressure.

The Elevator Pitch

Imagine that you're stuck in a lift with Sir Richard Branson or Bill Gates and have 30 seconds to convince them about your business before they're gone; what do you say? You give them the hook – the benefits – in a single paragraph and you *smile*.

Just as a singer stuck in a lift with Simon Cowell might be wise to sing the hook of the best song they've ever written and tell him quickly how he could sell lots of records if he gave them a shot (smiling, of course), you'd be wise to have a 30-second 'elevator pitch' prepared. You never know who you're going to meet, when or where that might be.

Think of all the benefits you offer to customers. What is the single most important one from their point of view?

Write your elevator pitch

Why should this time-starved person take an interest in your business idea or future? Give them one good reason to take your business card and call you.

> *'Luck is when preparedness meets opportunity.'* Oprah Winfrey

Be prepared for every opportunity and you could get very lucky indeed.

The elevator pitch

The premise – we make clothes with conscience.

The endorsement – so and so is on board.

◆ EXERCISE ◆

Write your elevator pitch here:

We make/we work with _____

Who have a problem with _____

We solve that problem by _____

So they can _____

Which means _____

We have _____ on board now too.

You can tailor your pitch to suit potential investors, customers or staff, tweaking it depending on what they most want to get from you and your business. Remember, what's in it for them?

Don't worry if your core benefits and values aren't unique enough. It's better to find a suitable selling proposition that fits your brand, business and abilities, than to struggle to search for one that is so unique you get away from the customer needs and spend lots of time and money in the process of your search for uniqueness.

Truly unique ideas are copied soon enough anyway. So find something unique if you can, but ultimately focus on what you are good at, as that in itself may be enough to differentiate you. First and foremost identify what solutions you provide to customers' problems – that deciding factor in their buying decision.

Find the trigger – unique or not – and you're onto a winner.

Capture the soul of your brand

Once you've captured the essence of your business personality, this clear message and snappy summary of your brand personality should be included in every customer contact, on your website, in your brochure and wherever you can think of including it.

Also make sure your staff and suppliers can contribute to the personality of your business and express the qualities of the brand. Essentially, you must be able to live your message and practise what you preach. As well as being your strapline/slogan, it must also form the backbone of your customer service policies, staffing and management policies and methods.

STEP 16: EMBLEMISE YOUR BRAND

Think Pink! Or Red or Blue or...

Now you have a name, a core message and a brand personality, it's time to translate your brand into an image. As well as shape, you will need to consider which colours reflect your brand personality and appeal to your target audience.

Is the personality energetic, exciting and interesting? Then you might opt for red, orange or yellow. If confidence needs conveying, neutrals can communicate that, while blue and green are seen as stable, calming colours. Are you targeting children or is the company environment likely to be fast-paced with speedy delivery? Primary colours can help you suggest that energy, as can the use of high-contrast opposite colours (such as Sainsbury's orange and blue or McDonalds' yellow and red). Are you targeting women? Is your brand personality feminine and stylish? Consider using classy pastels and low contrast colours and accents to create a solid and confident brand.

Weave it together

Once you've decided on a logo, with or without the company name or initials included, you should consider creating a style template for your company's communications. Detail which font faces and sizes should be used in headers and body text, then define print and web colour values for logos or backgrounds. Ask your logo designer if they can create a style guide or stationery template. All this presents a united brand persona to customers and staff, and can save time and reduce the margin for errors in documents that are dispatched.

◆ EXERCISE ◆

Iconic Icons

List logos that stick in your mind or you remember being impressed by. What do you like about them? Their simplicity, their style, their connotations? Are they icons that represent the brand (such as Apple computer's apple, or Nike's 'swoosh') or do they combine an icon with their company name in a striking font, like The Body Shop, ilikemusic.com or Feel Good Drinks Company?

_____

_____

1 Define your company's core values. Write a list of up to ten core values.
2 Translate them into an image. At this point you may wish to hire a designer or friend who's a graphic artist. Tell them your vision, the benefits, USP and values of the business. Tell them about the personality and any colours you've already considered. Show any relevant material in your Ideas and Inspiration book. Consider also having a go yourself, to see what ideas you can bring to the table. You may not be an artist but you could sketch something a designer may be able to bring to life professionally.
3 Think carefully about which font to use. Again, this may be something for a graphic design expert, but consider sans-serif fonts if you'll focus mainly on web marketing and using your logo on the web more than in printed format (and also opt for colours that are in the web-pallete of 256 colours). Pick serif fonts if you'll be focusing on using your brand in printed format and focusing on offline marketing and printed materials more than on the web.

The Good, the Bad and the Ugly

Let's take a peek at those brands we know well and those we'd rather forget.

The good

◆ Stelios Haji-Ioannou is owner of the easy brand (easyJet, easyCar, easyValue, easyMoney, easyInternetCafe and easyMusic) and self-confessed serial entrepreneur. Inspired by Branson and a company called Southwest in the US, Stelios did his research and launched easyJet as a budget option.

'In easyJet I had two assets, the airline and the brand,' explains Stelios. 'It was the fact that the name meant something to people, so I separated the brand from the airline.'

As a result, Stelios went on to start up his other businesses all connected to the easy brand and not to the airline. They shared common characteristics of outsourcing certain parts of the distribution to the customer and reducing cost to the customer as a result (enabling customers to print their own tickets, for example). By creating a brand that stood for making customers' lives easier, Stelios has built a good strong brand that goes a long way.

◆ Creative branding agency, SNOG, has a fantastic brand name and personality (they have to, it's what they do). It captures their youthful, funky exuberance in just one highly memorable word.

◆ Other good brands include any that are honest, from The Feel Good Drinks Company and organic fashion retailer HUG, to The Body Shop, Virgin and Coffee Republic.

'*There was no rocket science behind building the Coffee Republic brand*,' says Sahar Hashemi in *Anyone Can Do It* (which, by the way, I highly recommend that anyone starting their own business reads).

'*It was a brand built from the heart. It had acquired a soul and with it, a unique voice. Customers believed our voice because we lived up to our word. Honesty is more valuable than any marketing gimmick that money can buy. It is the foundation for a genuine dialogue with the customer.*'

Honesty is the best policy, in branding, business and life.

The bad

When I say 'the bad' I'm not referring to brands that were just plain bad, as nobody can remember them. Examples of The Bad include those who've made big bad branding boobs. Such as:

1. 'Introducing Monday', the brand that Price Waterhouse Coopers spent plenty on branding before checking the domain name, IntroducingMonday.com was available to buy for themselves. This was an error that cost them lots of embarrassment and wasted money.
2. The Post Office rebranded to Consignia, spent a fortune on this, then changed back to Royal Mail plc. Doh!

Learn from the big boys' mistakes. Only rebrand if really necessary and your customers want you to. By contrast, when research revealed that customers approved of rebranding – Freeserve went ahead and changed their name and brand to Wanadoo, and it's worked well, improving perception.

◆ EXERCISE ◆

It's time to revisit your business profile. In the meantime, complete the following sentences:

◆ I am:

_____

◆ I offer:

_____

◆ What makes my brand different is:

_____

STEP 17: PUTTING TOGETHER YOUR DREAM TEAM

Who You Are: Your Partners and Team

Of course, it's not all about you. Your business may need partners and you may need staff either from the outset or soon after. Having a good team is another ingredient necessary for success. And the people you choose to work with you to drive your vision forward will represent you and your brand. So how do you choose? (We look more into how to find the right people to join you in your mission in Chapter 12.)

In the meantime your task is to try to create a dream team where the unique experience and talents of each individual complement what's missing in others, including yourself.

Says Red Letter Days' Rachel Elnaugh,

'At Red Letter Days, it was only when we started to understand the DNA of the business and the brand, that the business really started to blossom. Because when you understand what you're about; totally understand your customer, your offering and your brand image, it's so much easier to make decisions, including who will best fit your organisation.'

In their book *The Beermat Entrepreneur*, Mike Southon and Chris West detail what they call the 'ideal line-up' for any successful business:

1. *The entrepreneur – vision and charisma.*
2. *The technical innovator – brains behind the product.*
3. *Delivery specialist.*
4. *Sales specialist to build revenue.*
5. *Financier, to keep costs under control.*

'*All should be equal shareholders,*' advise Mike and Chris.

This is so that each team member is as committed as you are, but brings their own special qualities and expertise to the table. You will also need to find suppliers and other partners who can complement your own talents.

For example, although the three co-founders (and equal shareholders) of Feel Good Drinks bring complementary skillsets together to work in their company, they've also set up a network of partners to deliver the operational infrastructure of the business, such as designing their liquids, making their glass bottles, packing their products and managing their storage and logistics functions.

◆ TOP TIP ◆

It's all about finding a great support network, both internally and externally, to get you to where you want to be. Even if you are setting up as a sole trader, you may still need to find partners to outsource work to. Focus on accessing the expertise your are lacking.

Perfect partnerships

Online celebration cards retailer Sharpcards.com founder Will Walsh knew nothing much about the web or card trade, so he went into business with people who did have knowledge in those areas.

Sharpcards.com managed to persuade Royal Mail and WHSmith to partner with them, so they could provide white label solutions to these big names. Most people wouldn't think of going to their biggest competitor, but it has worked out well for Sharpcards, because they can benefit from the advertising budget of their partners, and charge for licensing of their card-sending service – a clever proposition.

Sharpcards also focused on drumming up some business development partnerships with companies like Lastminute.com and BT. They did this by employing a very good salesman who sold the notion of card-sending as being entrenched in the British psyche, and therefore a perfect added value service for those companies. The salesman was thinking about what was in it for them. How could this offer add value to what BT or lastminute.com were already offering?

'It's all down to planning. You've got to plan who you want to make the partnership with, narrow that down to a manageable list, and then start pestering them. I got a meeting with Reuben Singh in Manchester, and he said the only reason we were there at all was because I'd e-mailed his secretary 15 times.' Will Walsh

- Plan a wish list of potential partners, narrow that down to a manageable list, and then start contacting them.
- Ask yourself what's in it for them. Listen, get feedback and find out how many loops there are to work through, then work on each of those. You need to work out what they want from you and change your offer to suit, because it usually will need changing.
- Make sure you convey clearly that your service is an added value service their customers will appreciate and why.

STEP 18: DECIDING ON BUSINESS STATUS

There are three types of business status in the UK:

1. Sole trader.
2. Limited company (includes limited companies and public limited companies, the latter are those that have been floated on the stock market).
3. Partnership.

Choosing The Business Structure

Sole trader

The majority of businesses operating in the UK are one person enterprises. The pros of going it alone as a sole trader include:

- straightforward registration
- simple record keeping
- keeping all profits after tax
- the chance to test your market.

However, as there is no distinction between you as an individual and the business, you are liable to pay for business failure out of your own pocket.

Limited company

If you opt instead to trade as a limited company, this means that if the business fails you are less at risk, because the business is viewed as a separate entity. If you are sued, it is the company being sued rather than you personally, and the owners are liable only for the amount invested if the business fails.

A limited company requires at least one director and a company secretary to follow the rules and maintain official records.

To set up a limited company you need a company name and UK address for your registered office, and make payment to Companies House. You can deal directly with Companies House www.companieshouse.gov.uk or have a specialist company set your business up for you. Part of the registration process includes stating details about your new business in the form of Memorandum and Articles of Association. These can be bought off the shelf from legal stationers, or drawn up by a solicitor.

Some companies have been established to set up companies for you. One such business is Quick Formations www.quickformations.com. This can save the hassle and cost of having a solicitor draw up your Memorandum and Articles of Association and other documents.

The obvious pros of setting up a limited company are your lowered financial liability, and the ability to transfer shares easily and even create mortgages to make it easier to borrow money. The company will be able to continue should anything happen to you.

However, as well as a great deal more paperwork to deal with, there are annual returns required by Companies House every year, and you will be liable to pay additional tax via Corporation Tax. Also, anyone can look at your company accounts or check your shareholders' identities should they wish to for a fee, which means your privacy is lessened.

Partnership

If you want to form a business with one or two other people as partners, you can set up a partnership. Each partner receives a percentage of the return of the business, depending on investment (of time and money).

Partners are liable for debts of the business, as is the case with sole traderships. And if one partner gets the business into debt, assets are liable to be seized from other partners to pay off debts if necessary. So be careful who you choose to go into business with. Make sure you know each other are competent and have complementary skills. Decision-making can take longer and there can be difficulties in agreeing on everything or having different visions for the company, but two heads can be more productive than one and can share the burden too.

- Will you be a sole trader? Will you form a limited company or a partnership? There are advantages and disadvantages for both.
- Call the Helpline for the Newly Self Employed on 08459 154515. You can register as self-employed straightaway, and get free one-on-one advice.
- If you have a business idea or name, check with Companies House if it is already in use and request a trademark registration pack from the Patent office, to see if your name is suitable as a trademark.

Keeping It Legal

You do not need to notify Companies House if you are operating as a sole trader. By law you have to notify the Inland Revenue within three months, or suffer the penalty of a £100 fine: www.inlandrevenue.gov.uk. However, before a sole trader chooses a name to trade under, they should check to see if it's already being used. Another sole trader could be using it, maybe even someone local. So new sole traders can still check for registered companies on the Companies House website, to see if a limited company is operating under their proposed name, and can use the internet and local phone directories to check if a sole trader is already using the name. Similarly, it's worth checking with the Patent Office to see if the name has been trademarked. This saves hassle, especially later on if you decide to become a limited company and register with Companies House.

By law, you must also display the name/s of the owners of the business and an address on all business stationery and at your premises (unless you are using your own name).

Now that you've cracked your brand and key messages, know which status your business will take (and some legalities), you're almost ready to create the right marketing materials and choose the appropriate strategies. But first you need to write your business plan and crunch some numbers.

Map out and mastermind your future, it's time for the business plan.

CHAPTER FIVE

How to Plot Your Findings and Map Out Your Future

,

Creating Your Living, Breathing, Organic Business Plan

By the end of this chapter you should be able to answer the following questions:

+ How will I get from where I am now to where I want to be?
+ How will my business operate?
+ What do I need to do and what finance am I likely to require?
+ Where do I go from here?

You'll also learn what to put in your business plan – an 'organic' business plan that will not only be used by you as a living and growing plan, but can be used to show your business off in a positive light, should the need arise for funding or exiting the business.

Why write a business plan?
It's easier to be passionate about the future if you can see where you are going and how you are going to get there.

Everybody needs a map, direction, a guide to help them get to where they are going. Your business is simply too important to leave to chance, just like your life. A plan is especially important if you intend to untie that safety net of a salary to jump into the abyss of self-employment. 'Jump and the net will appear' may be a valid quote, but it's best to have a plan A (and B).

You absolutely must know where you want your business to go and how it is going to get there.

You can do this by figuring out your destination and writing down what actions need to be taken and by whom, in order to achieve that goal and arrive at that destination.

Furthermore, facing the great unknown and all the challenges that go with it becomes so much easier by approaching it in manageable chunks, little by little.

Eating an elephant

As Bobby Hashemi of Coffee Republic says:

You can eat an elephant if you approach it one bite at a time.

A good business plan communicates ideas and tasks, goals and strategies, and enables focus and direction – by focusing your mind and defining long-term objectives.

Map out your idea. Write your recipe for success, your business blueprint. Only then will you know which ingredients to select, the tasks and actions you'll use to blend together into a successful small business. The business plan will clarify your data-dumped information.

Reinforce your belief

Keith Milsom, who runs AnythingLeft-Handed.co.uk, also uses plans to help reinforce his motivation and passion:

'*Know where you're going and have a clear plan and clear objectives with times and measurable outcomes. Have a clear business plan that tells you how you're going to get from where you are to where you want to be, plus some financial forecasts of what's going to happen on the way. Planning reinforces your passion too, because **it's easier to be passionate about the future if you can see where you're going and how you're going to get there.'***

You should write a business plan in order to:

◆ Set your objectives and goals, how you will achieve them and by when.
◆ Fine-tune the business and optimise time and resources by identifying priorities and discarding less crucial tasks.
◆ Benchmark the performance of the business.
◆ Persuade investors to invest or financiers to finance.
◆ Enter a business award to gain recognition and prize money.

And always write your own business plan. Feel free to use this template but create the guts of the plan yourself. This is crucial, otherwise you won't understand the plan.

STEP 19: CRAFTING YOUR BUSINESS PLAN

Be realistic when writing your business plan, because over-zealous projections can create problems later on and can damage credibility to those who can see through the generous forecasts.

What to Include In Your Business Plan

Your business plan needn't be packed with detail. You can elaborate in your marketing and operations plans. The business plan should be fairly short and concise.

◆ EXERCISE ◆

Your business plan

Include the following content:

1. **Name**, **address and contact details** of the business along with the **business status** (ie sole trader, partnership, limited company, franchise).
2. **Contents** page with page and section numbers.
3. **An executive summary** which defines your entire business proposal and details the key points, including the objectives and purpose of the business plan. Provide details of when you intend to start up, plus any track record within your industry. Although the executive summary is often the last part of the plan to be written, it goes on the first page and will be read by people unfamiliar with your business, so make it clear. Also bear in mind that some financiers will only ever read this section of the plan, so it needs to stand out and summarise everything clearly.

Sketch a rough executive summary here, referring back to your elevator pitch and business profile:

_____
_____
_____

4. **Business and products** – what progress do you perceive will be made once launched, and in which markets? Talk briefly about ownership and describe the product or service.
   ◆ What will make the business unique or different? How will it be differentiated from other similar products or services?
   ◆ What are the benefits you will offer to customers? Will you save them time or money, make their life easier or safer…?
   ◆ Are there any disadvantages or problems?
   ◆ How are you planning to develop and grow the business?

Refer back to your business profile.

My products/services are special because:

_____
_____
_____

5. **The market and competition**– explain which markets you will sell in and segment the market into groups that you will compete in.
   ◆ What is the size of each market segment and your intended share of it?
   ◆ Are there any noticeable market trends, changes in tastes or growing market areas?
   ◆ How might these affect your business?
   ◆ What drives the market?
   ◆ Are there any growth forecasts for the market segments in which you operate?
   ◆ What contribution to profit do you think each part of your business will make to the overall business?

- Give details about the primary competition. What do and don't they offer? Are there any windows of opportunity? Who supplies, distributes or partners them? Who are their biggest customers? How does their product or service compare to yours? What are the key differences and how do they market their business? (Use your competitive intelligence report notes about your competition from your fact-finding mission).

My market:

_____

_____

My competition:

_____

_____

The main advantages of my product/service over my competitors' are:

_____

_____

6. **Marketing and sales** – outline how you intend to reach your target markets and give details of price, product and positioning.
   - Where will your product or service be positioned in the marketplace – as a high quality item with a high price, or as a budget item or service? Is there high demand? How will you price your service/products?
   - What are the unique selling points of your product or service and which of these are of primary importance to your customer?
   - Who will be the end user?
   - How will you reach the end user and promote your business?
   - What selling methods will you be using: face to face, telesales, website sales…? Do you think your idea has a great angle that might get you some good PR – some local or national TV, press or radio coverage? Would the idea translate well to the internet for online selling, or would it sell best at exhibitions and events, or over the counter?

Revisit this part of your business plan once you've completed the chapter on marketing.

My customer:

_____

_____

My marketing:

_____

_____

7. **Management and personnel** – detail the proposed or existing management team structure and list management members' expertise. Outline any areas of weakness that could be improved, plus how they might be improved.

- ◆ How will you employ and train staff?
- ◆ What skillsets will you have in place and need?
- ◆ Who will work for you from the outset and what do they bring to the fore?

My dream team consists of:

_____

_____

The areas I will outsource or learn skills in are:

_____

_____

8. **Operations** – describe assets and premises that you have or intend to purchase.
   - ◆ What machinery, equipment or premises will you need to buy or do you own?
   - ◆ Will computers/IT be used within the business and how?
   - ◆ What communication, customer services and operations procedures and processes will you put in place?

My business location will be:

_____

Because:

_____

_____

9. **Financial performance** – include your financial forecasts and estimates of what you will be likely to pay out and receive for the first year.
   - ◆ List direct costs and outgoings as you see them.
   - ◆ Figure out cashflow by reviewing dates your payments will come out and ensuring that enough money will be coming in to the business to cover them.
   - ◆ If using the business plan to raise finance, use these figures to predict what cash you are likely to need (adding up to 20 per cent contingency to any funding requirement outlined in your forecasting).
   - ◆ Explain why the money is needed. Are you funding start-up? Are you funding growth? Acquiring new customers? How so?

Revisit this part of your business plan once you've completed the next chapter on cash flow and finance.

I will need the following assets to start up and throughout my first year:

_____

_____

_____

◆ **EXERCISE** *(cont)* ◆

I estimate the annual cost of employing staff/outsourcing to be:

_____

_____

_____

I intend to pay for these by:

_____

Grants

_____

Loans

_____

Own money

_____

Creditors

_____

I can obtain credit from the following suppliers:

Supplier:	Days' credit:	Monthly order estimate

To fund the business I need to borrow a total of:

_____

I can afford to pay the following per month in loan repayments:

_____

The security I can offer is:

_____

10. **SWOT analysis** – create a one-page analysis of the strengths, weaknesses, opportunities and threats for your business. Your market research will help. Refer back to the ACE assessment you've already made notes on. Outline briefly what you intend to do to make the most of your strengths and opportunities, and how you intend to smooth out creases and deal with threats.
    ◆ Strengths: you may have a great name, idea or niche product.
    ◆ Weaknesses: however, you might foresee low profit margins initially, problems recruiting decent staff or may rely on a few customers for the bulk of your sales.

▶▶

◆ EXERCISE *(cont)* ◆

◆ Opportunities: your biggest competitor may have gone out of business or you may have seen the chance to target a new and growing market.
◆ Threats: your biggest competitor may have grown or is now offering a unique service or product that you are unable to offer. A new competitor or economic pressure could also threaten your business start-up.

Strengths:
_____

Weaknesses:
_____

Opportunities:
_____

Threats:
_____

11. **Visualise the future** for your business and what you want to achieve. Then create objectives, tasks and actions. Refer back to your written goals.
   ◆ How do you intend to grow your business and achieve your targeted market share?
   ◆ Where do you want the business to be in one year, three years and five years?
   ◆ List what you want to achieve and by when. Note who will carry out the action or task to make this happen. Explain how you intend to reach these targets and exactly what needs to be done in order to do so.

My ultimate goal is to:
_____
_____

I expect to achieve the following over the coming years:

Year 1
_____
_____

Year 2
_____
_____

Year 3
_____
_____

◆ **EXERCISE** *(cont)* ◆

12. **Include an appendix** to add more detailed information, such as market research, company or product literature. You might also include more detailed financial forecasts in the appendix, along with CVs of key team members, target customer details or anything else that will add credibility to the business plan.

Show the plan to trusted friends and experts to get feedback. Find out if there were any parts of the plan that they didn't fully understand when they read it, and tweak accordingly.

Have you revealed the answers to these questions in your business plan:

◆ How will I get from where I am now to where I want to be?
◆ How will my business operate?
◆ What do I need to do and what finance am I likely to require?
◆ Where do I go from here?

'Study your idea on paper before launch,' advises easyGroup's Stelios. 'Stay hands-on in the early years and work hard.'

How Much Time Will You Need?

Now you've created the plan, you need to include a **task plan** to put into action. For example:

Action	Time or funds needed	Date due	Desired goal/target
Night class	£35 12-week course	June-Sept	Improve marketing know-how
Gather advice			
Market research			
Finalise business plan			
Check legislation			
Look for premises			
Obtain equipment			
Produce promotional material			

Obtain premises			
Obtain planning consent			
Register with authorities			
Formulate policies/ procedures			
Employ staff			
Open days			
Launch and manage business			

Getting Credible

Finally, remember that if your business is different and is challenging the status quo, being unconventional and 'on the side of the customer' can all make it harder to convince suppliers and financial institutions that your idea will work. Additionally, as a start-up you have no track record. Hence the importance of a great business plan backed up by valid research and the passionate determination of the people involved.

Do you believe in it? If you don't others won't. Your business plan must convince you that your idea has a chance of working, otherwise you'll be hard pushed to convince the gatekeepers of potential finance.

'Diligence is the mother of good luck.' Benjamin Franklin

Talking of finance, it's time for the maths bit. Sorry.

CHAPTER SIX

How Much? Figuring Out the Finance: Costs, Funding, Grants and Loans

The Biggest Obstacle – Money, Money, Money

Now that you've got an idea and a rough sketch of that idea, you need to find out how much you'll need to start your business up, get it off the ground and maintain it while you feed and clothe yourself and your family. This is must-have info, before you make the jump and start up, up and away!

Not only will you need to raise enough cash to get you started, up and running, you'll also need to be able to control cash flow of the business while it operates, including the management of working capital, while having a million-and-one other things to do.

This chapter examines what kinds of costs can be involved in business start-up, giving you a number of examples and providing details of resources for funding and grants for UK small business. Cashflow, keeping records, and profit and loss forecasting will also be examined, along with methods to keep costs down – a key to initial success.

Lack of cash flowing through the business and spare capital in times of need is *the* number one factor why most small businesses fail. Ultimately, understanding the money side of your business is a crucial success factor, regardless of your disdain for maths at school. (*Moi aussi* – I preferred French.)

The amount of attention you pay to cash flow can literally mean the difference between life and death for your business. *So take it seriously*!

Simon Woodroffe, CEO of Yo Sushi, Ambassador for UK Entrepreneurship and author of *The Book of Yo!*, echoes this:

'Cashflow is everything. In terms of small business there is only one rule to be very rich. And that is don't run out of cash, especially near wages day. Because, if you don't run out of cash you can carry on trading and then you have the capacity to get very rich.'

Questions you'll need to find answers to include:

1. How much money are you going to need to start up and what about ongoing overheads and expenditure?
2 Will you need to raise finance and borrow money?
3. When will you need that capital? How will you afford to pay it back?
4. What sources of finance are currently available to you?
5. How many sales/customers will you need to break even, be back to zero and starting to turn a profit?

STEP 20: KNOW HOW MUCH YOU NEED TO LAUNCH

If you are starting a business from scratch, your start-up costs will likely be more than if you start a business that is a franchise or a network marketing opportunity (where products and materials are generally provided). When tallying up the initial costs, you need to consider everything: where will your business be located and what costs will that entail? At home? If so, what equipment and additional costs will you incur, from postage, stationery and marketing materials to internet connections, tax and loan repayments, and so on. Or maybe you'd need to hire an office/shop outlet and pay for fittings and fixtures, rent and parking?

◆ EXERCISE ◆

Tally up your start up costs

- ◆ What will your start-up finance be spent on and how will it justify its expenditure?
- ◆ What will your sales cycle be? (From first contact to invoice and payment, how long will this be?)
- ◆ Will you have to lease a shop, if so what is the cost of that?
- ◆ Will you need shop fittings, to hire a designer or builder?
- ◆ What machines or equipment will you need?
- ◆ What will your initial stock cost (if selling products supplied elsewhere)?
- ◆ What will your product development and manufacturing costs be (if making your own products)?
- ◆ What time will be involved (if selling services)?
- ◆ How much packaging will you need and what are those costs?

List other miscellaneous items you can think of here.

_____

_____

When you've totalled up your start-up costs, consider how much working capital you'll need to keep afloat before sales take hold, and still afford to pay wages and loan repayments.

So now you need to focus on working out what cash will be coming in and what cash will be going out, long after the start-up period is over.

STEP 21: KNOW HOW MUCH YOU NEED TO EARN

I asked Dame Roddick if she found managing cashflow an obstacle when she first started out. She says:

'I had no understanding of what cashflow was. It was all about how much did it cost, how much could I sell it for and would what I got back pay the bills and put food in my mouth? I remember my husband, Gordon, before he went off travelling for two years, saying you'll have to do £300 per week to pay for the overheads of the shop, the mortgage and everything and put enough into the business for new products. That was my entire business acumen.'

Evidently, knowing how much you need to survive is the key figure. That lady with zero business acumen went on to turn her business into a £700million company with 2,000 shops across 12 timezones, and to be made a Dame of The British Empire. From small acorns, oak trees grow.

◆ TOP TIP ◆

> Be aware of how much cash you have and need – your incomings and outgoings, and be realistic when calculating how much you'll need to start up.

STEP 22: GET TO GRIPS WITH CASHFLOW

How many Sales/Customers will you Need to Break Even/Stay Afloat?

Before you look to sourcing additional finance you should try to get your head around cashflow and the basics of book-keeping.

Keeping control of your books is about making everything tally, by keeping good records that are clear and enable you to know exactly what money is coming in and out of the business and how things are going financially.

Cashflow, in essence, is the balance of all the money that flows into and out of your business on a daily basis. Cashflow is not the amount invoiced, or amount owed by your creditors or debtors. It is the actual payments that are received into the business and the actual payments that go out of the business.

Many businesses that are still profitable go out of business because they got into a cashflow crisis that caused them to close down.

By planning out your bank statements and forecasting your balance at any given time, you will be more prepared for dips and have longer to deal with potential problems, rather than facing a sudden nasty cashflow crisis and having to phone your bank manager in desperation every couple of weeks.

To track each penny that goes in and out of the business, you should use and adapt the monthly expenses worksheet below and use the cashflow forecast worksheet on page 99 as the basis for your own.

Cash inflow

Cash from sales and commissions – some retailers have good cashflow because they make purchases on credit and are paid by customers in cash. However, some businesses sell on credit, so that the inflow of cash is delayed until the payment is made. For these businesses credit control must be in place.

Monthly expenses worksheet

Monthly payments	Column A	Personal expenses	Column B
Rent/mortgage payments		Clothing/Shoes	
Groceries		Entertainment/CDs	
Council tax		Laundry	
Insurance (home)		Training/Education	
Insurance (life)		Memberships/Subscriptions	
Insurance (health)		Dental care/Prescriptions	
Insurance (vehicle)		Eating out	
Insurance (pet)		Travel (rail tickets/taxi fares)	
Car expenses (fuel, oil)		Birthday gifts/Charitable donations	
Loan repayments		Other	
Credit card payments			
Childcare		**Savings/Investments**	
Car payments (other finance)			
Other payments			
Home operational expenses		**Column B TOTAL**	
Broadband/Dial-upconnection			
Telephone		**Total monthly expenses (C):**	
TV licence		**(total of columns A + B**	
Digital TV subscription		*(use in cashflow forecast)	
Gas		**Total monthly non-business**	
Electricity		**income (D)**	
Water			
Household maintenance/Repair			
Household supplies			
Other			
Column A TOTAL		**C – D = MINIMUM INCOME REQUIRED FROM BUSINESS**	

Cashflow worksheet

	January	February	March	April	May	June	July	August	September	October	November	December	TOTALS
SALES INCOME/RECEIPTS													
All sales/invoiced													
Cash from debtors													
Capital introduced													
TOTAL SALES INCOME (a)													
VARIABLE COSTS/RECEIPTS													
Postage/printing/stationery													
Motor/travel													
Professional fees													
Bank interest/charges													
Tax to save													
VAT payable or refund													
Drawings													
Repairs/renewals													
TOTAL VARIABLE COSTS (c)													
Gross profit (a - c = B)													
FIXED COSTS/OVERHEADS													
Monthly non-business expenses*													
Rent/rates/water													
Payments to creditors													
Salaries/wages													
Insurance													
Heat/light/power													
Telephone													
Internet													
Web maintenance/metrics													
Web hosting													
Capital payments													
Other													
TOTAL FIXED COSTS (d)													
Net cashflow (B – D)													
Cumulative cashflow P/L													

* See page 98 (c)

Cash outflow

◆ General overheads and salaries.

◆ Stock and raw materials.

◆ Capital expenditure and work in progress (common for service businesses which do the work for a month or six months and are paid on completion).

◆ VAT and tax.

◆ Capital repayments to owners, investors and shareholders or lenders, such as the bank, including interest and any drawings/salary.

You need to make sure your estimates of sales are fairly accurate and that you estimate correctly how long it will take to achieve those sales. Always overestimate the time it will take to achieve a sale or task or goal, that's just the way it is in business. Make sure you also estimate overheads and costs as well as you can.

Things always take longer and cost more than you think they will, so plan for that in your estimations.

To arrive at your cumulative cashflow profit/loss figure, as marked * in the cashflow worksheet, you must add up or minus the preceding month's net cash flow figures.

For example, in both January and February net cashflow figures might reveal a loss each month of £200, which would make the cumulative figure for February -£400. If a £300 profit was seen in March's net cashflow, then the cumulative figure for March would be -£100 (a cumulative loss of £100). The aim is to ensure the final cumulative figure for the last column is a + figure rather than a - figure. In your first year of business, this may not be possible.

Consider 'what if scenarios' and adjust accordingly. For example, 'what if sales should drop by 10% for three months consecutively? How would that affect forecast figures?'

Work out how much you'll need to bring in to start showing a profit. This is your **break-even** point.

◆ TOP TIP ◆

Purchasing larger items just before the end of a VAT period, rather than at the start of a new one, can help with cashflow.

What Is Profit and Loss?

If a business has no profit, it would have to sell assets and seek finance to continue trading, so profit is paramount to a business in the short and long term.

A profit and loss account provides a snapshot of the company's actual trading performance over the last accounting period (a year) and reveals all sales and profits, costs, expenses and losses, plus tax provisions and payments. Everything is recorded when a sale is invoiced or a purchase is made.

As a small business, you can either outsource everything to an accountant, but learn the basics of book-keeping so you know how to record your paperwork for your accountant; or you can read a book and get to grips with the accounting yourself. Try:

◆ *Understanding Business Accounting for Dummies* – UK edition by Colin Barrow, John A. Tracy.
◆ *Book-keeping and Accounting for the Small Business* by Peter Taylor.
◆ *Understanding Small Business Accounting* by Phil Stone.

Keeping costs down

In the meantime, here's some advice from small business owners currently operating their own companies.

Beware hidden costs

Says Michael Parker of online sweet retailer, A Quarter Of:

'Keep things simple and keep your costs down. Create a model/plan on a spreadsheet for your business, and keep tweaking it to make sure things work. Plan for everything. When we first had the idea we worked out the costs and what we thought we'd make. The danger is that you think you're making money but you're not because of hidden costs. We worked out the cost of the sweets, how much we'd sell them for and the postage, but didn't take into account the cost of the box, or that the weight of the box might take it into the next postage level, or that a three kilo jar may make 11 rather than 12 bags of sweets, because you have to go slightly over rather than under, which means all your profit calculations go out the window.'

Tally up rather than down when estimating costs and down rather than up when estimating sales.

Stock and distribution

Alan Clayton of gourmet chocolate gift business, Choc Aid, explains:

'The most expensive cost for us is distribution. The bigger the manufacturer is, the smaller their distribution cost, because there are vast economies of scale. Whereas I'm trying to deliver small amounts of chocolate at the moment to lots of little shops, which is the most expensive way you can do it.

Stock when starting out is the biggest obstacle of the lot, because when you go out to buy the products from the manufacturers, they'll ask you how many you're going to sell and you don't know, so you almost inevitably end up buying whatever their minimum production run is, which means you probably won't get the price. We're lucky in a sense that chocolate has a shelf life of about a year, so we do have that grace.'

The lesson is to be prepared for hidden extras and find out what minimum stock orders are when you do your research.

Overheads

'Keep your overheads down. Focus on profits, not revenue.' Owen Weeks of IT consultancy business, SSS Ltd.

From start-up and beyond, keeping overheads down is worthwhile to get to the next stage of growth, but don't be so focused on doing so that you make mistakes. Sahar and Bobby Hashemi wisely hired a full-time store manager who had coffee bar experience for their launch shop (they made only one mistake with that, because she had not managed anyone before, but more on business leaders' collective mistakes later).

The upside was that the Hashemi siblings managed to keep their costs down by collecting bagels each morning and delivering French pastries themselves to nearby offices. They invited friends round to place stickers on cups because they couldn't afford cups printed with their logo at first.

More ways to cut costs

Think of ways you could keep your running and launch costs down.

To save money also consider the following:

- Buy furniture and equipment at garage sales and auctions.
- Barter and trade. In the past I've had stationery printed at a discounted rate in return for offering my services to them for a discounted rate. There are possibilities to trade and barter your services with those of others. So go out and find them. Networking on online communities is a good place to start.
- Recycle paper. Feed paper back through your printer and use the blank sides for rough drafts or to make small notepads.
- Look at cheaper providers for utilities, such as Telecom Plus or Skype.

STEP 23: KNOW WHERE YOU INTEND TO OPERATE FROM

Location, Location, Location

Running a business from home has many benefits – which explains why the number of people working from home has risen so dramatically in recent years. The UK has the highest number of homeworkers in Europe, with 7 million – almost a quarter of the entire workforce and, according to Datamonitor, that is expected to increase to 53%.

From missing that awful rush hour traffic and being able to sit in the garden and work when the sun makes an appearance, to being able to work flexible hours and keep costs down – the benefits of working from home are plenty.

Business benefits of working from home

◆ Home workers have a ten second commute to work, rather than a lengthy and sometimes stressful journey, saving them time and stress.

◆ There are generally fewer costs, no additional rent, petrol, parking or lunchtime drink costs.

◆ Home workers have more flexibility with working hours and can check their e-mail or do other work anytime, day or night, to fit in with their lifestyle. 'If I need to work late or check a late e-mail I don't have to go out of the house,' says freelance copy-writer Eppie Hutchings.

Business benefits of working from rented office space

◆ Self-employed professionals who work from home tend to work longer hours. This can be seen as a drawback or as a benefit. For those who are bogged under with workload, the ability to work anytime of day or night is a good thing, as it helps to get control of the workload. However friends and family may see overworking as a drawback.

◆ Despite the fact that societal attitudes, technology and the internet have made working from home more acceptable to clients than it used to be, there is still a notion of hiding the fact that you work from home (or alone) from your clients. Having a 'proper' office gets rid of this uneasiness about the professionalism of working from home and visually sets you up as a more legitimate company. However, some customers don't have a problem visiting businesses in a home, so it really does depend on your client base and their mindset. 'When my customers want a meeting, they come to my home, and we are able to have meetings in a relaxed comfortable space in the dining room or even in the garden,' says Eppie, who would rather buy a bigger house or convert her garage than move to a rented office. 'If sessions overrun, I can provide food without having to send out for something and, as a result, more of my clients are turning into social contacts as well as repeat-business customers, and my referral rates are also improved.'

◆ If your clients are more formal you can feel more confident about inviting them to your place of work, although there are many executive meeting rooms available for hire. This has been a particular benefit to Sherry Madera of ionicadvisors.com. 'We found immense benefit from the "correct" address on the letterhead for building credibility with our client base,' says Sherry. 'We moved into an office space with a W1 area code for the express reason that it reflects the nature of our firm and many of our clients would assume our offices would be in the West End.'

◆ Generally there are fewer distractions, and establishing a cut-off point between work and home is much easier. It's psychologically less taxing if you can physically leave your office at night to go home and relax. Artist Diana Janicki agrees, 'for me the benefits of moving to office space outside the home include a more disciplined daily schedule and a healthier social interaction on a daily basis, plus an opportunity to network and create more business, and to brainstorm and collaborate on projects more effectively.'

Decide whether you need to rent or lease space or can work from home.

If you need to lease a shop, you'd be best advised to find a surveyor. It took Coffee Republic seven months from receiving a loan letter from their bank to securing the lease on their first outlet, so be prepared for a long search.

Consider the square footage and cost, the history of the location, the availability of parking, area crime rates, notes from touring the area on foot, quality of public services nearby, local business climate and neighbouring shops plus utilities. Also evaluate your prospective site in relation to your competitors' locations.

STEP 24: KNOW IF YOU NEED TO RAISE FUNDS, WHEN AND HOW

Consider the risks and consider how much of your own capital you're willing to risk on your business venture. Do you have any savings or non-work related income already? Many banks will only loan capital if you are showing commitment by putting in some of the cash yourself.

If you're not prepared to risk some of your own readies, then you can't expect anyone else to risk their money, bank included. And the least expensive money to use for anything is your own money; it comes without interest. It costs you more long-term to borrow from banks or loan schemes and even more from venture capitalists and private lenders.

If you have savings, use them first.

If you do need to take out some kind of loan, make sure you read the small print, know how much interest you are paying and how much per month your repayments will be, to help you decide whether you can realistically afford them. Don't shoot yourself in the foot before you've begun.

How to Finance the Business

There are two key types of finance. Private sector and public sector, excluding your own money and cash borrowed from friends or relatives.

1. Private sector finance consists of lending from banks and equity finance from Venture Capitalists or Business Angels. If you're seeking £1,000 to £1 million, consider the Enterprise Finance Guarantee (EFG) which replaced the Small Business Loan Guarantee Scheme or pitching to Venture Capitalists (VC's) and Business Angels (BA's). If you need much less to get your business off the ground, your own money, cash borrowed from friends, relatives, seeking out soft loans or approaching the banks will be more viable (and will help ensure you retain control of your business, rather than being governed by VCs and BAs.)

2. Public sector finance consists of grants and loans. So, before you approach anyone for seed capital, you should look into the possibility of receiving a grant (money you needn't pay back) or a loan (money you do pay back, with interest). See the Useful Resources chapter at the end of the book to find details of websites that help you search for relevant grants.

So, you can borrow cash from friends or relatives, the bank, from venture capitalists or business angels, commercial finance houses, or Enterprise Finance Guarantee (www.bis.gov.uk).

Your particular business location (eg near to the docks) or industry (eg IT training or childcare) might have specific funding or grant schemes, particularly if you are undertaking any kind of research and development. Other sources of finance include equity in assets, such as your home or car.

◆ TIP FROM THE TOP ◆

Your family may not be able to lend you the money you need, but a member of your family could act as a guarantor for any loan you take out, so look into this option if necessary.

Grants

Grants generally depend on the kind of business/industry, the location of the business and what the money is to be used for. There are many grants available for research and development, or you may qualify for a New Business Grant in some areas of the UK (for example, see www.buildingupbusiness.com).

Some Enterprise Trusts and Government bodies provide grants to help towards the costs of a new or redesigned website, or can subsidise other areas of your business, such as marketing or grants to help pay for training.

As a potential employer you may be eligible for a grant that will help towards paying staff wages and NI contributions, or may find an industry body that provides grants on the basis of job creation.

And let's not forget the trusty overdraft; ideal for short-term financing, when you need to buy some equipment this month and have plenty of sales guaranteed for next month, but don't have the cash right now to finance the equipment purchase.

A combination of an overdraft, grant money, soft loans and equity could give you what you need for your start-up and working capital.

So consider all the options before approaching the kind of deep-pocketed financiers who'll expect a chunk of your business in exchange for putting their hands in their pockets. Retain control by being wise about finance.

Finding grants

To source potential grants, loans and other finance for your business:

◆ Sign up to www.j4b.co.uk, a grant-finding service.
◆ Phone your local Business Link and ask if they can help you source some grants that might be available to you.

- ◆ Contact the Department of Trade and Industry (DTI) to see if you might be eligible to apply for a Regional Enterprise or Investment grant, or a grant for Innovation or Research and Development Support.
- ◆ Contact your local authority and TECs/LECs to see if they can provide you with a marketing, training or employment grant.
- ◆ Search the web for details of local philanthropists who you might be able to persuade to become sole investors.
- ◆ Search the web for specific sources, such as the European Social Fund, or the Youth Incentive Scheme (see www.esf.gov.uk).
- ◆ If you are aged between 16 and 30 contact the Princes Trust to see if you are eligible for any funding from them (visit www.princes-trust.org.uk).
- ◆ See if your business fits the criteria for the Government Small Firms Loan Guarantee Scheme.
- ◆ Apply for Start Up Awards that offer cash prizes, and much-coveted publicity that goes with winning, such as Shell LiveWIRE, HSBC Start Up Star or www.startupawards.co.uk.

Soft loans

The following authorities may be able to provide you with a soft loan, where you can receive a capital repayment holiday for the first few months (during start-up phase) and can generally borrow £5,000 to £10,000 unsecured:

- ◆ local authorities
- ◆ Local Enterprise Trusts
- ◆ TECs/LECs
- ◆ industry associations, such as British Steel and British Coal.

Government assistance

Sharpcards had to change their global domination plan into a plan of natural organic growth, when the internet crash happened and they lost half their staff. They fortunately had a solid business, so redid the numbers and managed to secure £200,000 from their original seed capital investors, but the third round of funding would have been even harder to secure, until Will heard about the Government's Small Firms Loan Guarantee Scheme (which has since been replaced by the Enterprise Finance Guarantee and lends to viable businesses with an annual turnover of up to £25 million).

'Every loan you get from a bank means you usually have to give some kind of private guarantee, and what the Government has done is, if you're not in a position to give a guarantee, they will guarantee 70-85% of a loan on your behalf.'

Straightforward retailing is not within their scheme, so Sharpcards applied under the licensing area.

'We ended up getting £100,000 through that scheme. I wasn't in a position to guarantee that sum, as I'm sure many people aren't. It's a really good scheme and we pay 3.5 per cent interest and then another one per cent to the Government.'

If you need large capital but don't have a guarantee or guarantor, this option is worth a try.

◆ TOP TIP ◆

Some accountants advise that loans be used instead of shares where possible to raise extra finance. Loan interest is seen as an allowable expense against profits, but dividends on shares are not.

Private sector – venture capitalists and business angels

So what if you need a large sum to start your business and don't get anywhere with the Small Business Loan Guarantee Scheme? How do you approach that? Julie Meyer, founder of First Tuesday and Ariadne Capital advises:

'You've got to be a great ambassador for your business if you want to raise finance for it. You need to be out there going to networking events and at every private investors' event. Be out there telling people what you're doing. It's a job for an extrovert, a communicator, and when someone says they might be interested in investing, you need to know how to close them. What's it going to take to get them to invest that £100,000 into your business? What can you do to incentivise them, discount on the next round evaluation? Find out. You have to get people to like you and want to work with you, and then you have to know how to get them to part with their money.

There can be a great business idea or venture that would not make a good venture capital investment. For venture capitalists, and this is where some of the problems happened during the dotcom era, they really need to see how they can make ten times their money inside of three years, and that's just not possible for a lot of businesses. So that's where friends' and family's money, angel investors or Government loans can source businesses that don't fit that criteria.'

Coffee Nation's Martyn Dawes used his belief in himself and his idea to secure the money he needed to kick-start his business. His last chance to attempt to raise seed capital took place five years ago when Martyn 'gave it his all' in front of 'business angels' in Cambridge. He left with pledges for £100,000 in seed capital. Dawes says:

'It was a huge turning point. Back then, the company essentially consisted of four coffee machines. Now we're seeing turnover of nearly £10 million a year from our units in shops and garages and we've signed a big contract with Tesco, which means that Coffee Nation has really arrived.'

He offered his investors 20 per cent of the company – which meant that he valued himself and the firm at £500,000 on the back of four coffee machines and his passionate vision.

'They're backing you. You've got to convince your investors that you won't give up. That day was about my passion for Coffee Nation: you've got to create a vision for your backers.'

Equity finance

If you do need to sell some of your equity in your proposed business in order to secure the finance you need, seek equity partners who have skills you are lacking in and can really bring something to the business. If their skills and knowledge base complements your own, an equity partnership can reap rewards. When speaking to potential business partners, always go with your gut feeling and ensure they have a measurable track record in doing what you need them to do within your business.

Take retail chief Philip Green's advice and seek out investors who can add value other than monetary value to your business:

'My first port of call, if I was trying to get money, would be to someone who could add another dimension or leg to the business rather than a purely financial party.'

That's exactly what Sarah McVittie and Thomas Roberts of Texperts.com did, giving shares to a web developer friend who then built their software at no cost. He will reap the benefits along with the founders and it gave him an added reason for being as committed to the project as the co-founders.

With thousands of users, many corporate accounts and some great publicity, Sarah and Tom are in profit just a couple of years in, and are more than covering their low fixed costs, which include renting the number, paying their team and for text messages sent.

Dame Roddick also sold a chunk of The Body Shop's equity in return for a private investment that would enable her to franchise the business.

Don't bank on it

The bank should be your last port of call before approaching equity finance and after trying to find grants and soft loans or your own/family money, as banks charge high interest and are in business themselves to make money out of you. The bank is very useful to secure overdrafts, but take small manageable loans only after you've looked into the other potential sources.

Don't be disheartened if you do visit the banks and find them not interested. The main banks all rejected Coffee Republic for a variety of rather pathetic reasons, such as 'coffee is a fad' or 'too inexperienced in catering', but after months of persevering a branch of NatWest wrote to the Hashemis to agree in principle to their loan request, on condition the manager could approve the site.

Similarly, Sally Preston of frozen baby food company, Babylicious, got knocked back from the banks.

'We were unable to raise finance on what I felt were acceptable terms. It was deemed by banks to be a very good idea, but a bit too obvious. So I ended up walking away from a salary and remortgaging my house. With two small children who are six and eight now, that's a huge risk, so I've needed buckets of self-belief and the support of my partner.' Sally Preston after leaving her consultancy job to start up Babylicious in 2001

Dame Roddick too was refused a bank loan implicitly. So her husband Gordon went to the same bank and got a £6,000 loan without a problem, before handing the money to his wife. She says:

'Nothing has changed much there. It's still easier for a woman to raise money for a new kitchen than it is for a business. Banks are just housekeepers of money. It's just about control and getting their money back. So in terms of finding ways to finance your new venture, you have to be more creative.'

To Risk or Not to Risk

CASE STUDY
Yo Sushi

Simon Woodroffe was certainly creative when coming up with ways to finance Yo Sushi while the grand opening took place.

'When Yo Sushi opened, I didn't have the money, but we had a lot of people coming in through the door, so it looked good but I owed an awful lot of money to builders. Luckily I'd got these sponsors on the door – none of them had given me very much, in fact Honda just left me one motorbike for six months. But I said thanks very much and called them my sponsors,' Simon explains.

'I heard that one of the big building companies who I owed £250,000 said "give Simon the credit he's asking for, because if it all goes wrong, those big Japanese giants who are behind him will pay up." So I was very lucky – it was a good perception, I got away with it, and we managed to pay all the bills. A year later we didn't have any of those equity people there.'

Simon funded Yo Sushi with the help of private investors and through mortgaging his house. He was risking big money, but it paid off.

'I funded it with my entire assets and life savings, everything I had in the whole world – my flat and everything, which was £150,000 at the time (having got divorced). I put the entire amount in – putting myself completely on the line. I had £100,000 from the Government loan guarantee scheme and £50,000 from a private investor, plus some very expensive leasing. But if you add all that up, it still only came to half the money I needed.

'I didn't want to start up a small restaurant, I wanted to start something that was a big deal. So I went ahead and signed the lease and got the whole thing going, with less than half the money I needed. I had various equity investors hovering around in the background. So I put myself right on the line.'

Luckily, the risk paid off and Yo Sushi now has 45 sites in the UK and is expanding internationally. Simon retained 22% of the business, which was sold in 2003 for £10 million. Primary Capital has since sold Yo Sushi and Simon no longer owns a share in the company. He has since received an OBE and launched the YOTEL brand.

It's not about how much you're prepared to risk, as every entrepreneur I've spoken to has taken some element of risk, with many remortgaging their homes, it's also about speed. How fast or slow do you want to grow?

Fast or slow? Manic or organic?

STEP 25: LOOK AT THE POSSIBILITIES FOR GROWTH

Growth will involve strengthening your team, your suppliers, hiring an operations manager or managing director, writing a new business plan and seeking new finance. It's a question of whether you grow organically or manically. Coffee Republic did the latter, so did Yo Sushi, others have grown organically by funding their business via sales and profits only, avoiding borrowing large sums of cash. Let's look at some examples of both.

Manic Growth

> **CASE STUDY**
> **Coffee Republic**
>
> *'The key isn't just bringing the dream to life,'* says Sahar Hashemi in *Anyone Can Do It. 'It's about creating a living business and managing the inevitable questions about growth that follow.'*
>
> Coffee Republic grew from one to 1,000 stores in five years and was quoted by Deloitte and Touche as the second fastest growing company in the UK in 2002. They were opening a new store every two weeks, so had to hire a property manager and project manager to handle the store fittings, and a training manager to bring staff up to speed.
>
> They planned that they needed £600,000 to grow the business to six stores within one year, and would therefore need to sell some of the equity. After taking out an advert in the Venture Capital Report, they found a sole investor and were able to start paying themselves salaries. At the 13 store mark, the Hashemis were able to meet their initial long-term aim of introducing a 'sip and browse' concept to the UK by opening outlets in Waterstones book stores – growth was helping them achieve their dreams, and fast.
>
> Their third business plan was to have 35 stores up and running within two years, and to meet this objective they calculated £4.5 million was now needed. An old friend of their father's was able to invest, and suggested they float the company and reverse it into an existing shell company already listed on AIM. This left them with 2 per cent of what was now a group, rather than a limited company, a long-term investment. With this, Coffee Republic became a PLC, with a finance director, HR director and receptionist at HQ. And with a public company comes all the trappings: a board of directors and board meetings, shareholders, advisors… and, ultimately a loss of personality or control.
>
> *'The focus shifted from external (customers) to internal.'* Bobby and Sahar exited the business in 2001 but have since returned.
>
> *'Suddenly, the business given life by your personality needs you to become all the things that would have hindered success at the outset,'* says Sahar.

Speed kills. If you or your company aren't ready for growth and move too fast, your business could suffer the consequences. If you do grow, prepare yourself well for it – wear your seatbelt!

Growth can be very difficult to manage. If you create lots of overheads, get in more staff and end up operating under capacity you can run the risk of undertrading, or you could find the opposite risk of having too much business to be able to handle. Getting the balance right is the critical part.

Says Rachel Elnaugh:

'I think of the two, your business is probably slightly safer errring on the side of overtrading rather than operating unprofitably. Because it's much easier to bring in resources and add to your business than it is to scale it back. As Simon Woodroffe always says, "Before you go to your next stage of expansion always be bursting at the seams, so don't scale up until that." That's a much safer way of growing than predicting over the next five years years we're going to triple in size and therefore we're going to get big new offices now and lots of staff and structure, and then find that the business doesn't come in to meet it.'

And that's partly what happened to Red Letter Days. Ironically, a few months after speaking with Rachel, her business, Red Letter Days went into administration. Part of this was due to the rapid growth and subsequent overspending by a new CEO, the appointment of whom Rachel now admits was a mistake.

On returning to the business in 2003, Rachel did all she could to rescue the business from the debts it had incurred, but it was too late. Now, you may wonder why you should take advice from someone whose business has failed, but crucially, someone who has been *both* hugely successful *and* has also failed, can pass on what they've learned. For that reason, and because of her incredible determination, I've re-interviewed Rachel since the Red Letter Days collapse and you can read her story on page 228.

Another risk of growth is to duplicate mistakes from your first business model.

'Pay attention to the detail of a business, those mistakes in the business model may be small now but they are compounded by growth.' Stelios Haji-Ioannou, easyJet

Each stage of the growing process must be planned for strategically and monitored. You need systems and checks in place. Especially if you opt for manic fast growth.

Of course, just because you think big doesn't mean you have to subsequently think fast, as this can create challenges and move your business out of your control.

'Speed is a major obstacle', says Dame Anita Roddick, 'You want to rush, you want to open up more shops. There should be lessons on how to be more reflective, which you never are when you're successful. You don't stop and think or reflect. Reflection and time to reflect is something you tend to lose when you are successful. It becomes so seductive, there's this hurry sickness which is the modus operandi of growth, but in reality you never question yourself and ask why you should grow.

Should we have stopped at 100 shops and just had a great life? We should never have gone onto the stock market, we would have been wealthier, more independent, more political, had we not gone down that route, but it would have taken us four or five years to get to where we were. Looking back now I would never have gone that route and would have gone for organic growth'.

Organic Growth

Just as some people profit from thinking big and growing fast, some people (often pure dotcoms) avoid taking risks, which also pays off.

CASE STUDIES

The Garden Pharmacy

Having researched the likely footfall and competition, Harry Ganz set up The Garden Pharmacy in Covent Garden, funded with a very small bank loan.

'We started off very modestly and it's been our principle for the past 20 years to reinvest into the business, and not rely too much on loans, so as soon as we could pay off the bank loan we did. We've never spent more on the website than the website generates, so the advertising spend has increased by 30-40 per cent only in line with the turnover.'

This playing it safe strategy is about quality of life as much as it is business success, for Harry.

'Apart from the fact that many businesses fail because they do spend more than they've got, if you spend in line with increasing profits it takes a lot of pressure off you and you can be more relaxed in running the business,' he explains.

'Watch your overheads and don't let them run away, and that's the most important thing in terms of making sure you're always financially viable.'

'See your expenditure as business-building investments rather than as costs. If your expenditure is made up of costs and not investments, you need to rethink and avoid investing in costs.'

Heaven @ Home

Amanda Strowbridge of beauty business Heaven@Home took out a personal loan and got her credit rating right up to fund her product development and business growth.

'That's the most important thing you can do if you haven't got investors on board, you need to make sure your credit rating is fantastic, because then you can borrow,' advises Amanda. She says to any small business owner or start up, 'you cannot be scared of debt, that's the main thing. If you're scared of debt, don't even go into business.'

'Be prepared to remortgage your house at some point, which I'm doing at the moment.'

Despite taking risks to grow the business, Amanda has taken a slower approach to this than Simon Woodroffe's rapid growth model.

If an idea is a winner but you don't have the necessary funds, organic growth can be the best way forward. 'We've had to hold back,' says Amanda. 'Sometimes you can be a victim of your own success, because we get a lot of phone calls already. We could go out and market the business heavily, but literally not be able to fulfil those orders, and then you've got a company that doesn't make its customers happy. So it's been organic growth as I'd rather go slowly but surely.'

Three years after launch and Amanda's business is doing well. *'It's just coming good now. You start off and you get busier and find that you're doing 15 jobs, and that's the hardest part, two years in when you're doing all the roles, and you haven't got any investors on board.'*

A year after that difficult phase, growth and development are firmly on Amanda's agenda, and she now has two investors in the business, has reduced her outgoings by ten per cent having restructured her debt, and has developed a product range of her very own – the Heaven@Home brand.

Dreams

Some entrepreneurs grow organically but still take risks, because they want to retain control and full ownership of their business. Take Mike Clare. He financed his first Dreams Bed store by selling his prize MG, using his house as collateral against an £8,000 bank loan, and borrowing £4,000 on his credit card (telling them it was for an extension to his kitchen).

Each evening Mike would deliver the beds he sold himself. Nearly 20 years later and Dreams is a £100 million sales business and he owns 100 per cent of the company. He's achieved his dreams without losing control to outside investors or a board and has avoided the stock market. A dream business indeed.

If you want to grow organically rather than securing large sums of finance, consider what risks you can take and then:

- Focus on finding more paying customers.
- Persuade them to buy more frequently (via a monthly retainer, with some kind of loyalty incentive).
- Persuade them to spend more each time they do buy.
- Invest profits back into the business.

Many 'small' businesses, with less than 50 staff, fear that growth to a medium sized business, with 50-249 employees, will mean losing control of 'their baby', as is quite often the case. However, there are strong benefits to growth, be it manic or organic.

Embracing Growth

Improved credibility

Improved credibility and stronger suppliers are benefits of growth.

'There's very much a tipping point in business. When you're tiny you have to do all the chasing and nobody wants to know you, because your orders will be small. It's not even economical for the post office to collect from you, so you have to take everything to them. But when you get to a certain size, suddenly the local post office, couriers and manufacturers are more interested in you, and the manufacturers will ring to ask you to stock their goods which makes life a lot easier.' Michael Parker of online sweet retailer, A Quarter Of.

Of course, in growing you are increasing the workload (two shops = double the work) and it's still a roller-coaster ride of risk. But you can minimise it by ensuring you are ready to grow effectively.

Clone what works

Once you've hit upon a strong business model that is working, having broken even and proved your idea, you may be ready to embrace growth. This means you clone what you have; clone everything that made it successful and roll it out. If you've kept in tune with the detail in the first business/store, you won't be cloning mistakes. If you're not ready, you'll make repetitive and costly ones.

Whichever route you take to growing your business – organic or manic – make sure you take time out to reflect; to smell the roses and enjoy the journey. Remember success is just as much about the journey as the destination, so live it, breathe it and enjoy it.

◆ EXERCISE ◆

List how you might obtain funding. What approaches will you take? List possible sources here.

_____

_____

_____

List how you might find a suitable equity partner. Refer back to your personal assessment and Chapter 4 on branding. Review your weaknesses and seek out partners who are strong in these areas.

_____

_____

_____

◆ TOP TIP ◆

You can get tax relief on loans, so as a sole trader or partner any interest paid on a business loan is an allowable expense as a deduction against tax, when working out your taxable profits (which means you are allowed to deduct this interest from your turnover).

Running the Business Finances

Tips to manage and improve your cashflow:

1. Agree terms before taking on work. Be aware of new late payments legislation for small business. See Bepaidontime.co.uk or Promptpayers.com to learn more.

2. Lease or rent/hire where possible as paying instalments can conserve immediate cashflow.

3. Check you can afford large purchases in good time, and that you have the funds to grow the business. Figure out the working capital that would be needed to fund a ten or 20 per cent monthly sales increase, so that your business only grows at a rate that you can afford to finance comfortably. Restrict growth or seek additional working capital where necessary.

4. Invoice as soon as possible and say thank you for early payments. One trick is to send a sweet with the invoice to entice early payment, or include a stamp or SAE.

5. Improve cashflow in the short term by offering time-sensitive incentives to customers to buy sooner rather than later, or pay quickly (discounts or freebies).

6. Focus on lead generation rather than brand awareness when marketing.

7. Pay commission on receipt of payment rather than receipt of order or invoice, to delay payment of the commission and encourage customers to pay promptly.

8. Don't give out more credit than you could afford to lose as a bad debt. Monitor late payments.

9. Identify seasonal peaks and troughs and aim for good stock control, keeping just enough stock to service your customers. Aim to speed up stock delivery times and sell off any old or unused stock if necessary, to raise extra cash during periods of poor cashflow.

10. Speak to your accountant about any tax breaks, such as capital allowance claims for IT expenditure or computers. Also see if your local authority provides grants for broadband.

11. Reduce costs, increase your prices, sell more, or try all three.

STEP 26: UNDERSTAND BOOK-KEEPING

Book-keeping Essentials

If left to pile up, paperwork can be the bane of a business's existence. Decide on a method of recording your 'books'. Book-keeping simply makes your paperwork easier to deal with by providing a system that tells both you and your accountant exactly what is going on in terms of incomings to the business and outgoings from it. This, in turn, helps you keep track of where your business is ultimately going (and makes it much easier, when it comes to tax self-assessment).

All money coming in (incomings) and going out (outgoings) must be recorded in order to keep track of your cashflow situation and to keep tax records (by law). This means you need to keep a record of every sale and every purchase.

Keep:

1. Sales records
2. Purchasing records
3. Bank statements.

How to keep sales records

File **Sales paid** and **Sales unpaid** invoices in two separate files.

Create a simple procedure as routine, to keep track of all sales you make.

1. For each sale you make, issue an invoice with an original number and keep a copy for your files and place in the Sales Unpaid folder.
2. Once paid, pay the cheque into your bank account and write the invoice number, payment date and amounts on the paying in slip stub.
3. Remove the invoice from the Sales Unpaid file and write 'paid' and the date it was paid in the top right-hand corner.
4. Place the invoice in the Sales Paid folder with the most recent paid invoice at the top, so invoices will appear in order they were paid, rather than in order they were issued.

If you receive any non-sales income, such as grants, tax rebates and so on, simply enter them in the cash book underneath the entries for Sales Income.

Cash sales

Shops that take cash from sales and spend it on wages can lose track of their accounts and the tax and VAT office will be more suspicious.

To avoid complications:

1. Use till rolls or EPoS cash summaries as sales invoices.
2. Keep records of money going in and out of the till and reconcile daily.
3. Keep any receipts from purchases made using money from the till.

At the end of the month, check both cash book balance and bank statement balance are the same and correct any errors.

Purchases

Receipts or invoices must also be kept for each purchase made, including cash purchases. Keep a cash book to record all cash payments you make and keep any receipts for cash purchases in a box file labelled Petty Cash, or on a spike.

You and your accountant can decide on suitable headings for your cash book, which, computerised or hard-copy, will record all the money coming into and going out of your bank account.

Tax

As a self-employed person you need to pay tax. If forming a limited company you should hire an accountant to do your more complex accounts and work out corporation taxes. However, if a sole trader, you will need to complete a self-assessment once a year and send it to the Inland Revenue. You will also need to save some of your profits each month to pay the tax bill the following January. There are penalties for missing the deadline.

As you register with the Inland Revenue you will automatically receive your Self Assessment Tax Return in good time. Telephone the Inland Revenue helpline for Newly Self-Employed on 0845 915 4515 for more information.

STEP 27: UNDERSTAND VAT, PAYROLL AND BANKING

VAT

The registration threshold is £70,000 so you don't have to register until you are making that turnover. Being registered for VAT means that you must also charge VAT on all goods and services that you provide, and enables you to claim back VAT that you pay on your own purchases. If your customers are mostly VAT-registered it might be advisable for you to register for VAT voluntarily.

VAT can be described in three steps.

1. You buy supplies at a price that includes input tax.
2. You sell goods or services at a price that includes output tax.
3. You deduct the input tax from the output tax and pay the difference to Customs and Excise or receive a refund if the input tax paid is more than the output tax received.

For more information on VAT call 0845 010 9000 or visit www.hmce.gov.uk

At the end of each month or quarter (accounting period) businesses registered for VAT must complete a one-page VAT return for Customs and Excise. VAT returns and money owed must be sent to Customs and Excise within a month of the end of the VAT accounting period.

How to register for VAT
Download and print form VAT 1 from the Customs and Excise website: www.hmce.gov.uk/business/vat/vatregist.htm

What Is Payroll?
Payroll is a method used to calculate and produce payslips. At its most complex there are a range of complications involved, including:

◆ processing statutory sick pay and maternity pay
◆ pension contributions
◆ family tax credits
◆ personal or student loans.

Where can I find help?

Find out details of PAYE deadlines and which forms need to be filed by when, along with other useful advice and information on PAYE and payroll at a variety of resources:

♦ Employers' helpline – 08457 143143.
♦ Inland Revenue website – www.inlandrevenue.gov.uk
♦ The Institute of Payroll and Pensions Management – www.ippm.org or 0121 712 1000.
♦ Your own accountancy firm. I can recommend Dawkins Lewis and Soar at www.dlsa.co.uk and Cranleys Accountants at www.cranleys.co.uk, both based in Hampshire.

Opening a Bank Account

You will need a business bank account. Before you open one, compare them and see which offers suit you best, and which charges are the most competitive. You can find out at www.bba.org.uk or www.moneyfacts.co.uk Choose wisely and you could save yourself a lot of money and hassle later on. You may already have a good relationship with your existing bank, and they may offer a good small business banking service. It is still worth checking out the alternatives.

Questions to ask banks when comparing

♦ What is their charging period (monthly or quarterly)?
♦ What are their standing charges?
♦ Do they provide interest if in credit?
♦ Do they offer a cheque card and/or debit card/ATM card?
♦ Do they provide telephone banking and/or internet banking?
♦ What are the charges for debits, standing orders and credits?
♦ What are their overdraft arrangement fees?
♦ What rates of interest do they offer?
♦ Can they offer you negotiable terms to give you a better deal?

Questions to ask yourself

♦ Will you be making many deposits or withdrawals each month?
♦ How will you transact: over the phone, online, or at your local branch?
♦ Who do you know who runs their own business? Can you ask them who they bank with and whether they're happy?

Now that you've evaluated the money situation in detail, it's time to pick and mix your marketing strategies and collate your materials, so you are ready to shout from the rooftops about your new business as soon as it's launched.

CHAPTER SEVEN

How to Sell – Marketing and Selling Your Products and Services

It's all very well having a great product or service, but if you can't find a simple way to communicate your idea to your audience, you won't be selling very much.

By the end of this chapter you should be able to answer the following questions:

- How are you going to find new clients?
- How will you market and sell your products or services?
- How will you build a customer base?
- How will you generate repeat business?

This chapter examines the different methods of marketing and selling, from writing a press release and networking, to using customer testimonials and referrals. Practical exercises will help you sharpen your strapline, your list of benefits and high quality marketing literature that will encourage action. Plus, successful entrepreneurs reveal which marketing strategies have given the best return for them on their marketing spend.

Where will you begin? It's not just a case of distributing a few flyers, running an ad in the local paper or sending a press release out. Telling people what you do, in essence, is what marketing is all about. If you've completed the exercises in the previous chapters you'll be able to tell people exactly what you do.

Marketing is simply doing this – informing people – and keeping them informed. Whether you tell people what you do over the phone, through the media, face-to-face or in writing, you have to partake in this telling people activity, and then, once you've told them, you need to tell them again and remind them – a constant exercise.

As the public, we are used to being bombarded with millions of marketing messages, each with its own promise. This means that it is not quite as simple as just telling people. Your message needs to stand out from the rest in order for the audience to remember it, so your marketing message needs to be memorable and give its audience a reason to listen up, pay attention and take action.

Furthermore, that message needs to be repeated through various means to maximise impact and have people remember you.

◆ EXERCISE ◆

Which marketing messages can you remember? Are there any that stick out? Are they recent or old messages that have stuck in your mind? List them here.

_____

_____

_____

_____

Consider why they might have been memorable. What medium was used? What words? What perception do you have of that brand as a result? Did they use a catchy slogan, music or memorable imagery?

_____

_____

The Marketing Pie

You've already worked out the benefits of your product or service and identified your unique selling point (USP). You should also have some ideas for a strapline and have a compelling elevator pitch prepared. So now you are ready to pick the marketing strategies that will suit your business and objectives best. Following that you can craft your marketing messages to suit.

STEP 28: FIGURE OUT WHICH SLICE OF THE MARKETING PIE YOU NEED

Before you write your marketing literature and key messages you need to choose which of the various marketing strategies will make up your marketing 'circle'.

You need to figure out:
◆ What slice of the marketing pie or 'circle' you are on.
◆ What ingredients or tools you will need.
◆ Which strategies you should use that best suit that position in the circle (ie your objectives).

To do that you need to consider which of these objectives holds the most importance for you and your business at any given time. Do you need to:

1. Find and attract prospects and customers, make contacts, gather leads, collect referrals? Having enough numbers to call and e-mails to e-mail is **slice one** of the marketing pie.
2. Convince the prospective customer to book an appointment to allow you to present to them or persuade them to enter your offline or virtual store by getting their attention is **slice two**.
3. Closing the deal and getting the sale once you have their attention is **slice three**.

4. Providing the service or product and then following-up contact to request a referral or testimonial from the customer is **slice four**.

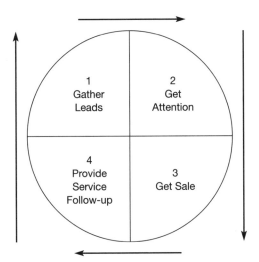

As you begin to follow up and contact each customer again to seek repeat business,
you are then gathering more leads to go back to slice one.

As a brand new start-up business you will almost definitely need to begin with **slice one**
of the marketing circle. You need to attract prospects – names, faces, leads, contacts –
people to get in touch with, likely customers. This is the first part of the circle. Attracting
prospects to you and making first contact. Part of this lead generation process should
include launching a website and driving traffic to it through web promotion.

If you already have a collection of business cards from people you have not spoken to
since you met them, have leads or e-mails you have not yet replied to, or prospects
who said call me back in a few months – then you need to focus your efforts on following up 'slice four'.

If, however, you find that following up doesn't tend to lead to many appointments or
repeat sales, or find prospects are already using your main competitor, then you will
need to focus on **slice two**. Get their attention, appeal to their needs and wants, lower
prices or offer added value, do whatever it takes to compel them to act.

If you find yourself getting plenty of meetings, but minimal sales as a result, or have
plenty of customers entering your store but few buying, or don't know where you stand
with new clients, you need to focus on **slice three**, closing the deal and getting the sale.

Whichever needs the most work at any given time is the part of the pie you should focus on.

Once the sale is closed, the order fulfilled, the customer is satisfied and you've gathered
more contacts from that customer by way of referral, you can start over again at **slice one**.

STEP 29: PICK AND MIX YOUR MARKETING STRATEGIES

Marketing Strategies

Sir Richard Branson's trademark is outlandish publicity stunts. He will do pretty much anything to promote the Virgin brand, be that driving a tank down Fifth Avenue in New York to introduce Virgin Cola™ to Americans, playing a drowning man in Baywatch, or flying his hot air balloon across the globe.

The majority of us don't have the budgets that Branson has (and I'm not sure if a tank would fit down my road), so it's time to figure out what strategies are viable for you and your budget.

Of course, which marketing strategies, ingredients and tools you use will depend on which slice of the pie you are on, and what your objectives are.

Here's a list of marketing strategies to pick and mix, depending on your objectives:

- Writing: articles, checklists, reports, tip lists, newsletters.
- PR/publications: press release submission to targeted media.
- Public speaking: at seminars, workshops, conferences, meetings.
- Direct mail: sending sales letters and printed materials through the post.
- Telemarketing: contacting prospective customers over the phone.
- E-mail contact: e-mail updates or e-newsletters.
- Referrals: happy customers refer someone they know to you/recommend/pass on leads.
- Testimonials (happy customers put their review of your services/products in writing).
- Networking (mixing and swapping contact details/information/advice with others) including business and social networking via ecademy.com, Linked In and Facebook.
- Trade Shows/Exhibitions/Events (taking a stand to sell products, get feedback, gather leads).
- Giveaways (using competitions and prize draws to incentivise action).
- Face to face selling (once appointment is booked, to persuade a prospect to buy).
- Via website (directing leads to the website).

What are your objectives?

- To raise awareness of your brand or new product/service? Then you'd use articles, a promotional event, sponsorship or targeted advertising – plus PR.
- To raise credibility and have people trust you? Then you'd try public speaking and articles, networking and running seminars or workshops for your target audience, or collecting testimonials and case studies from happy customers to use as evidence of how good you are.
- To generate leads, referrals and sales? You'd focus on networking, direct contact, follow up, phone and e-mail marketing and giveaways.

Let's examine these strategies in more detail.

Networking

If you are at **slice one** of the marketing pie and your objectives are to make new contacts, get leads and referrals, source expertise or create a support network of skills and knowledge, networking is a great idea/strategy.

However, networking should become an integral part of your overall annual marketing plan, as it will improve your chances of success. Here's why.

In his book *The Luck Factor*, Richard Wiseman deduces from many years of research that 'lucky' people tend to do the following more than 'unlucky' people:

1. Smile
2. Use eye contact and open body language
3. Relax
4. Listen
5. Stay in touch with contacts
6. Network.

In terms of networking, it's because the more people you meet, the greater chance you'll have of bumping into someone who will affect your life in a positive way.

Richard Wiseman explains:

'By chatting to Sue, you are only a handshake away from the 300 people she knows on first name terms. But it doesn't end there. Each of Sue's friends also knows 300 people on first name terms. Sue might introduce you to someone who is likely to know someone else who is interested in referring business your way, hiring you, becoming your partner, and so on. You are only two handshakes away from roughly 300x300 people – 90,000 new possibilities for a chance opportunity, just by saying hello to Sue.'

From *The Luck Factor* by Richard Wiseman, published by Arrow Books. Reprinted by permission of the Random House Group Ltd.

So get out there and interact with people.

> *'"People buy from people" should be engraved on the door of every start-up.'*
> Mike Southon and Chris West, authors of *The Beermat Entrepreneur*

You need to get your face in front of other people and be likeable. Network. Refer business to others, chat and broaden your contact base. Just don't forget to smile!

Going online and joining networking groups on the web can be a great way to learn networking if face to face networking makes you cringe.

Which specific area, market or industry would you do well to have connections in? Go on the web to search for forums, networks and discussion boards that focus on these areas, where people are likely to be discussing topics you can comment or advise on.

I only realised myself that I should take time out to brush up on my own networking skills when I was nominated as one of Internet Decade's Top 100 'Movers and Shakers' in the last decade of the internet. A dark champagne-filled hotel foyer was the scene, and I did manage to boldly walk up to some people whom I'd added to my wish list earlier. But I did waste some of that networking opportunity, sitting on my own figuring out what to say. I could have used the opportunity much more than I did, had I known what I know now.

So take action:

◆ Brush up on your networking (and listening) skills.
◆ Join online networking groups.
◆ Attend networking events and free seminars to meet others who might be able to help your business. Try local business agencies and chambers of commerce first.
◆ Keep an objective in mind when networking. Is it to find a book publisher? Find a venue for an event? To find more customers in a certain area? Focus on your objectives.

Build relationships

Grow your network on a regular basis for the long-term. Just a little bit of effort each week will add up over time. Focus on **quality** rather than quantity. Low quality efforts in high quantity just create a poor reputation that lots of people hear about. Better to spend the time to build a quality relationship with the right person over time, focusing on their needs first.

As you grow your network, politely ask for referrals from your support network. Consider who you want to target. The idea is not necessarily to approach them directly (unless you have the gift of the gab), but to have one of your support network warmly introduce you.

Give introductions, information and advice of your own within your area of knowledge and support network. See more about networking online in Chapter 11.

Referrals

When you first start up in business you won't necessarily have any existing customers to get referrals from, so ask friends and family, local tradespeople and shop owners; go online and seek referrals from members of networks, from your bank manager or accountant, club and society members and people at the local pub or club. Ask journalists and suppliers or potential suppliers for referred business. 'If you don't ask you don't get' is just as valid a concept in business as it is in life.

◆ Ask people you know to introduce you to others who might benefit from your products or service.
◆ Ask customers for referrals, they may not think of doing so themselves but may be more than happy to recommend you or give you leads, if you remind them occasionally.

Then, when you have a clutch of customers, communicate regularly with them. Tell them you would like more business or are looking for new business and want their referrals or testimonials. Show them exactly how they can recommend you; give them the tools to do so.

◆ TOP TIP ◆

Catalogues and many online stores offer vouchers to those who refer a friend to them. You could offer an incentive or rely on the quality of your product or service. On the internet this concept has grown with **affiliate marketing**, where 'referrals' come from sites related to yours who then earn a commission on any sales that come via their link to your website. We'll look at this in more detail in Chapter 11.

Articles

Raise your credibility and position yourself as an expert in your field by writing articles and sending them to e-zine and website publishers, along with regular magazines. Your article should be useful to readers and include a link to your website. That way, wherever your articles are posted, you can get website traffic from there. Secondly, those who click to your site from an article will already see you as a credible source of information.

◆ EXERCISE ◆

1. Write a regular column/article and/or newsletter filled with witty observations or useful tips and advice, such as ten tips on finding a babysitter to suit you, or seven ways to improve your website. It could be part commentary, part information and resources. Upload this to your website, post it on online forums and networks and/or submit it for publication in targeted publications. This is one of the best ways of establishing yourself as an expert in your field.
2. Include a good signature line at the end of your article, eg 'Written by author, writer and web consultant Cheryl Rickman of www.webcopywriter.co.uk'
3. Submit your article to relevant offline and online publications including those listed in your media file with your permission granted for them to reprint the entire articles, including the contact details, copyright notice and signature line.

If you 'can't write for toffee', as one of my clients once said of his writing skills, consider hiring a writer.

- ◆ Source a directory of freelance writers or, when networking, keep a lookout for a local freelance writer who writes about your field/market/industry.
- ◆ Make contact with your story or self/business profile, but make it interesting. Writers need a good source of contacts for articles they write, both now or in the future. Some will even be able to 'ghost write' for you – write or revamp an article as if written by you, with your byline for submission to targeted publications to build credibility and raise awareness.

Advertising

You will notice that I rarely discuss actual advertising in this chapter. This is simply due to my own personal experience of advertising not working (offline) and the experience of every single business person I've ever interviewed who says 'advertising doesn't work', excluding three (Pants4him.com who successfully advertised in gay and male grooming publications and on taxis, Feel Good Drinks who had a successful campaign running 30-second TV adverts on the plasma screens that are now installed on London buses and Lastminute.com who advertised on London buses when they launched).

The many other people I've spoken to have found advertising to be expensive with minimal or zero return.

PR is free, and you get better exposure than if you advertise. You can generate thousands of pounds worth of free advertising by getting editorial coverage in a daily newspaper, so it's worth investigating using PR and articles as strategies to potentially save you money. Furthermore, editorial coverage holds much more credibility than blatant advertising and can therefore achieve a much better return on a much smaller investment.

If, however, you've done your research and know that a good deal of your customers do find your product or service through advertising, then consider the options. See how your competitors advertise – where, how often?

I know an accountant who has discovered that he can earn a decent enough living and grow his business 'organically', simply by selling his services to vets, doctors and medical related companies in a certain radius of his home. So he advertises in targeted vet/medical trade publications and local newspapers and generates good business as a result. He's carved out a niche audience, so has a wealth of expertise servicing that, creating more business from new targeted prospects who see his credibility and expertise within their profession as a bonus. So targeted advertising works for him. Referrals also work well for him too.

◆ TOP TIP ◆

If you do advertise, you must track each response you get to see which advertising is working. So make asking how customers found you/heard about you an integral part of your first communication with the customer.

PR and publications

PR is one of the best marketing tools at your disposal if you get it right. By sending snappy news items to newspapers and other media, you could get some free publicity for your business.

'PR is the cheapest marketing tool available. If you have an innovative service which reduces prices to consumers, you can shout about it and contest the established players. Both consumers and the media

enjoy hearing about a new, good deal or seeing the overpriced and inefficient practices of incumbents being exposed.' Stelios Haji-Ioannu, easyJet

♦ Get quoted. Next time you see an expert quote in a newspaper or magazine and it's something you could have said, on your area of expertise, write a letter to the editor outlining your experience and provide your own comment on the article you've seen.
♦ Draw up a PR calendar and invest in a wall planner to indicate when to send your releases to your list of targeted media and publications. Use the internet to find dates that you can tie into your own business.

Remember that glossy magazines on the news-stands work months in advance, so if you are sending a press release about an activity or date happening in the New Year, you'd need to send your press release to the glossies three months prior to the event or date in order for it to make the New Year issue.

Sign up to a PR course. Paula Gardner at DoyourownPR.com has a superb online newsletter and PR course by e-mail that I can highly recommend for any business start-up. Here's just one of Paula's tips:

'Choose five of your dream magazines, newspapers or trade publications and really get to grips with the content. Read with your PR head on and think to yourself 'Why did they do a story about her – what makes her so interesting?' 'What is the hook of the story? What makes this story news?' And then … can I come up with an angle or story that is even better than that?'

Once you've written a snappy press release, following the 'who, what, why, when, where and how' format of news stories, submit to targeted publications as you find them, along with your media list.

Also submit using a free service, such as www.prweb.com or www.click2newsites.com/press.htm and www.pressbox.co.uk or pay a small fee to submit your release at www.responsesource.com

STEP 30: CRAFT YOUR MARKETING PLAN

The Marketing Plan

Give yourself a monthly strategy plan. This way you can focus on using just two or three strategies per month (eg referral building and networking, or getting PR and net-working) – and these are wholly dependent on your objectives for that given month. A plan will help you know where to start, and what materials and strategies to use at any given time (slice of the pie) – whether to focus on a brochure, generating leads or following up leads, for example.

Create a marketing plan annually to include raising brand awareness, sales targets, growth actions, costings, resources and strategies. Use a variation of the action plan on page 93 to plan your tasks and goals in terms of marketing or the marketing worksheet on page 139.

You will certainly need to know where in the 'circle' you are when you implement any marketing action plan, as this will directly affect which strategies you choose to use.

◆ EXERCISE ◆

Write the marketing strategies you've chosen in your plan (eg direct contact/follow up plus writing/PR)

_____

_____

Write down which slice of the marketing pie you are on currently – what you have and what you want (in terms of business), eg about to launch business, have no clients (two prospective), have list of leads to make first contact with.

_____

_____

Write down your goals for the end of **month one** and **month three** and write down what achieving those goals would get you (eg retail therapy or investing into the business to enable you to employ staff). It's important to have goals and rewards in all your plans, eg to have seven clients by the end of month one and 20 clients by the end of month three. I would have enough money to get more stock (month one) and could go on a break to Paris and pay off the Visa (month three). Have clear goals such as more appointments booked or quotes supplied, more orders or hours invoiced, and so on.

_____

_____

At the start of each month write a list of daily and weekly actions to implement the marketing plan, complete your marketing pie, reach your goals and objectives, eg make three calls each day, practise selling in the evening, solicit a testimonial from a happy customer and/or referral from another, visualise success and spend time on preparing materials.

_____   _____

_____

You will need to take care of your daily actions as soon as you can each day during your marketing plan focus period. If there is time left over you can focus your efforts on website promotion, admin, or other areas such as lead generation.

STEP 31: SELECT THE MATERIALS YOU'LL NEED

Marketing Materials

What slice of the pie/circle you're at and your objectives will determine which strategies you use; and which strategies you use will determine what materials you'll need. So if you add networking to your marketing menu one month, in terms of materials you'll need business cards, a website to direct people to and a polished elevator pitch.

What you want to achieve will affect which strategies and marketing materials you will need to focus on at any given time.

Marketing kit

You should now have written your customer profile, elevator pitch and a business idea profile. Plus you've brainstormed words and language, created a logo, found yourself a good name and written a strapline. You also know what your objectives are, what slice of the marketing pie you need to be on and what you plan to do. So before you write your materials, you need to know what else to include in your marketing kit.

You'll need to have a 'kit' ready in case those people you call want more information from you. You won't need to have all of the items listed below in your kit. It all depends on the kind of information you want to present and the kind of impact you want your materials to have. So pick and mix depending on your chosen strategies.

Your marketing kit:

1. A website to point people towards.
2. An offline traditional brochure can be a worthwhile investment.
3. A telephone script for calls in and calls out and/or telesales staff.
4. Business cards and stationery.
5. A snappy press release.
6. Posters and flyers.
7. A newsletter.
8. A direct mail packed with punchy headlines, a great opening paragraph, benefit-rich text and the main benefits repeated in the PS.
9. Reward/loyalty cards.
10. Gift certificates or vouchers.
11. Stickers, bumper stickers.
12. A CD-Rom or video presentation.
13. Reports, articles and white papers.
14. Inserts.
15. Postcards.
16. Invitations.
17. Free samples.

18. An 0800 number.
19. T-shirts and promotional items, including bags (avoid the plastic variety to save the environment).
20. A list of speaking venues, topics and a speaker's biography.
21. A letter to the editor.

Now pick and mix which materials you will use for this marketing plan that support your chosen strategies. Tick the ones you'll use from the list above.

Remember, the key to successful marketing from the outset is to always be clear about what your objectives are and what part of the pie you are on, so you know what materials to invest in and which strategies to employ.

Your marketing literature must entice your prospect and make them want to investigate your offer further.

Your literature needs to look professional. You may opt to hire a professional copywriter (they generally charge around £40 per hour for copywriting/£15 for proofreading) or do it yourself, if you have the skills.

STEP 32: CRAFT YOUR MARKETING MESSAGES

Crafting Your Message

You should now be well aware that all your customers care about is what's in it for them. Tell them benefits, offer proof of problems solved via case studies, examples of reliability or quality, and details on how to order or make contact with you.

Here are a few tips on crafting an effective message.

♦ Litter your website and marketing materials with clear and concise benefits, as it's those that make people spend their money, not features. Focus your words on solving a problem that your customer/prospect has. What can you do for them and exactly how? You need to spell out these benefits loud and clear. What do I really get from this purchase?

♦ Don't be sensational as there's plenty of hype and over-promising these days. Consumers are worn out with it all and can see through sensationalist claims. Only include benefits you can back up with proof and results/testimonials.

♦ Grab your readers' attention with a good headline and opening paragraph. The headline should be benefit-rich and concise – it should make your reader want to read more and it should never end with a full stop. You don't want your reader to stop.

♦ Use testimonials where possible in all sales literature, including on your website. Quotes from happy customers work very well in convincing similar people with similar needs to go ahead and buy something. As part of your marketing plan include time to contact existing/past customers for testimonials and referrals.

♦ Use a PS – this is as important as the headline and must be benefit-rich.

◆ Include calls to action. Tell your customer exactly what you want them to do and when: for example, phone today to secure your place on a course that will transform your leadership skills, call now to take advantage of the early bird discount.

Each single element of a whole campaign – the message, copy, design, layout, media used – everything should appeal to the target's self-interest. It must do this, while also highlighting a company's brand personality and unique strengths. To create a campaign that focuses on audience self-interest and the key brand message, you need to establish which of your unique strengths your customers value the most. You will have uncovered them from your customer survey, now is your chance to use that knowledge to your advantage.

Remove the risk

Give a guarantee. If this is a viable option you should do it. Guarantees have been proven to increase sales by as much as 200 per cent.

Having absolutely nothing to lose when making a purchase is the ultimate sales trigger. It illustrates confidence in the product or service and removes all the risk from the buyer, placing it back on you. Why would I want to place the risk back on me, you may well be thinking. Because, if your product really is as good as you say it is, you will see far more additional sales as a result of implementing a guarantee, than you will receive returns. The majority of people don't claim under guarantees, even when they feel they are within their rights to. Most people simply won't. Of course some people are dishonest and will try to claim their money back fraudulently. But sales do increase with a good guarantee, providing other elements of your marketing and sales messages are working together and if your product/service is good enough.

Test

Test and track your marketing efforts. Test different messages and different materials and roll-out with the most successful strategies. Give each strategy and each piece of marketing literature a source code, and give customers a source code once they've ordered, so you know how you got them. Always ask fresh leads where they heard about you: from a friend, website link, search engine, flyer. Use this information to see where you should be spending your marketing pounds.

◆ TOP TIP ◆

◆ As a general rule, 20 per cent of customers generate 80 per cent of profits. So as your business grows you'll be able to focus your attention, marketing strategies and materials on those customers and increase profits and return on your marketing investment as a result.

◆ With the mass of marketing material and strategies to choose from, it can take some time to find out which of these work best for you. So it's worth learning what can work exceptionally well from successful entrepreneurs in the meantime.

Take a leaf out of Dame Anita Roddick's book

Be resourceful and interesting

'We never had a marketing department – we didn't even know what it was. We just got lots of awards because we knew how to promote and enchant. We went in the opposite way to other firms. When we floated on the stock market, we set up a human rights department and a community department because we were still basically activists.'

Be cheeky and court controversy

'All of the campaigns have been fantastic, but a really interesting one for The Body Shop was when we started to support industrial hemp. It did everything, it had thousands of uses, didn't need pesticides. But it was vilified by the agro-chemical industry because it didn't use pesticides and looked like marijuana, so everything about it was vilified, and yet it was a saviour.

I loved being able to support that plant and break down on any level the myth that says you can't put industrial hemp oil on your skin because you might get high. You found a collective wave of such stupidity from the organisations and the media and Health Canada, oh but it was such fun. So that in terms of the product was the most fascinating, because you knew that you were right, you knew you were more intelligent. You didn't think that stupidity was sustainable until you went to America and realised it was. So I loved that campaign because it was so cheeky.'

Find something worth spending your marketing budget on

'The Self Esteem campaign was another favourite, because you've got such terrorism of body shape within the fashion industry. So we've taken all the marketing skills we've had and put them into these campaigns, and have done a terrific job of it.'

We might not all have the desire to use our campaigns to help free prisoners of conscience from certain death, change the law or defend human rights (although it's great for business if you try – see Chapter 9), but we can learn to create interesting honest campaigns that fire the public imagination and get good press and media coverage.

The direct and sometimes controversial campaigns orchestrated by Benetton didn't always make me go and buy their clothes, but it certainly raised my awareness of their brand, what they stood for and what kind of clothes they sold. Some of their adverts were banned which created even more publicity for the company.

So be interesting, be resourceful, be cheeky and even controversial.

Use every blank space possible and make yourself useful

'When I got to know Ben Cohen from Ben and Jerry, he gave me some amazing advice – he said a blank space is an opportunity for a message.

You don't have to have huge budgets either. I used to put messages on the side of my car and then we translated that to trucks, so we had all these trucks going up and down the highways and motorways with messages about missing children on them.'

The Body Shop even painted messages on to elephants in India to raise awareness about HIV and AIDS.

'You've got to use every blank space and, once you've got your great idea, product or service and have separated it from everyone else's, you need to shout about those differences from the rooftops.

We had a fleet of 12 vehicles that travelled around Britain that acted like moving billboards, educating or entertaining the public. I'm not talking about advertising a logo here. I'm talking about things that really matter – like missing children. The first time we did it, we painted the faces of four missing children onto our trucks, along with the names of at least a dozen others who had disappeared and the number of a telephone helpline.

More than 30,000 calls were made to the helpline and some of those children were found. A girl who had been missing for more than two years was discovered in Marseilles because her face was printed on one of our trucks. That was about being useful to the community.'

The Feel Good Factor

It's not only activists like Dame Roddick who are doing good while getting their brands out there. Cause-related marketing can be great for business and is certainly great for karma!

Co-founder of the Feel Good Drinks Company, Dave Wallwork, uses Storm PR agency in London and has found this to be true:

'We launched my favourite juice, the Naturally Fundraising Pink Grapefruit Juice Drink, in September, just ahead of the Breast Cancer Awareness Month in October, so that got a lot of publicity for us and the charity, and made our customers feel good. We're giving 10p a bottle to the charity which has contributed to the £10,000 cheque we've presented to them – a nice way to get our consumers involved.'

Dave and his team have also worked really hard to build up good relationships with the press.

'We did things like send a team of masseurs into the head office of one of the big magazine companies when we did our launch, so they could taste the drink while having a head and shoulder massage, and feeling really good, because that's what it's all about.'

Other Marketing Ideas from the Top

◆ Feel Good Drinks offered sampling through their Feel Good Lounge at targeted events such as London Fashion Week.
◆ The Ministry of Sound club famously beamed a large image of the lovely Gail Porter butt-naked onto the Houses of Parliament. Fabulous publicity generator. Didn't do any damage to Gail Porter's public image either.
◆ Coffee Republic focused mainly on PR, as like most new businesses, they couldn't afford to advertise. The marketing they did was to leaflet nearby offices, provide free samples outside the shops and offer customers loyalty cards. Later Coffee Republic hired Elite PR, who had Versace and Tag Heuer as clients. They also used themselves as marketing tools by getting personality profiles and interviews in leading

newspapers. But, once again, it was the quality of the product that generated the best PR, winning taste awards time after time. Their Baby Cap generated immense press coverage – by creating a quality fake cappuccino (hot chocolate with foam) they amassed thousands of pounds worth of PR. Job done! As the company grew they also focused their marketing internally, creating a company newsletter including company news, views and trivia, including 'celeb spotting' where staff could mention any famous faces frequenting their shops.

◆ Brent Hoberman, co-founder and chief executive of online travel site Lastminute.com, the online retailer, is an advocate of targeted marketing. '*We did a very big campaign on buses. But we did it only in London and in very central areas. Because of the impact, people thought we had done a national campaign. It made the company appear a lot bigger than it was.*'

Unfortunately, we don't all have the budgetary capabilities to advertise on London buses. But we can still be creative with what we have.

◆ James Campbell, founder of painting and decorating business Finishing Touches, and winner of a recent NES award, got creative with his van.

'The best decision I've made so far is my van! You've got to see it to believe it as it's like a rolling advert. It's so clear and colourful that people come up to me in the street and ask me for a leaflet. In big bold letters on all four sides of the van it says 'Renovate, Build, Manage and Maintain' then 'Finishing Touches' and then my slogan is 'Renovating the Past, Building Your Future', which I've had copyrighted.'

Think creatively about spaces to fill. What could you put your message on? Cars, vans, lorries … elephants?

'In India, we placed signs on the flanks of an elephant. And this project was described by the World Health Organisation as one of the most effective grassroots AIDS education campaigns they had ever seen.

The elephant walked down the streets of towns in Tirumangalam in Tamil Nadu with information on its side in Tamil and English about where to go for information on sexually-transmitted diseases and how to get free condoms.' Dame Anita Roddick

---

◆ **TOP TIP** ◆

- ◆ Hire an agency for launch PR to target the nationals.
- ◆ Think creatively, with targeted competitions and e-mail viral marketing.
- ◆ Consider a theme or calendar event/date you can tie your PR materials into.
- ◆ Get what you do right before promoting your wares.
- ◆ Treat the press – think creatively!
- ◆ Harness the power of celebrity and seek out good angles for media coverage.
- ◆ Provide customers with loyalty cards so they get a freebie after making a certain amount of purchases, or whereby you partner with other local businesses to give your customers discounts at those places on presentation of your loyalty card.

Harness the power of celebrity and PR

Feel Good Drinks have auctioned celebrity photographs online to make money for charity.

The CakeStore.com have also put this PR strategy to good use:

'We've done a lot of celebrity cakes and are quite in with The Sun *newspaper. When Jordan came out of the jungle we sent Peter Andre a cake of her boobs from* The Sun, *and they were so pleased with it they gave us a mention. A small business like us cannot afford to advertise in the national press, so by causing a bit of a stir you get free publicity. We also get a few requests from TV companies to make cakes, and made the biggest Yule log for Jim'll Fix It. And the product advertises itself. Mums, dads, wedding guests, they always ask where our customers got the cake from, and we label them too.'* Tim and Kevin of The CakeStore.com

TheCakeStore.com has had a good amount of national PR, having a whole page article in *The Times* after a happy customer wrote in to share their experience. *The Evening Standard* did a two-page Day in the Life of a Cake Decorator feature.

Sally Preston of Babylicious also got in on the celebrity hook. She wrote to Victoria Beckham, who became a Babylicious customer as a result.

'I wrote to Victoria and said 'you're a mum, here is our product, would you like to try it?' I met her mother and sister recently at the Baby Show, as her mum came up and found me for a chat.'

Mentioning this fact in a press release could be the paragraph that swings the balance and secures some editorial coverage in a national.

Generating interest

Most of Heaven@Home's business comes from PR in national media and from referrals from happy customers, all thanks to a great idea and some clever PR.

'At the start nobody knows who you are, so your PR person is out there pushing, and then people actually phone you. We've had a couple of TV appearances. The programme Shattered about people staying awake on TV recently, the person doing the massage was me! And we've had quite a few celebrities. We do Tara Palmer-Tomkinson and Patsy Palmer, The Appletons and Donna Air. We also did Meera Syal's birthday as she'd been recommended to try us by a friend.' Amanda of Heaven@Home

Clearly celebrity clients can be worth their weight in gold.

'Tara Palmer-Tomkinson is such a nice girl, and she's gone all out to promote us, beyond what she needed to do. She's mentioned us on lots of programmes. And we've had some great features. The Saturday Times *did a whole page on us and in advertising terms that's £120,000 worth. You magazine, did a half page feature. We had 180 phone calls from that alone. The phone started ringing at 7am and I hadn't even had a chance to read the thing myself!'*

Amanda has been lucky to find a good PR consultant with as much belief in the business as she has.

'I would always advise PR over advertising. In terms of endorsement it's worth so much more. There's always a risk because you don't know if journalists are going to write about you – but that's a test of whether the idea is a good one, and whether the angle is clear to them in your press release.'

Amanda's tips:

- Focus your efforts on PR and getting referrals and repeat business. 'The PR we've gained would have cost us thousands in advertising and generated lower results'. If you have a good idea that journalists will like, you can spend your marketing pounds far more sensibly by taking on a PR person or agency.
- Target locally with leaflets and local magazine and press editorial.
- Grab the opportunity to let the product promote itself with cards, stickers and labels on your products.

Rachel Elnaugh also champions PR over advertising as being the most successful strategies for Red Letter Days when at the helm.

'In the early days of the business we got three paragraphs of editorial in the Mail on Saturday on the Femail page saying "How to make someone's day", which I wasn't expecting.

I just happened to pop into the office to collect some papers and all the phones were ringing. I wondered why the answer phone wasn't on, but checked and saw that both were full. So I turned over the tapes and sat down literally taking calls all day long one hour after the other. We ended up receiving around 3000 calls from that one piece of PR. So that's probably the most successful thing we've ever done even including TV, so PR is incredibly powerful.'

Whats more, PR is a necessity when it comes to persuading retail buyers to stock your products.

'It's one thing to get a product into the shops, but the main thing is sell-through for the buyer,' advises Rachel. *'They don't want to stock something unless you can demonstrate that you've got a marketing/PR campaign that will pull the product through. There's nothing worse than slow moving stock. So that's a big part of the pitch to a potential buyer what PR you've had, or are planning on getting.'*

Latch on to a theme

Around 2,000 unique visitors per day visit Michael Parker's retro sweet shop website – AquarterOf.co.uk. Most of this traffic is driven there by word of mouth, backed by prime search engine rankings, plus a successful PR campaign.

The Times did a quarter page about the website, and *The Telegraph* followed suit with three pages in their magazine. '*As soon as you get seen in those papers lots of other people approach you,*' explains Michael. '*The Sun did a page shortly after that and then we had radio, TV and all sorts, so it's worked fantastically well for us.*'

AQuarterOf has also managed to get itself in front of the expat community through word of mouth and a couple of interviews on English speaking radio in Spain, although they haven't consciously gone after that market yet.

A Win Your Weight in Sweets competition and promotional campaign did well on handbag.com, while a viral marketing campaign created an online buzz around retro sweets via the distribution of a branded 'How 80s are you?' e-mail that was forwarded to journalists, friends and family.

Despite the clear results that have come from this PR, Michael believes it's more important to get what you do right to ensure consistent results and repeat business.

'I think it's more important to get what you do right than to go out shouting about what you do. Actions speak louder than words. So if you obsess about getting publicity you won't. By the time we'd got publicity we'd spent 18 months getting right what we do, and had not tried to go round shouting about it.'

When Michael started they had 50 sweets in the shop and now stock around 500, with the large range of suppliers growing as a result of the PR. 'With the recent publicity we've had, we've been approached by a lot more suppliers.'

An innovative idea for Sally Preston has been to promote Babylicious in partnership with other baby products, such as leaflets in baby cups and labels on nappy packs, to raise product awareness.

'Something we worked out quite quickly was that there are a lot of complementary products that mothers buy at the same time as baby food, such as nappies, cups, spoons and so on. We've also discovered the internet is a very powerful tool and that people use links to get from site to site, so we've built relationships with other companies in the same market.'

Babylicious also advertises in local magazines and has done some tried-and-tested editorial pieces.

'For example, we've been in Prima Baby, *the second largest baby magazine in the country, and featured as the 'mum's choice' of products, beating the jars.*

We've done it on a miniscule budget, through 'guerilla marketing' and through bartering, so I've written articles and editorials for magazines in exchange for free publicity.'

ilikemusic.com also chose to cross-promote by providing competition prizes to a new digital music channel in 2003 – Channel U. Both shared the same target audience but weren't competing, so ilikemusic.com provided Tupac DVDs as competition prizes for free in exchange for a free advert created by the TV channel. Channel U profited from the premium rate competition entries via the channel, while ilikemusic.com benefited from free promotion on a TV station that was already getting more than one million viewers a day.

- Think laterally and cross-promote.
- Send samples of your products to journalists and review panels.
- Write articles.
- Cross-promote with like-minded brands which can add value.

Keep a Record of Publicity

Use the publicity record (page 139) and a variation of the action plan (page 93) to plan and record your marketing and publicity efforts, or use the additional marketing worksheet on page 139.

◆ EXERCISE ◆

List your lead sources, places or people you know that you can get lead information from. Get out your customer profile sheet. Who do you already know or have details of who fits your profile? List them. You will be able to add more leads once you've completed your research and start putting your marketing strategies into practice. Draw up your first prospect list. Write down everyone, including personal contacts you rarely talk business with.

_____

_____

_____

_____

Now you know how to attract customers and what materials and strategies you'll be using, it's time to learn how to keep those customers with great service. Deliver!

PUBLICITY RECORD

Media name	Web address	Contact name	E-mail/tel	Sent material	Follow-up	Result
Example: New consumer	www.newconsumer.co.uk	W. Martin	info@	Nov 15	Nov 22	editorial in feb issue

MARKETING WORKSHEET

Objectives	Pie Slice (1–4)	Strategies	Materials	Results/Further Action
Example: To gain credibility and leads	One	Networking Article writing E-mail marketing	Business cards Media and press list E-newsletter Press Release	1cust +1referral Publshd imd.net

CHAPTER EIGHT

How to Sell – The Importance of Good Customer Service

Apparently those big corporate telecommunications companies and similar corporations 'value my custom.' That's what they tell me repeatedly as I'm left on hold for minutes, before being passed to another wrong department, my problem still not resolved. We all have customer service horror stories. The telephone line at the local Royal Mail depot is left unanswered – always. There are too few staff, so they leave the phone to ring off, preventing customers who can't collect undelivered recorded mail from arranging redelivery. These experiences don't make me feel good as a customer, they just frustrate me. And we tend to tell more people about our bad experiences than we do about our good ones. This being a case in point. I told you, didn't I?

As a business, you want to avoid being on the other side of that criticism with you getting it wrong.

Encourage complaints by making it easy for customers to do so, but strive to make your customer service shine so complaints aren't frequent.

As a consumer culture businesses are forever telling consumers how much they value our custom (even if they don't always value our time) especially when being left on hold on the phone. But what do businesses really do to prove that customers are genuinely valued?

By the end of this chapter you should be able to answer the following questions:

◆ What are the basics of good customer service?
◆ What customer relationship management software options are available?
◆ How have successful entrepreneurs managed to keep customers happy?

'It is high time the ideal of success should be replaced with the idea of service.' Albert Einstein

'Under-promise so that you can over-deliver.' Stelios Haji-Ioannu, easyJet

The Customer is King

The customer is always right is a well known business mantra, because without customers you have no business, it is their needs that feed a business's sales. Getting business from your existing customers is less costly and unpredictable than attracting new ones, so retaining customers is vital for businesses, both new and old, small and mammoth.

Happy customers will recommend you to their personal network, while unhappy ones will grumble to all and sundry about how disappointed they were with your service. Small businesses can't rely on big budget ad spends to push their brands in front of the public consciousness. So maintaining a positive reputation becomes even more crucial. Ensuring that you are getting positive comments from word of mouth, rather than groans and moans, is one of the most important things you can focus on.

'The secret of success is to do the common things uncommonly well.' John D Rockerfeller Jnr

Hotels sometimes ring customers to say room service is on its way, or a GP rings a patient at home to check on their recovery. A hotel or event management company might send its customers audio maps to listen to in the car as they approach, while a contract cleaning firm could valet its customers' cars while they're in a meeting, or place expensive perfume and sweets in the WC.

Coffee Republic relied on the quality of their customer experience and word of mouth initially to market their business. Virgin focuses on the customer experience, and the experience of its staff. People – be they your customers or your staff – are what drives your business, you are simply the initiator.

'As part of our service we actually handwrite the card and send it for the customer. Sometimes with a bit of confetti sprinkled in it, and that's quite popular, especially with expats or people who aren't near a card shop.' Will Walsh, Sharpcards.com

Wild West Foods sells beef jerky over the web (www.wildwestjerky.co.uk) and has a great customer base, with thousands of people having ordered from the site. Hundreds of those are repeat customers. Founder Richard Davies puts his success down to honesty and good customer service:

'If I make any mistakes I replace the order with double, and I put extra bags in if people order a lot. I also keep the postage low and make a loss on it, if anything.

I like to have that ethic of the corner shop from childhood memory, with the helpful lady behind the counter. I write handwritten thank-yous on my invoices, and I'm honest with my customers always.'

It certainly seems to be working. Richard has found a lot of his customers arrive on his site via word of mouth. In fact, Richard's customers' loyalty is so strong that they even tell Richard when his competitors get in touch. He says:

'A lot of businesses would do well to remember that customer service ethic. So many internet sites ignore customer service and take months to deliver, which gives internet shopping a bad name. I get a lot of e-mails from people saying 'thank you' because I put the customer first, and there's no reason why other internet sites and traditional businesses can't do that.'

Treat customers as you'd like to be treated

When Sir Richard Branson set up Virgin Atlantic, he had two things in mind: lower prices and better service. He wanted to serve quality meals, provide enthusiastic flight crews, entertainment and an all round better experience for those flying. He wanted it to be fun for both staff and customers, so he ensures that his customers are treated as he himself would wish to be.

The industry has been well and truly shaken up by Virgin's innovative entertainments and quality service. Massages, manicures, spas and putting greens are the order of the day at Virgin hub airports. The result is that other airlines have had to fight harder to keep their customers, while Virgin have kept on winning customers by putting them first.

Talking of airlines, Jan Carlzon from Scandinavian Airlines famously said, 'coffee stains on the flip trays tell the customer that we don't service our engines properly.'

What will your service and attention to detail be telling your customers?

The bottom line? Make yourself and your business attractive to buy stuff from. Buying from you should be an enjoyable and rewarding experience. It should be fun and satisfying. Would you enjoy shopping at your shop or website? If not, why not? Strive to improve all areas consistently and treat customers as you'd like to be treated.

Another example of clear-cut focus on the customer is The Body Shop. While at the helm before handing over the reins, Dame Roddick explains just how focused they were.

'I think there are few companies in the world that can claim to enjoy the strong, enduring relationship with customers that The Body Shop has enjoyed. We brought our customers into the heart of the company, we thought of them as family, we invited and encouraged them to participate in everything we did. None of our competitors have been able to match us in this.

But the single most effective way of communicating with customers, after years of suggestion boxes or focus groups, has been the newly burgeoning The Body Shop At Home. Some 3,000 consultants hold on average 100,000 parties with more than one million customers each year and bring back anecdotes, spontaneous reactions and stories. Nothing in the history of this company has been more profound or focused than that two-way conversation in people's homes in terms of letting us know whether or not we live up to our customers' expectations.'

But even the most honest and customer-centric businesses can make customer service errors. Dame Roddick shared one of The Body Shop's with me:

'A few years ago we were designing a bubble bath/shower gel and the design department made the bottle look like a fruit juice bottle, and called it Fruit Juice. We were stuffed, because the company then (even though I didn't like what they were doing) put a huge amount of money into tooling up these bottles so they did look too much like fruit juices that kids would drink, and of course it was banned in most countries for that reason. So that was a huge economic foul up – the customers really complained too, and rightly so.'

STEP 33: CREATE A CUSTOMER SERVICE POLICY

Customer Service Checklist

So how can you ensure you tick the quality control box in terms of customer service and retain those valuable customers?

1. Get feedback and try to retain customers. Ask your customers to score your service and other elements of your business out of ten. Work on areas that score lower but don't ignore those areas your customers rate highly. Offer plenty of methods for your customers to complain if they need to. By hearing what your customers don't like and would prefer changed you can make appropriate changes and turn a disgruntled customer into a happy one. Go the extra mile and don't argue with your customers because they'll take their business elsewhere. Create a problem-solving platform from complaints you receive. Solve your customers' problem and they'll be back, again and again, with friends.

'If you replace products because you think customers are bored of them, you forget there's always a few out there who love that product and won't accept it.

To this day I'm still getting letters. You can try to keep every single customer happy, but it's not easy. What can do is relate to them. If they phone up screaming at you, you've got to be patient and how you relate to your customers when the shit hits the fan is really important. You don't close your eyes, you don't ignore it, you spend a lot of time, because you can regain that customer.' Dame Anita Roddick

   Handling complaints well can turn a dissatisfied customer into a loyal one. So put systems in place to figure out where you lose customers, and why, to ensure that future customers won't have that reason to become part of your customer losses statistic. Commit yourself to high quality customer service with clear processes for all staff to follow, and you'll find it much easier to monitor where you've lost a customer.

2. Make sure your customers always have an interesting and enjoyable experience and strive for high satisfaction levels. It must be worthwhile to them, they must value your service just as you value their trade. Think of ways you can create that perfect customer experience.

3. Be transparent and communicate with your customers frequently and honestly. Make sure your customers understand your philosophy and ethos. Show them

respect and you'll be granted the same. Be transparent and honest. Tell your customers your beliefs as a company, because honesty begets loyalty. Create a healthy community built on trust. Promote reality rather than false promises and you'll reap the benefits.

4. Commit yourself to a strong, clear customer service programme that is possible to implement by all staff, with a focus on high quality. Implement this consistently and track where you lose and gain customers and why so. Test how well the programme is working, and tweak the programme or train staff where necessary. Set some delivery measures (eg return calls within two hours, answer e-mail requests within 24 hours).

5. Go the extra mile. Exceed expectations as often as you can. This can be a relatively painless exercise, as you can give your customer a delivery deadline that you know you'll reach before deadline. By delivering early rather than 'on-time' you look like you've gone the extra mile even if you haven't.

'It's not difficult to provide good customer service. It's all about expectations, we don't say next day delivery because we rely on the postal system and they don't always get it there the next day, so we say three days. When they get it the next day our customers are very impressed.' Will Walsh, Sharpcards.com

6. Spend a day in the life of your customer as soon as you launch your business to the world, and at regular intervals after that. Walk in your customers' shoes for a day and have members of staff do the same.

Phone in with enquiries or requests for contacts; send in a complaint and see how you're treated. Take the journey your customers take, browse your store or go through the process of ordering items online. Do you notice any areas of frustration that could be smoothed out? Make a sales enquiry or place an order. Once your items are delivered what shape are they in? Does the packaging cast the products in a good light? Where could improvements be made?

7. Provide bonuses and freebies to show your customers you value them.

8. Always make sure somebody is available to take phone calls.

9. Develop a promise, and keep it. If you claim to offer quick turnaround time or high quality service at affordable prices, make sure that you live up to your word. Don't disappoint.

10. Train staff in customer service skills adequately. Help them understand why they should value the customer, rather than saying, 'oi, they pay your wages, they do!'

11. Listen to customers and staff – practise doing this in order to be able to make positive changes and improvements to the business, policies, products and services.

12. Invite customers to participate in product or service development and brainstorming. Get a customer focus group together or provide suggestion boxes for customers and staff. The Feel Good Drinks Company had some of their customers involved at product development stage, and rightly so. I'm currently addicted to the Naturally Uplifting Apple and Blueberry Juice Drink!

13. Smile. A friendly attitude and warm, genuine smile can leave a lasting impression. And it costs you nothing.
14. Create a good impression by making your reception area, shop or website home page welcoming. Also use packaging, proposal letters and other bits of collateral that the customer receives to create a good impression of your business.

◆ EXERCISE ◆

How can you go the extra mile for your customers? Brainstorm innovative ways of saying thank you and pay attention to how you're treated as a customer. Note good experiences and bad. List how you can bend over backwards to satisfy your customers' requirements at all times.

_____

_____

_____

Customer Relationship Management

To have a business model that is sustainable, you need repeat business and recurring sales. A big mistake in business is to simply file away a customer order once their product or service has been delivered. The best thing you can do in business is to follow up your existing customers, because you've already acquired them and spent your money doing so.

Your customer base is the best asset to your business.

Consider investing in software built for **customer relationship management (CRM)** such as ACT or Goldmine, to help record your contacts and ensure every member of staff stays on top of client relationships. The better you record your communications with customers, the more you will sell, as you'll be able to create better profiles from your data, therefore enabling more defined and accurate targeting when you are trying to attract new customers.

Remember, it's much easier to sell to someone who's already bought something from you than to someone who hasn't, so make customer retention a high priority in the daily management of your business. Constant revenue streams from repeat customers can be the lifeblood of your business, so treat customers well and harness the power of your database. Use it, work it, profit from it.

Try to focus on upselling additional products and services to the 20 per cent of people on your client/prospect data base who are your best, most valuable repeat customers. Target those on your database with products and services they have not yet purchased or with products they have previously bought within a certain time period. They might be ready to re-order.

Record every contact you make with them, along with all their contact information and responses. Note down objections, feedback, what they've bought and when, plus why they've bought and where they heard of you.

Listen – Learn – Impress

Dazzling customer service is the only way to guarantee customer loyalty. And an increase in repeat business can really make profits sparkle.

So go on. Dazzle!

CHAPTER NINE

How to Behave – The Case for Ethical Business and Social Responsibility

eth·i·cal adj. *adhering to ethical and moral principles; being honourable and moral.*

This chapter reveals how it is not only large corporations that should understand corporate social responsibility. There is demonstrable commercial benefit to being responsible and trading fairly. Ethical business is not only good for the planet and human race, but is also great for business. The importance of ethical business in today's world will therefore be evaluated in this chapter, with case studies including Ben & Jerry's and The Body Shop, along with responsible smaller businesses that focus on a purpose. As public confidence in corporations erodes more and more, the rise in vigilante consumerism is also covered in this chapter which also inlcudes a social responsibility checklist.

By the end of this chapter you should be able to answer the following questions:

- How can small businesses be ethical in terms of choosing suppliers, promoting sustainability and serving the community, without breaking the bank? (In fact, quite the opposite).
- What do you need to know about fair trade globalisation.
- How can you implement an ethical, green and socially responsible business model, while still increasing your bottom line?

What Is Corporate Social Responsibility (CSR)?

In a nutshell, it's the act of 'giving back' to the community through local projects or helpful working practice. It's about being honest, being aware of the impact your business has on the environment and on the local and global community.

In today's fractured economic climate, businesses large and small must win the support of a sceptical public through honest methods that don't involve manipulation. With increased globalisation, oil and energy resources running out, outcry over child labour in supply chains and poor working conditions, corporate social responsibility has become a buzz-word among the large corporations which have faced mass boycotts and protests from customers and suppliers alike. The face of business is changing. But ethical business isn't just a model for large companies.

Business in 2010 and beyond must have ethical foundations and conduct responsible and responsive business. And that applies to businesses of all shapes and sizes, large and small.

Says Chairman of Business In The Community, David Varney:

'The success of our economic system has always depended on the goodwill between the business sector and society. Until recently, the glue that bound us together was trust. Unfortunately, that trust has been undermined by business scandals, the uncertainties of the marketplace, fears about the control of big corporations over everyday life, and a growing cynicism about business practices.

I define corporate responsibility as a company's positive impact on society and the environment through its operations, products or services and through its interaction with key groups such as employees, investors, customers, communities and suppliers.

Even ex-Prime Minister, Gordon Brown, has said:

'Corporate responsibility is a belief that economic, social and environmental objectives can be pursued together and in harmony, and in particular that corporate self-interest and corporate responsibility are not irreconcilable opposites, but can move forward in unison. It is a recognition that when business loses trust it is at its most vulnerable.'

The current situation: commerce without conscience

'Ours is a world of nuclear giants and ethical infants.' Omar N. Bradley

In her book *Business As Unusual*, Dame Roddick explains the current situation and some facts that most people don't realise:

- Half of everything spent by British consumers goes into the coffers of just 250 companies.
- Only 27 countries have a turnover greater than the combined sales of Shell and Exon.
- The combined wealth of the seven most wealthy businessmen could clear world debt and destroy poverty.
- The world has 30-50 years' supply of oil – then that's it!
- Water shortages are intensifying.
- Climate changes, population levels, affluent lifestyles are all increasing.
- Infectious diseases are killing millions, denied treatment through high drug prices set by wealthy drug companies.
- Tariffs and subsidies lock out producers whose goods are cheaper from developing countries.

- Computers, fridges, nappies and cars are dumped in landfill sites, polluting our soil.
- Air travel is on the increase and is the fastest-growing contributor to greenhouse gas, while the airline industry pays no duty on fuel and no VAT on tickets.
- Supermarkets dominate, small suppliers go out of business, and the focal point of the community, the local corner shop, is under threat.

'The new nomadic capital never sets down roots, never builds communities. It leaves behind toxic wastes, embittered workers and indigenous communities driven out of existence. There is no more powerful a stimulator in society than business. It is more important than ever before for business to assume a moral leadership in society.' Dame Anita Roddick

It is certainly clear from these facts that conscience is completely void in the global market, but it is just that – conscience – that holds the key to an end to this globalisation and unfair trade.

Businesses across the globe need to stop and think. They need to get informed, be aware and take action. Even the most evil tycoon could benefit from getting informed and taking an ethical approach. Being ethical is good for business, an ethos that has been proven time and time again. And it certainly beats having your brand dragged through the mud or your products boycotted.

Fortunately, that message is starting to be heard. The UK now has an Ethical Trading Initiative, and The Council on Economic Priorities has created an auditable social accounting standard (SA8000). There has been a Government minister for Corporate Social Responsibility since 2005. According to EIRIS, UK ethical investment hit a record high of £9.5 billion in 2010, up from £2.5 billion when I first wrote this chapter back in 2005. A variety of initiatives and organizations have been created, such as CORE (Corporate Responsibility Coalition).

Brand managers who fear consumer boycotts are taking notice. Unfortunately though, the majority of businesses, big and small, still focus primarily on the bottom line above all else, including having principles and embracing social responsibility. This is despite the proof that being ethical in business can result in an improved bottom line in any case.

Why be ethical?

Ever heard of karma? Or the term 'you reap what you sow'? Then it probably won't surprise you to know that acting responsibly and responsively is *good* for business – profits included. That in itself, coupled with the growing market for ethical businesses and goods that are fairly traded, is a good enough reason to be ethical in business – big or small.

Kindness = real profit (financial and human profit)

There are a great many benefits to setting up a business with a strand of honour underpinning decisions, processes and the purpose of your business.

Research published by the Co-operative Bank reveals the total value of ethical consumption in the UK is now almost £20 billion, while sales of ethical goods have grown 13 per cent during 2002, when the economy grew at 1.3%.

One only needs to look at examples of multinational businesses which have benefited from their stance on corporate social responsibility to see why a business should think ethical.

'I think the majority of people come out of the womb wanting to be a good person, lead a good life and be honourable, so why that changes when you put on a business coat really baffles me. I am, in my skin, an activist – I am trying to free guys in prison in America and stop sweatshops. When I went into business, I didn't think you had to leave yourself and your beliefs at the door.' Dame Anita Roddick

♦ The Co-Operative Bank too have benefited from their ethical stance, cornering the market in ethical investing. The Fairtrade brand, buying directly from farmers in developing countries and paying a guaranteed above-market price, has seen the Co-Op's profits rocket.
♦ Waitrose saw a like-for-like sales increase of 12 per cent in 2003, while it aggressively promoted its commitment to ethical global sourcing. So if making and maintaining money are your main motivators, following the lead of these companies will help you generate more of what you want and will go further to keeping your customers happy.

As the DTI puts it:

'Companies which take these issues seriously not only achieve benefits to society; they can also enhance their reputation, improve competitiveness and strengthen their risk management.'

There is now a mountain of evidence that businesses can boost their reputation, and even demand for services, by supporting local regeneration projects, sports teams or community centres, for example. Ethical and socially responsible business, no matter what size, can also have a big impact on the quality and retention of staff. According to a study by accountancy group Ernst and Young, four in ten jobseekers take into consideration prospective employers' CSR track record.

Furthermore, being a responsible business reduces risk and can help to secure the future of a company in terms of achieving sustainable profits. Being responsible has impacted companies to their advantage, with share prices of computer companies that managed risks well outperforming those of companies that didn't by nearly 20 per cent.

John Downy, parliamentary officer for the Federation of Small Businesses, says:

'Businesses can make lots of savings by improving their environmental performance and complying with environmental legislation.'

We look in more detail at some case studies of corporate social responsibility in the business world later in the chapter, so you can get a real understanding of why you should behave morally in business.

So what about small businesses?

According to Bibby Financial Services (survey 2004), three in ten small-medium enterprises (SMEs) have no formal policy when it comes to environmental management, equal opportunities, ethical investment or corporate governance. Most of these businesses without a policy thought they were too small for it to benefit them, while 20 per cent said they were more concerned with key business goals. (The good news is that seven in ten did have an ethical policy.)

However, NetRegs research revealed that from the 8,600 businesses they polled, only 19 per cent could name any environmental legislation affecting their business.

In order to deal with this lack of awareness and misplaced objections to behaving ethically in business, we'll deal with them one by one.

First those businesses should consider one of Dame Anita Roddick's famous slogans:

'If you think you're too small to be effective, try going to bed with a mosquito!'

CHOCaid and HUG are examples of small businesses making their independent voices heard in a corporate industry while doing their bit to make a difference.

The secret of The Body Shop's huge success in terms of growth was that it embraced the cottage industry mindset with a powerful and unique message. This is what beat all their competition and drove the company forward. So what's your purpose? Review the exercises you did in Chapter 4 and add kind, ethical and purposeful to your list.

Furthermore, 'reaching business goals' and increasing sales and profits, raising awareness, getting more clients can all be helped rather than hindered by focusing some time on social responsibility and ethical business practices and principles.

Fortunately, just over half of the small businesses surveyed by Bibby said they made a conscious effort to protect the environment by minimising waste and more than two-thirds had donated money to a charitable cause in the last 12 months. Seventeen per cent of respondents had sought advice on ethical business practices during that period. So the tide is clearly turning.

The bottom line is that by implementing an ethical and socially responsible policy, and having clear principles, people are more likely to buy from and work for you. And, of course, if you aren't doing this, your competition will be doing so, quicker than you can say Body Shop body butter!

The rise of the vigilante consumer

Today's business landscape is testament to changes in the world. Today the impact of business on society and planet are scrutinised more than ever. Customer trust has been eroded with years of half-truths and over-marketing. Social and environmental costs are rarely taken into account, and if they are they are the costs often passed onto the consumers.

A recent poll by Mori found that 86 per cent of consumers think about ethical issues when choosing products.

Four out of ten consumers around the world responded in some way against actions they thought were unethical during 1999, according to PriceWaterhouse Coopers research, and since then consumers are becoming more and more 'savvy' in reacting against unethical actions, companies and products.

Consumers are expecting moral decisions and, equally, they understand that their purchases are moral choices too. 'Vigilante consumers' set out to punish companies that get out of line by refusing to buy shares or buying shares to hijack the AGM. They are doing the groundwork, but regular customers are also fed up with being manipulated.

'The fact is, businesses can not longer hide behind consumer ignorance or indifference. Customers are hyped out and cynical. They've been overmarketed. They crave knowledge and want honest information.'
Dame Anita Roddick

Public trust has sunk to an all time low and all that can be done to restore it is to be honest, ethical and improve performance in customers' and investors' eyes. Stakeholder pressure for improved environmental performance has also dramatically increased since the 1990s.

So what can you do about it?

♦ Provide your customers with all the information they need. Tell them every ingredient, every process and tell them your story.
♦ Be honest and encourage feedback. Don't build a PR wall and talk down to your customers. Open up channels – listen and respond. If you choose the smokescreen option your customers will be watching and waiting.

Waste Management

According to NetRegs, the online environmental advice service, businesses in the UK are losing 4.5 per cent of their revenue by not managing their waste and could save around £1,000 per employee through simple energy efficiency programmes or by switching off unused lights.

Businesses in Scotland alone produce 15 million tonnes of waste each year and are some of the worst culprits, according to the research. Indeed the average person in the

UK consumes around one tonne of materials per year. Eleven tonnes of materials are consumed by industry to produce than one tonne.

This waste includes:

◆ consumables
◆ damaged or redundant equipment
◆ office waste
◆ canteen waste
◆ maintenance waste.

Greenbusiness.org.uk reports that the total cost to UK industry of wastes, whether solid, liquid or gas, amounts to at least £15 billion annually, or approximately 4.5 per cent of total turnover. This figure does not include wasted heat and lighting energy through inefficient use, water use, excessive use of raw material or time. These are the 'hidden costs' of waste.

What can be done?

Recent measures have been put in place to impose taxes to promote more efficient use of resources, and there has been an increase in liabilities to those who ignore them.

◆ TOP TIP ◆

Inefficient waste management can be expensive and pollution results in fines, so it's more cost-effective to manage waste efficiently.

'*Savings can be as much as 1 per cent of turnover, enhancing profits,*' says Green Business.

Globalisation: How It Affects You and Your Suppliers

'*Globalisation is now considered as a new religion. Economic corporate globalisation is the most undemocratic, the most secretive, the most evil organisation of this belief that only a few companies, mostly Western, can control the world. What it doesn't realise is that globalisation fans violence, it fans tension, it increases poverty. What we need is an economic system that embraces the weak and the frail, and is not just making money off the backs of the weak and the frail.*' Dame Anita Roddick, in *Business As Unusual*

You may be able to import products from overseas or source the cheapest supplier, but make sure you do your homework and know their policies. Similarly be wary when working with/for large corporations as they may be part of a chain of power that is creating a wider divide between Westerners and the rest of the world.

Being ethical is also about being honest about what you're buying.

'If you've got suppliers, be wary of the cheapest, because it could be made using sweatshop labour. Build your relationships with your suppliers, because they depend on you for their survival and you depend on them.' Dame Anita Roddick

Julie Meyer, founder of First Tuesday and Ariadne Capital, agrees that there is no need to either profit from unfair trading or go for the jugular.

'You do not need to be successful at the expense of others. There is enough out there for us all – I can be successful and help you to be successful too. Greed, jealousy and incompetence are a deadly combination.'

Don't focus on the lowest cost solution if it means outsourcing your call centre operation to India (à la BT) or using sweatshops (as Nike/Walmart have been alleged to) as this will create public indignation and will not be good for business.

◆ EXERCISE ◆

Revisit your purpose. Recognise your significance and that of your business. Recognise what you represent. Might you include any of these words in your description of your purpose or values?

Ethical
Moral
Decent
Fair
Noble
Respectable
Right-minded
Upstanding
Virtuous
Honourable
Prudent
Charitable
Genuine
True/honest
Dependable

_____

_____

'Business must be run at a profit, else it will die. But when anyone tries to run a business solely for profit... then also the business must die, for it no longer has a reason for existence.'
Henry Ford

Following the Lead of Ethical Companies

'Corporate social responsibility and ethical business are not new issues' explains Dame Anita Roddick. *The Quakers were deeply smart business people and enormously wealthy. But they never stole, never lied and never cheated. Can you imagine that in business now? They respected and protected their community of workers, built towns and schools, even villages. They had a moral imperative in everything they did. I think we can learn from people and groups like that.'*

Business may have become hypnotised by the bottom line and forgotten their moral obligations to civil society, but it is now necessary to snap out of the destructive business acumen of profits over principles and follow the lead of many businesses that are already profiting from their principles, while helping to solve issues of a social and economic nature.

The Pioneers and Followers of Ethical Business Thinking

The Body Shop

Set up by Dame Anita Roddick in 1976 and launched selling 20 products that she knocked together in her garage and packed in urine sample bottles. That creative thinking has been instrumental in growing The Body Shop to where it is today, with over 2,000 shops across 12 time zones.

In 1984 the company went public, and at its height The Body Shop was worth £700 million. Despite some initial boardroom acrimony when Anita's successors took over, The Body Shop continues to be profitable today. The company sold to L'Oreal in 2006 after the chairman introduced himself to Anita and said, 'I wanted to shake the hand of the one female in my life who's caused me more trouble than any other.' Anita and her husband decided that persuading such a cosmetics giant to retain The Body Shop's core values was a worthwhile move and negotiated a deal for £652m in March 2006. The £130m which The Roddicks reportedly made from the deal has been invested into social enterprises and donated to causes, continuing to do good. Anita passed away in 2007. Her legacy lives on.

How? By shaping business to be kinder; supporting and campaigning on issues and promoting community trade and self-esteem.

'The Body Shop currently support 39 projects spanning the globe. In Ghana we support the cooperatives, we trade honourably and we get great products. They get wells, medical care, education and veterinary care. We support the sesame farmers in Nicaragua and grassroots farming in Brazil. It is really supporting the small-scale family farmer. We pay the right amount of money for their goods rather than beat them down to the lowest price. It's a very interesting and worthwhile purchasing policy we have. We also support Amnesty International, Native American tribes, projects in Peru and India. At a personal level, we support women and children suffering from HIV and Aids.

I think The Body Shop has been brilliant. We tried so many experiments and one of them was shaping business to be kinder. It proved you can run a very high powered organisation, open 150 shops a year, collect for the community, campaign for animal rights and speak out about social problems in the community as well as do the things that businesses are traditionally measured by.' Dame Anita Roddick

Anita has always challenged the status quo and done so very effectively. She's challenged how business should be done and how society should work and continues to do so with her communications company, AnitaRoddick.com and activist portal, TakeItPersonally.org.uk.

'I am proudest of the campaigns we ran at The Body Shop against Shell, after the execution of the playwright Ken Saro-Wiwa. But we've campaigned on missing children, on the undermining of women by the cosmetics industry, on climate change – and lots of other things.'

While at The Body Shop, Anita Roddick measured her company each year 'by how brave we'd been.' Today with Anita Roddick Publications Ltd, even after her untimely death, Anita continues to challenge the status quo. Anita's human spirit was enriched from travelling, campaigning, being active, getting involved, implementing change, saving lives and turning tables. More businesses of all shapes and sizes should do the same and learn from the example of ethical businesses such as hers.

On the other hand, it was this politics of consciousness – and this alone – that distinguished The Body Shop from most other companies. '*Our competitors never followed us there. The vast majority of companies never have.*'

Ben & Jerry's Homemade, Inc.

The Vermont-based manufacturer of ice cream, frozen yogurt and sorbet was founded in 1978 in a renovated gas station in Burlington, Vermont, by childhood friends Ben Cohen and Jerry Greenfield, with a $12,000 investment ($4,000 of which was borrowed). In 2000 they announced the company's acquisition by Unilever for $326 million.

How? By giving back to the community, promoting peace and committing to social responsibility, ethical business and responsible packaging.

'*Business has a responsibility to give back to the community,*' says co-founder of Ben & Jerry's ice cream, Ben Cohen.

Ben & Jerry's has committed a great many efforts to social responsibility and ethical business. These include their PartnerShop Programme social enterprise, a growing movement in which non-profit organisations use the power of business for community benefit. PartnerShops are Ben & Jerry's scoop shops that are independently owned and operated by community-based non-profit organisations. Ben & Jerry's waives the standard franchise fees and provides additional support to help non-profits operate strong businesses.

The ice cream factory provides factory tours and supports a variety of campaigns and causes, most recently helping to fight global warming by teaming up with Dave

Matthews Band and Saveourenvironment.org plus a coalition of advocates to create One Sweet Whirled. 'It's a new flavour, but also a campaign to try to inspire change to the way we impact our world,' says Ben.

Ben & Jerry's promotes responsible business practices that respect the earth and the environment and has an economic mission:

'To operate the company on a sustainable financial basis of profitable growth, increasing value for our stakeholders and expanding opportunities for development and career growth for our employees.'

The business also has a social mission:

'To operate the company in a way that actively recognises the central role that business plays in society by initiating innovative ways to improve the quality of life locally, nationally and internationally.
Our focus is on children and families, the environment and sustainable agriculture on family farms.'

In 1998, Ben & Jerry's introduced the ice cream industry's first pint container made from unbleached paperboard, a new 'eco-pint' carton.

By minimising waste, innovating eco-friendly packaging solutions, supporting sustainable food production, family farms and rural communities, Ben & Jerry are still living up to their 1998 Corporate Giving award for donating 7.5 per cent of their pre-tax profits to nonprofit organisations through the Ben & Jerry's Foundation.

The Co-operative Bank
How? by being customer led, ethically guided the banks own strapline.

The bank's ethical policy was introduced in 1992 to set out precisely what ethical standards would govern the types of businesses the bank would and would not offer services to. The bank chose to base its ethical policy on the concerns of its customers, on the basis that it is generally their money that is being used, and they should have a say in how it is used.

More than a decade later, the bank continues to be the only high street bank that gives customers a say in how their money is used and which encourages their input into the ongoing development of its ethical policy.

'When we launched the policy, more than 80 per cent of customers thought that it was a good idea to have a set of ethical principles guiding our investments. By 2001, this support had increased to 97 per cent of customers who participated in the review. This level of support provides the bank with a clear mandate to implement the ethical policy and we have committed to consult with our customers every three years to obtain a new mandate.'

Why not let your customers help define your policies and help choose your suppliers?

Levi Strauss

How? By pioneering an employee volunteer effort called Community Involvement Teams as far back as 1968, with 79 teams now operating globally.

The Levi Strauss Foundation provides innovative 'sourcing' grants to local, regional or global non-profit organisations to support programmes that themselves support education and human rights programmes.

Levi Strauss, who devoted substantial time and resources to charitable and philanthropic activities, set his corporate values as empathy, originality and integrity and they still underline how Levi Strauss behaves as a business.

In 1991, they became the first worldwide company to establish a comprehensive ethical code of conduct for manufacturing and finishing contractors working with the company.

Since then they've launched The Levi Strauss Foundation which provides grants to community-based organisations working to create meaningful social change. There is also a focus on corporate giving and employee community involvement and volunteer schemes.

PATAGONIA

Patagonia is a sportswear and equipment company 'committed to the core' to the soul of the sport, environmental action, uncommon culture and innovative design.

How? By building products and working with processes that cause the least harm to the environment, funding support groups, and donating to the natural environment.

'*We believe in using business to inspire solutions to the environmental crisis,*' say Patagonia on their website.

Not only do Patagonia use quality cotton from sustainable sources. They've created a Patagonia child care centre for their staff, built an innovative and environmentally-friendly customer service centre in Reno, Nevada and have set up a number of environmental initiatives using their business to promote restoration of the environment.

HUG

HUG (www.hug.co.uk) – make organic cotton clothes for women, men, children and babies.

How? HUG's mission is 'to make fair trade fashion and to make fair trade fashionable.' They do this by using only certified organic cotton, a guaranteed price for the farmers who grow it, and good labour conditions in the garment factory they contract with (like a 48 hour week, redundancy, maternity and sick pay).

All HUG clothing is made using a special long-fibre certified organic cotton from Peru, which is noticeably softer than the cottons used by even the best fashion brands. This, and the use of high-tech Swiss-made ecological dyes, makes their tops beautifully soft.

'*Being ethical doesn't mean you can bypass the laws of economics,*' advises Nick Pecorelli, founder of HUG. '*Thousands die every year from pesticide use on cotton. Beautiful fashion doesn't need to cause death,*' says Nick, advising start-ups looking for growing opportunities to consider the ethical option.

'*There are plenty of people out there waiting for ethical businesses that get the design, quality and customer service right too.*'

Vodafone

How? Vodafone train their senior executives on corporate responsibility and run forums on responsible purchasing, handset recycling, ozone depletion, energy efficiency, responsible marketing and transparency on the radio-frequency issue.

They're developing innovative speaking phones for the visually impaired and mobile technology for diabetic-monitoring purposes.

Says Charlotte Green, director of Corporate Responsibility at Vodafone:

'*Vodafone is donating wind-up and solar-powered radios to give African children access to information and supporting a measles vaccination programme, also in Africa. Corporate responsibility will have to become a cornerstone for those companies that want to be around for the long haul.*'

Other ethical businesses

♦ JJB had sourced some clothes from Burma but now manages its supply chain much more effectively. They now get any Far Eastern suppliers to sign a 'socially responsible trading policy' which sets requirements governing working conditions and environmental/social impact.

♦ Tesco has a few hundred foreign suppliers (on top of almost 4,000 in the UK). They have helped set up the Ethical Trading Initiative to agree fair pay and workers' rights.

♦ Barclays Bank has created a staff volunteering scheme whereby a quarter of their staff volunteer in some way, from educating locals about HIV/Aids in Africa to mentoring young offenders in West London. Staff are given two days' paid leave to get involved in some form of voluntary activity. The bank also offers staff up to £1,000 to set up employee-volunteer groups.

♦ Comet have come up with an innovative scheme to save waste, serve the local community and raise their public profile. They've trained long-term unemployed local people to strip down electrical goods that have been returned, fix them and give them away or sell for substantial discounts to disadvantaged local families.

♦ Scottish Power turned unhappy customers into thrilled ones by investing in a £20 million community-based tree-clearing initiative, working with local communities to fell trees in preparation for forecasted storms. The result was limited damage to the homes of locals and restricted power loss (along with happy customers). The year before was quite the contrary however, with some Scottish Power customers being left without power for as long as six days, damaging the company's reputation for customer care significantly. Since then, Scottish Power invested in protecting the community and taking preventative measures and have reaped the rewards, through improved customer loyalty, customer numbers and by winning The Business in The Community Company of The Year Award in 2002-3.

STEP 34: GET ETHICAL – CONSIDER YOUR LOCAL AND GLOBAL COMMUNITIES AND PLANET

Social Responsibility Checklist

So are you ready to set your business up as a socially responsible one? Here's a checklist to help you make a difference.

◆ Be honest – make transparency vital in all areas.

'If you've got a small business just don't tell lies. That's almost unheard of in business now. Be honest and open to your employees and those you work alongside. Be honest to your suppliers and your customers. Honesty. Can you imagine in the cosmetics industry where the modus operandi is just to lie about what products can do? I think honesty will stand you apart from anyone else, and so will humour.' Dame Anita Roddick

◆ Network.

'They're out there, so connect up. If you're moved by something, you should always network and connect up and say thank you and get involved.' Dame Anita Roddick

◆ Support your global community by sourcing only fairly traded goods.
◆ Use organic supplies and manage your supply chain.
◆ Have suppliers sign a socially responsible trading policy.
◆ Create voluntary community schemes for staff ranging from skill sharing to regenerating wasteland. Community involvement will instill a sense of pride in your workforce.
◆ Save waste by fixing returned goods.
◆ Recycle paper, waste, water, cans, plastics.
◆ Develop innovative products that create change.
◆ Donate to good causes: donate time, services, goods or funds.
◆ Create positive partnerships within your local community; with customers and suppliers.
◆ Spread the word and campaign for issues of importance to you.
◆ Commit to targets and report on your progress.
◆ Fundraise to help your local community or a campaign close to your heart.
◆ Network with others to exchange best practices and ideas.
◆ Consider regeneration. If you are moving your office, consider moving to an area you might not have previously considered to provide opportunities for those without.
◆ Encourage local education, fund education programmes. 'Invest in the success of others; the more you give, the more you get,' says Julie Meyer.

- Work with local producers to develop sustainable local supplies.
- Embrace the notion of creating a micro-community within your own local community, especially if you run any kind of entertainment establishment, café, restaurant, bar. It should be a hub of activity that creates a great experience for your customer. Lift your community's spirit, watch them form relationships, introduce people, smile and build an atmosphere.
- Build long-lasting markets by seeking out sources that are currently maltreated or undiscovered.
- Avoid entering markets in countries that have poor human rights records (unless of course you are actively campaigning to change those human rights).
- Pull your community together to work towards a common goal and watch your business profit.

'Support your local community in whichever way you can. Taking a high profile in the community is a far better marketing strategy than trying to outspend the competition, if for no other reason than the positive impact on staff morale.

Find something that outrages you, that moves you to act. Pick any issue, whether it's waste, whether it's the environment, whatever makes you angry should also make you act and get involved. You can't be informed if you're passive and sitting in watching TV, you've got to see the control. Find out where the local Government office is. Follow the money and influence, and find out why this is being put there, who's funding it, who's behind it? It's a terrific sense of real investigation into where the real power lies. People forget that the power is within themselves, but the system is relying on apathy. It's apathy that's making things we don't want happen. It's the biggest dilemma in our society. So just get involved where you can.'
Dame Anita Roddick

- Make your business a force for positive social change. Use your products as conduits for it. Does your playgroup business use unsafe materials? Do you make something that could provide an alternative? Could you help solve the graffiti problem in your area or educate youngsters in the area?
- Make your finances transparent. Include in your measure of success enough to sustain communities, cultures and families.
- Pay your corporation and/or self-assessment tax.
- Commit to a common purpose and watch the good it does your company. Produce a sustainability action plan for the business and as part of every staff member's development plan to promote sustainability in their work.
- Think about the story behind any product or service your company sells or purchases.
- Don't use plastic bags for packaging or general use.
- Don't provide bottled water in plastic bottles.
- Recyle your paper, your rubbish and use recyclable packaging materials. Create recycling processes and use both sides of each piece of paper.
- Safeguard the environment by conserving energy and resources. Elevate conservation over consumption.

- Practise good environmental office cleaning and clean up mess responsibly.
- Use energy efficient light bulbs.
- Cut carbon emissions in your factory. Tom Delay, head of the Carbon Trust says, *'those that act now by cutting carbon emissions will be tomorrow's winners, whereas those that wait are risking their future business success.'*
- Plant trees.
- Share your journey to work – share your car or get a lift with a colleague. Take turns.
- Recycle office furniture and coffee machine cups.
- Reuse redundant or returned goods in some way. Deal with waste effectively.
- Offer doorstep collection for customers who want to return goods on dedicated days throughout the year, or have amnesty days to encourage recycling.
- Conserve water. Consider alternative landscaping, fix leaks and install water-saving devices.
- Economise on car use. Do as many things as possible on one trip. Keep your car tuned up.
- Compost food products.
- Turn off lights, heaters and fans when not in use.
- Have a 'litterless lunch' as often as possible.
- Consider using the principles of industrial ecology in manufacturing.
- Use a mug instead of a plastic cup.

And let's leave the last word to an expert on the subject of ethical honest and true business:

'My vision, my hope, is simply this: that many business leaders will come to see a primary role of business as incubators of the human spirit, rather than factories for the production of more material goods and services. The business of business should not just be about money, it should be about responsibility. It should be about public good, not private greed.' Dame Anita Roddick

Inaction is no longer an option – if *we* don't act, who will?

Be responsible: take action.

CHAPTER TEN

Your Website – Planning and Creating a Website that Works

The internet is not just an information superhighway and search tool. It's an excellent marketing tool for your business, a tool that allows you to control the whole online marketing process. Low costs, combined with multimedia capabilities and the rise in internet usage, make the web a very dynamic marketing channel indeed.

You can reach millions of customers and prospects on the web; it's fast and effective; you can establish one-to-one communication; you can automate messages to customers and you can receive feedback to help amend and fine-tune marketing messages and campaigns.

This chapter looks at the benefits of having a website, what's involved and how to effectively plan and create a website that visitors will use, buy from and return to. We'll walk through the planning of the website, from content (what people will be able to read on your website) and navigation (how people browse the website) to the words, layout and design. Resources to help you build your own website or have it designed professionally are also included, with details of what to look for in a web designer. You can also learn from the case studies of successful pure dotcoms and those whose websites have proved to be a profitable extension of their regular business.

Why Web?

E-tail or online retail has grown year on year with and accounting for 10% of all retail sales, according to IMRG. Ample room for you and your business to harness the power of the web to increase profits, target specific niche markets or generate fresh leads. In fact, according to the Centre for Retail Research (CRR), UK consumers spent £38bn online in 2009, an average of £1,102 per shopper and more than anywhere else in Europe.

The benefits of doing business on the internet are:

◆ You can sell your products/services 24 hours a day, seven days a week and awake to see how much money you've made while you slept. Nice touch!
◆ You have a global reach. I have US clients and European clients I'd never have had the opportunity to sell my services to without the web. No need to rely on passing footfall trade.
◆ It is easier to target niche audiences online via a plethora of websites and targeted groups.

♦ Marketing can be quick and cheap. E-mail costs nothing but time and your web connection costs.

♦ It makes working from home a more viable option.

♦ There's less initial outlay than if you are leasing a shop or office space.

There are a multitude of reasons for taking your business online – in fact, some businesses operate as pure dotcoms, with no 'bricks and mortar' side at all. These include Amazon.com, Iwantoneofthose.com, Sharpcards.com and ilikemusic.com.

Other regular businesses – retail outlets, service business – use the web as a natural extension of their offline operation: as an online brochure, lead generation or sales tool. Some websites enable sales to take place there and then and are e-commerce enabled with shopping carts.

So let's look at successful businesses that have used the web as an extension of their offline business and seen their profits leap up as a direct result.

CASE STUDIES

Teambuilding.co.uk

'*In 1995 a friend called me and told me that the internet was going to be big,*' says James Coakes. '*I listened and managed to buy the domain name www.teambuilding.co.uk for about £20. Since then our website has sat high in the search engines. It brings in around half of our business each year and has taken me from £250,000 to £1.2 million in eight years.*'

Garden.co.uk

For Harry Ganz of The Garden Pharmacy, www.garden.co.uk, the business was looking to increase turnover and profit beyond passing footfall. With rents soaring (the shop is currently paying 25 times the original rent), the business, based in Covent Garden, London, was seeking a strong strategy to help them achieve their objectives, and the web provided the ideal opportunity.

'*Online business has one big advantage over offline business as the sky's the limit. There's only a certain number of people who can come through the door to buy from you in an offline shop, and maybe a handful more you can persuade to come into the store via promotions, but there is a limit. Whereas you don't have that limit on the web – 95 per cent of our customers are national and local (UK) with five per cent coming from the US and Japan.*'

Harry comments, '*since the first e-commerce site was established in 1999 with an investment of £5,000, the volume of orders has increased dramatically, and continues to do so. 2000 saw an increase of 90 per cent over 1999. Our internet revenue has now become more than a sideline to the bricks and mortar business – it accounts for 40 per cent of total turnover and, of our 28 staff, three are full-time on mail and web order processing.*'

'*The bricks and mortar side takes more work and you're more dependent on your staff. But without the bricks and mortar we wouldn't have the clicks and mortar online business,*' adds Harry.

Anythingleft-handed.co.uk

Founded in the late 1960s Anything Left-Handed has successfully taken a niche bricks and mortar business to clicks and mortar, and its Director, Keith Milsom, has become somewhat of an expert on running an internet business. With an E-Commerce Award in the bag, an average of 50 website orders per day, a healthy visitor to purchase conversion rate and 60 per cent of sales now coming from www.anythingleft-handed.co.uk.

'Anything Left-Handed had all the attributes needed to succeed online,' explains Keith. *'It was an established brand that was quite well known worldwide, we've got a good range of globally generic products, which are physically small enough that they can be put into bags and sent by mail all over the world.'* Not only that, the product was already proven through the existing mail order business and shop, so demand was already evident.

Wildwestjerky.co.uk

From fishing guide in the Outer Hebrides to internet entrepreneur – Richard Davies is a one-man testament to the power of the internet. Now his company, Wild West Foods, is bringing in over £5,000 a month and winning top food awards.

'Without the Internet I wouldn't have a business,' says Richard. And he's absolutely right. *'Five years ago, an American fishing friend brought some beef jerky over, and I absolutely loved it. The problem was, I couldn't find or buy it anywhere,'* Richard explains.

Using the free internet services at his Local Enterprise Council, 30 miles away, Richard began to research his idea and set off to the States. Despite US companies not wanting to share their recipes or contacts, Richard returned home and logged on to the web. Within minutes he'd found what he needed, a distributor who already exported to Germany. And because, between them, Richard and his German colleagues buy enough meat for Germany, Denmark and the UK in one go, they are able to share the cost of shipping.

He got himself a £1,500 loan and additional £1,000 grant from The Princes Trust and his Local Enterprise Agency helped out with the cost of the website, due to Government funding available to rural businesses going online. Using his £2,000 overdraft until cashflow improved, Richard was ready to launch forth.

A level playing field

The beauty of the internet is that it means small businesses can compete effectively – nobody knows the size of your company from a web address (URL).

> *'One of the nice things is that you can start off small and people don't know you're small.'*
> Michael Parker of AQuarterOf.co.uk

Communications toolkit

Most successful business people are now making the most of the web as a perfect communications vehicle for their business. It gets you out there. Dame Roddick is no exception.

'I'm an obsessional communicator. Whether it's the billboard, audio or visual, or electronic information like the web, then for me I use every medium to get my messages across; the web offers another choice.

It's also a way to get my ideas across that's not through the mainstream media. These ideas in the media are consistently censored by indifference, or if it's not celebrity or entertainment it's not included. For me the web is absolutely major at getting my information. Finding the truth on the web is much easier than finding it within the mainstream media.'

Quite literally you can publish your own news within minutes, rather than waiting for the mainstream press to write about you. Dame Roddick airs her views, features human rights news and provides educational insight into global issues at www.anita roddick.com and www.takeitpersonally.org.uk.

CASE STUDY
A bun deal – Thecakestore.com

The web has literally saved businesses from going under too. Local supermarkets were squeezing the life out of Tim and Kevin Slatter's family bakery business, with profits dropping each year as customers opted for the convenience of the supermarkets.

The internet has helped them to triple turnover and has given them acres of publicity in the national press.

They focused on a product area where these giants can't compete and harnessed the web at the same time. They fought back with The Cake Store, selling imaginatively decorated, mouth-watering celebration and wedding cakes, with a resulting tripled turnover since re-branding and going online.

Slatters Bakery began life as just one bakery shop 70 years ago, established by Tim and Kevin's grandfather, with their father expanding to five shops and even supplying wholesale. But times have changed. No longer do mums nip out for their bread twice a day. It's all about saving time and money. Twenty years ago all bakers' shops were busy, and we ate fresh cream cakes regularly, but not these days.

Crunch time was early 2001. Tim and Kevin were co-running their struggling bakery business with four shops in south London, but local superstores were undercutting their bread prices. Food habits and bakery products were changing; the era of take-aways, health food, wider choice and the rise of one-stop supermarket shopping were creating problems for Slatters Bakery.

'*Whatever we did sales weren't going up on bread and pastries,*' recalls Kevin. '*We were getting clobbered by the supermarkets for about ten years,*' adds Tim.

'*It's impossible to compete with the supermarkets because they do a good job and sell bread for 10-30p as a loss leader, but people think that's how much it costs, so our £1 bread might not sell when people can buy it for 30p and stick it in the freezer – we had to offer something they couldn't compete with instead.*'

Something needed to be done.

Specialising in a product that supermarkets only provided as standard (rather than spectacular) and in something their dad had specialised in years earlier, celebration cakes seemed the ideal product to specialise in. And unlike their dad's six-weeks-in-production-competition-winning cake creations, theirs would be stunning yet commercially viable.

'*Everyone has a birthday every year, and there's so many people in London, certainly enough to target, plus many other occasions, such as anniversaries, weddings and christenings,*' says Kevin, '*so the market was definitely there.*'

They found an ace up their sleeve with a dynamic cake decorator called Steven Howard. 'His skills were totally unexploited. So, with Steve making a spectacular range of cakes and my brother Kevin running the business, I began developing our website www.thecakestore.com which we launched in October 2001,' explains Tim.

'*It would have cost an absolute fortune to hit that marketplace. With the internet the customers come to you through search engines and links and they know what they want. If you type "birthday cake London" we come up top in the search engines.*'

So, with Tim already doing all the business accounts, having converted them from his dad's manual system, he started off on his computer and website learning curve.

Now, nearly three years later, there are over 450 different types of cake on offer from simply decorated, themed birthday cakes at £22, up to ornate 22-tier wedding towers costing £900+. The total bricks plus clicks turnover is now £1million with around 160 sales per month coming from the web store at an average of £55 each. This is a major turn around for the business that had £300,000 less revenue *and* higher overheads when it was a high street only set up. '*There's no doubt that e-commerce saved us,*' says Tim. '*Turnover's risen despite downsizing the offline operation to two stores,*' adds Kevin.

Getting Your Website Right

Of course, there are crystal clear benefits why any person in their right mind in business should have a website. But, like anything in business, creating a website that doesn't achieve a good return on investment or meet your objectives (or the needs of your customers) can be an expensive mistake. That's why you need to plan.

Understand what the web can do for your business, and get ready to harness the power of the internet.

You need to get it right. Research by BT Openworld shows that a quarter of small firms are at risk of losing customers by relying on out-of-date company websites. So it's not a case of sticking a website up and that's it, job done. You need to promote it and keep it fresh by updating it regularly.

In January 2003 the Interactive Bureau found that the corporate websites of the UK's top 100 companies had improved in the past year, but 'many are still wallowing in mediocrity.' The company's latest study has found that more than half of FTSE's 100s' websites have serious problems that need fixing – while 16 are so badly designed they should be taken down! Pretty harsh stuff.

The IB found that 24 per cent of these websites that had been redesigned are worse than before. Luckily 76 per cent had improved. But the simple fact is that many web designers don't know or care enough about the end user when designing sites for customers. After all, web designers generally are creative designers and technical coders, not usability, copywriting or CRM experts. Obviously this isn't always the case – there are some web design agencies which also specialise in usability but they are few and far between.

By understanding the basics of a good website you can avoid wasting money on the web. Regardless of numbers and statistics the average web user – be they customer using the web or employee using an intranet – visits a website **to access information** or **perform tasks** as **quickly** and **easily** as possible.

Sounds simple enough doesn't it? If you can create a website that enables users to access information or perform tasks quickly and easily – bingo.

Unfortunately, it's not as simple as that! Why?

Because... there are so many variables involved in making a website really perform. Each of these variables needs to be reviewed and revised to really make your website work for you, and ultimately optimise its performance/results.

Success criteria/variables:

1. **Navigation/information hierarchy/usability** – the order in which you place information and allow users to browse your site.
2. **Content** – must be useful enough to encourage return visits from your visitors.
3. **Copywriting** – the message must be clear, crisp and web-friendly.
4. **Design and appearance** – needs to create the right perception.
5. **Search engine readiness** – must be indexable and likely to get a good ranking in the search engines.
6. **Targeted marketing** – needs to market to the right people at the right time.
7. **Accessibility** – must be accessible by all, including blind and disabled users using screen readers and other technology to browse websites.
8. **Legality/security** – must have all the necessary privacy policies, terms and conditions.
9. **Web metrics/competitive intelligence** – should track your visitors and keep an eye on what the online competition are doing.
10. **Customer satisfaction** – must keep your online customers satisfied by timely response and quick service/delivery.

Each variable is crucial to get right to make the most of your website. You might have all of the above variables working for you, except for the search engine readiness, so you'd experience low traffic despite having a fantastic website. Or you might have a site that is search engine ready but has a confusing message. So you might get plenty of visitors, but few enquiries and no sales.

The majority of people who have websites built for them are not aware of this fact: that all these variables must work together to maximise website conversion rates (how many sales or enquiries you get). So you already have a head start.

STEP 35: PLAN YOUR REASONS/OBJECTIVES FOR HAVING A WEBSITE

By planning how often you'll add fresh content to the site, what your customers want and what you want to achieve, you'll be better equipped to profit online.

The first step is to decide the purpose and objectives of your website. Will it make an excellent additional sales platform to generate revenue and sales directly (via e-commerce and an online catalogue)? Would you like your website to be a stand-alone business in its own right? Or do you see it merely as an online brochure – somewhere to point interested prospects to that reveals what you do and how to get in touch?

These decisions will help guide the design, the content and the whole functionality of your website. If you want the site to be a sales vehicle with a catalogue of products that people can buy direct online, the cost and time needed to develop an e-commerce site and set yourself up so you can accept credit cards will be more than if you opt for a basic 'html' brochure site with no real functionality other than a link for people to e-mail you directly from the site.

Selling Online

There are three ways that you can become a 'merchant' and accept credit cards from your website.

1. By capturing card details securely, transmitting them to your desktop and then processing them through a normal PDQ facility. (For bank approved e-commerce software only.)
2. To process card payments from your site. Service providers include NetBanx, Protx, Secure Trading, WorldPay, Secpay, Datacash and many others. You pay more and generally have to wait for the money, but they process everything on your behalf.
3. A 'bureau' type service. If you are unable to acquire your own merchant account, the providers listed above will transact the funds on your behalf – a useful service for some, but not cheap.

Do you want to sell online? If so, examine the three options above or visit www.electronic-payments.co.uk to view options available

Plan Your Website

Before you build your website you need to plan it – and you need to plan it really well. Believe me, by spending time on the planning stage you'll save time, money and frustrations later on, when it could prove costly to make changes.

1. Revisit your list of USPs. What differentiates you from the competition? List why it will benefit your traditional customers to be able to access you via the web. Why would they want to use your website rather than a traditional shop? To find info, contact you or buy stuff. Is it quicker, more accessible, cheaper, offering more choice? Write what will trigger your offline customers to visit your website here.

2. Browse the web, look at your competitors' websites, jot down what you like and dislike. See what they are doing and aren't doing on their website. List ways you might satisfy unfulfilled wants or needs or future requirements of your customers. Seek out windows of opportunity online. List them. Also browse the web from your customers' perspective. Put yourself in their shoes. If you were them, where would you go online to find the information and products you wanted? List these websites and anything you like or dislike about them. Remember to save any relevant news and publication sites you discover into your media list.

3. Competitive intelligence – know your online competition:
   ◆ Who are your three main online competitors?
   ◆ What do they offer on their websites?
   ◆ Are there any gaps in their offerings?
   ◆ Are there any 'windows of opportunity'?
   ◆ How do your competitors market themselves?
   ◆ Who links to your competitors?

   The competition are literally only a click away, so you need to keep a firm eye on what your competitors are doing online. Is there anything that they are not doing that your customers want or need? Any windows of opportunity? How can you satisfy those needs on your own website?

4. Consider your budget. This will depend on how much control you want over your website. You have a few options. The first is to learn how to build your own website(s). This takes time and could cost a fair amount of money in training materials, but is the best way to retain complete control over your website without having to rely on anyone else (except the hosting company where your website will 'live'). The two other options involve having a web design and development firm create a website for you. A development firm can either design and develop a website for you that they update (so you pay for the design and development, plus a monthly retainer to cover their hourly rate for updating your website).

Or, for a larger cost initially, but no monthly fees to pay, they can design you a site that you'll be able to update yourself without any web programming knowledge. This involves the web team creating a content management system (CMS) that enables you to add text and images, and whatever content you like to the site. However, you'll need to have considered every angle of content, navigation and what you'll need to update before briefing an agency to design such a site. If you are considering making your website the port of call for your industry, with up-to-date news and regularly updated content, you'd be wise to invest in a CMS. Be careful who you choose however. I've used CMSs designed by four different web development firms. Surprisingly, the two most 'technical' firms built systems with many glitches and flaws, that took a long time to load and created many areas of frustration from a user's perspective. The two most creative firms built systems that were easy-to-use and didn't go wrong; solid, usable content management systems – how they should be built. These two firms are Bluebit.co.uk and ZebedeeCreations.com, and these are the only two web design and development firms that I can wholly recommend, except for Vivid-Image.co.uk, another great web design company.

5. Consider from the start whether you wish to sell your wares from your website. Professional e-commerce software is available for under £1,000, even under £500 (Actinic). You will need a merchant account and will need to pay set up fees and charges, plus transaction fees.

6. Ideally, when would you like your website be live for the world to see? Estimate this and then double or treble it, as web development nearly always takes longer than planned. Sometimes you won't have all the content and images you want to use ready to supply to your design team (frustrating for them) or they may be juggling many other projects. Know this and be prepared.

7. Will your market be international? Will you need to have translated versions of the site? The Little Experience secured a grant from Sussex Enterprise to help fund the translation of their children's activity kits and website into five languages. See if you can get funding for language translations (and hence, growth).

8. Gather some relevant web use statistics for your target market. Try www.emarketer.com, www.nua.ie, www.cyberatlas.com and see what's selling best online, what the size of your possible market is, how many UK internet users there are, and so on.

9. Evaluate what works. Which websites have you bought from and gone back to or recommended to friends? List them. What methods are they using that really work? How might you incorporate similar features into your own site?

◆ TOP TIP ◆

Know the difference between web design and web development. A web designer designs the 'front end' – the bit people will see. The web development team will code and programme the 'back end' of the site, the technical, invisible bit that makes it work and function correctly.

Web design is like graphic design but for the web. If you are a dab hand at Adobe Photoshop or know someone who is, consider having them design the site as an image to hand over to the development team.

After being let down by their second development team, ilikemusic.com did just that. The founder designed the site how he'd always wanted it to look as an image and handed it over to the developer who worked wonders creating a content management system and 'back end' to the site. The founder worked with a web usability specialist and the new developer to create a usable site that could be found in search engines – something their previous developers had not bothered about.

Give customers what they want

Once you have a basic understanding of what you want your site to achieve, your approximate budget and other elements, you need to plan further by considering your customers' requirements.

The secret to success both online and offline is to find out what people want and give it to them. Tim Booth of iwantoneofthose.com gives this advice:

1. Make your site live up to your word of mouth and make word of mouth/viral marketing central to your marketing (recommendations are better than suggestions, even editorial).
2. If you can, build your site as a consumer rather than a retailer. Thinking like your audience is crucial. Always be as customer-centric as possible.
3. Tweak your site, products, offers, etc based on customer feedback.

Establish online customer categories: geographic, cultural, job title, industry, age, spending power, values, beliefs, knowledge, lifestyle, media used. These may differ from your traditional offline customers. Use the Focus Group Survey on page 173 to find out more about your online clientele and what they think of your site.

STEP 36: WRITE YOUR WEBSITE BRIEF

Now it's time to plan your website in detail. Include in your brief:

◆ A brief summary of the company and brand image, plus your domain name.
◆ A brief summary outlining your objectives for having a website.
◆ A brief summary (web addresses) of competitors' websites, including those websites (competing or otherwise) that you like, and why you like them.
◆ Any no-nos in terms of design (eg please avoid using images of smiling ladies).
◆ A list of products and services broken down into categories.
◆ Your USP and list of benefits (of using your site and buying your wares).
◆ Mandatory inclusions, such as your e-mail address, contact information, privacy policy, the fact you want the site to be usable, accessible to all and not be built using frames. That the site must be indexable on search engines, and so on.

USER FOCUS GROUP SURVEY

ABOUT YOU   **Date**
Name
E-mail
Contact no
Business

What search terms are you most likely to use to find a site such as ours?

What solutions are you looking for when you visit our site?

Which solutions have you found best suit your needs?

What magazines and online e-zines do you read/subscribe to?

List your six favourite, regularly visited websites
1   2   3
4   5   6

Of the following, which are you most interested in doing?
◆ Saving time
◆ Saving money
◆ Only buying highest quality (price not an issue)
◆ List other benefits here

Website User Testing

Area	Task problems	Result	Page ref	Browser used
General	Visit each area of the site and check all links Perform a search Check that you receive e-mail when expected or advised			
Home page	Sign up to receive newsletter Book an event Register Log on/update profile Submit news Submit feedback form			

- Details of what action you want your website visitors to take and how they should contact you. Do you want them to join your opt-in e-mail list? Register as a full member? Buy your products online? Phone you to place an order or ask questions? Use your chat room and revisit often? Send you an e-mail?
- Ideas on packaging and web prices (will it be cheaper to buy online?).
- Details of product positioning in relation to price and competition.
- A summary of your key target audience segments and where they go online (note, you will also need a strategy to reach that audience, but we'll cover that in the following chapter).
- Details of how you intend to implement a customer service strategy online.
- Delivery and fulfillment requirements. Where will you house stock? How will you deliver? What will that cost you/the customer?
- Details of your timescale.
- Details of your approximate budget.
- Details of navigation, layout, design, content and copy (which we'll look at before the end of the chapter).

Examine these now, before the work begins. Stave off potential problems by reviewing your priority list and determining if resources and budget are in sync.

Once your website plan and actions list is complete, you'll need to list what resources you and your team will need to meet those actionable objectives.

What Will You Put On Your Site?

Content

What you put on your website is the most important thing as it's the glue that keeps visitors there for long enough to retain interest and take action, or possibly revisit.

Most web users find the following to be the most important features of a good website they will use and return to:

✓ Quick load speed
✓ Easy to use
✓ Good, fresh content.

Design and images are secondary. It's what you can do for your visitors and the way you convey this to them that is the key.

What does good content do?

1. Encourages return visits, as visitors see your site as a useful resource worth returning to.
2. Encourages word of mouth (see above).
3. Builds visitor confidence and improves credibility and trust by positioning yourself/site as an expert in your field.

So make your site **useful**. By making your website engaging you will encourage repeat traffic. You'll also build credibility – something of crucial importance on the web.

◆ EXERCISE ◆

Site content

Plan content – what will you include and where will you put it? Do you plan to just display 'brochure' content, ie your contact information, benefits list and information about your business? Or do you want to become *the* resource on your subject matter? If so you'll need a good stock of fresh and up to date content, such as articles, reports, e-books, news, links to other sites and so on.

_____

_____

How will you display your site content, in what formats, and how will your visitors be able to respond or enquire?

_____

_____

Think about how your visitors will prefer to view information: on web pages, as downloadable documents, or in another formats.

_____

_____

Web content ingredients to choose from for inclusion on your website:

◆ A tagline is a must for the what's-in-it-for-me mindset. This is your **online value proposition.**
◆ Prices (including p&p).
◆ A well planned and intuitive navigation system that includes links to a home page, about us page, page detailing your products/services, a page listing customer testimonials, a contact us page including your phone number, a shopping page(s).
◆ Useful content: a good balance between informative and promotional content.
◆ A useful links page, to add value and make it easier for you to collect reciprocal inbound links to your own website.
◆ An opt-in mechanism so you can collect e-mail addresses from interested visitors and build a good prospect list.
◆ Clear privacy statements, and a summary about security.

- Calls to action and contact information. Tell visitors what you want them to do next and give them the means to do so.
- About us information on a dedicated page (not the home page, that's where the benefits go).
- A newsletter.
- Testimonials and case studies to back up your 'benefit' claims.
- Site maps, help, FAQ, search function.
- Articles, reports, white papers.
- E-books and guides.
- Checklists.
- Currency calculators.
- Useful industry statistics.
- Newsfeeds from content providers.
- A directory.
- Downloadable catalogues.
- A guestbook for visitor comments.
- Games.
- Polls and online surveys. Limit them to ten questions. Yes/no and multiple choice answers are the easiest to analyse.
- Communities and discussion boards to provide information and add value.
- Customised log-ins.
- Personalised shopping carts and ordering assistance.

What to avoid:

- Complex sentence structures.
- Large chunks of text.
- Jargon.
- Images of smiling ladies talking on the phone.
- Moving interface elements.

Web content rules
1. Create a site with substance.
2. Display prices and contact information clearly.
3. Make content easy to digest, informative and useful.
4. Keep content fresh and up-to-date.
5. Create an enjoyable visitor experience.
6. Make your home page interesting.
7. Include what you can from the content ingredients list to whip up your own recipe for online success.

Navigation

Once you know what content/products you want to include on your website, you need to figure out how best to display them.

Business on the web is similar to offline business but seems heightened and magnified. If a customer comes to your store and can't find what they're looking for, or can't find someone to speak to, they'll leave and won't return. Similarly, if they have that experience online, they'll click to your competitors' websites before you can say 'world wide web', and they too are unlikely to ever return.

So your site must be easy to use and move around. It must contain up to date information. A bad impression will lose sales. And the last thing you want to do is have your website visitors frustrated by getting lost and not being able to fulfil that all important objective of accessing information quickly and easily.

So layout – known as information architecture, the way information is displayed within your website navigation – does matter. A commercial website should inform, educate and **persuade, but must also be intuitive to move around.**

The key to keeping navigation easy to use and intuitive is to **keep everything relevant.** Every click must provide relevance to the visitor or they won't click at all, except off to another site. Plan navigation – generally a side bar with menu buttons and links (see diagram below).

Map out how you want to guide your website visitors through their buying decision.

To create a usable hierarchy of information you need to think like your user. This is where user focus groups come in handy.

Home	
Link 1	
Link 2	
Link 3	
Link 4	
Link 5	
Link 6	
Link 7	
Home – Terms and Conditions – About Us – Contact Us – Privacy Policy	

A typical website layout.

Who are your visitors?

There are four types of site visitors:

1. Arrive by accident.
2. Know exactly what they want to find.
3. Have a rough idea what they want (this is the typical shopper).
4. Window shoppers, no intention of buying really, just browsing unless something really catches their eye.

With four main types of website visitor, you can decide on the navigation and order of the navigation links displayed, by focusing on displaying your information in the way that will guide each type of customer through to taking action. It's all about relevance!

It's not easy though. You need to try to anticipate visitors' frame of mind, plan the action you want them to take, and tell them what they need to know before they can take that action.

Which part of the search are they at? Have they just realised they need something to help them solve a problem, or are they searching for information, evaluating alternatives, making a decision to buy, buying, evaluating the purchase after it's been bought?

Too much detail early on can kill a sale; not enough information later in the process can kill it just as surely.

Talk to the right person, say the right thing, say it in the right way and say it at the right time.

A good way to keep navigation relevant is to make it task-based. What do your visitors want to do today? Think. Do they want to find information about your company, browse services, download tools? If so, your navigation could consist of Services – Downloads – About Us, and so on.

Navigation rules

◆ Keep it simple. Don't overcomplicate.
◆ Keep content to the three-click rule, so useful content is no more than three clicks away from the home page.
◆ Include a link to the home page from every page on the site.
◆ Keep navigation consistent across the site, so it's the same on each page.
◆ Create either a side bar navigation or top bar navigation with text links along the bottom if you wish.
◆ Keep links in your navigation menu bar to a maximum of seven to nine.
◆ Consider having a site search engine built so your users can search your site for what they need.
◆ Alternatively or additionally, include a site map with text links to offer visitors another method of browsing.
◆ Keep pages short and avoid long scrolling pages, especially left to right scrolling.

Design rules

◆ Position a sharp logo and headline/strapline at the top.
◆ Avoid using in site frames design. Search engines don't like them and they are not necessary.
◆ Make sure the site looks professional.
◆ Make the design clear and simple.
◆ Include plenty of white space with a light background to enhance readability.
◆ Keep colours consistent.
◆ Make sure the site is not too image/graphic heavy so it remains quick to load. Avoid oversized bulky files.

Search Engine Readiness

Your site might be easy to use, and well designed with top notch navigation in place and some great content, but it also needs to be found on the web.

You website must be ready for search engines to find and index, so when people search for 'training services' or whatever your site offers, your site should be listed (hopefully in the first few pages).

Imagine the web as a large village and each house represents a website. Those that come up high on search engines are the houses on the high street or main road. Customers will find them easily enough and stop by. Those who don't appear in the first few pages of search engine results, if at all, are the unreachable houses with unpassable gravel tracks, or houses positioned in the middle of the woods. Customers give up searching for them, or get lost or distracted and turn back.

◆ TOP TIP ◆

If you were opening a traditional retail shop, you'd probably opt for a good position on a high street with plenty of passing footfall. Give your website the same chance by making it search-engine friendly.

Avoid restricting access and avoid splash pages and gimmicks which could have visitors leaving without even stepping 'foot' inside.

The majority of website users find sites via search engines or links from other websites. So these are the two areas to focus your web marketing on. But there's a certain amount you can do at the website design stage to make this easier, including making your site indexable.

Search engine readiness

We'll look in more detail at these in the next chapter, but it's crucial to consider when planning the content, text and design of your website that you consider:

- How you'll make your site indexable. Some rules to consider are avoiding the use of frames, making sure that your website search terms/keywords appear in the body copy of your home page and giving page titles that are meaningful.
- How you'll generate links in. You should plan to have a links/resources page on your website so you can link to other websites. Make sure all links out to other sites open in a new browser window so visitors can remain on your site, even if they click other links to other sites.

Web Copy
Word choice
Try to select words that increase believability, stimulate action and generate interest. After writing your copy, see if any words could be replaced with better, more interesting or active words.

To really maximise the potential of the words you use, you can try prioritising each of your keywords using four criteria:

- Traffic potential – how much traffic would those words be likely to generate in terms of 'search terms' (eg 'getting more customers' might generate higher traffic than 'customer satisfaction improvements', depending on your target audience's needs and language.
- Prospect's intention (eg 'getting more customers' fits with this, as the prospect's intention is to get more customers).
- Stage in the buying process. It's difficult to know this, but some of your prospects will know little about what they want or need (be it a product, service or the right information), whereas others will know exactly what they need and just need to know price or availability. Keywords that satisfy them will include 'web design prices' whereas other visitors, not quite at that stage in their buying process, would use words such as 'find a web designer' or 'creating a usable website'.
- Likelihood to convert – your choice of words could make or break a conversion. So any of your keywords and search terms that are the most likely to convert (inspire your reader to take action) should be prioritised at the top of your list.

Prioritising your keywords and search terms helps determine the value of your keywords too.

Checklist to fine-tune copy for word choice
- Do words stimulate action, generate interest and increase believability?
- Could any words be replaced to encourage action?

Your words and message
Your aim is to convey the benefits of your product/service/website clearly and concisely and compel visitors to act before they click away.

So your message must be effective and compelling, clearly targeted at the right people, accurate (no spelling errors) and should abide by the following rules.

Web friendly writing rules
Make sure you include:

1. Clear, relevant message with clear benefits.
2. A tagline/unique value proposition.
3. 'You' copy, not 'we' copy. Instead of 'we provide the following services', choose 'you can access the following services'.
4. No jargon.
5. Calls to action.
6. Bullet points and numbered lists to break up the text.
7. Highlighted text (in bold) to improve page 'scannability'.
8. Short paragraphs and sentences and no large chunks of text, to improve readability.
9. Page titles, headings and sub-headings to act as signposts to the scanning reader.

Web readability: scannability
According to eye-tracking studies by the Poynter Institute, website visitors look first at text, then at photographs, and at graphics last. It also reported that 79 per cent of website visitors scan web pages for bits of interest and rarely read word for word. The study, along with other usability studies, also concluded that reading from a screen is 20 per cent slower than reading from a printed page. Therefore there are a number of copywriting strategies that have been devised to increase readability and scannability of copy to make it more web-friendly.

When writing copy for your website, ask yourself:

◆ Are magnetic attention-grabbing headlines and sub-headings in place?
◆ Are bulleted and/or numbered lists used?
◆ Have key words and terms been highlighted liberally in bold text to help the scanning eye of the web user? The aim here is that they don't have to read every word to understand your message – so highlight key words in bold with this in mind.
◆ Are sentences and paragraphs short and concise? There should be no large blocks of text.
◆ Is only one point made per paragraph, with the most important point made first?
◆ Is jargon avoided? Use customer language. Not only does this help in terms of relevance and understanding, but in terms of search engine readiness too.

Accessibility
Use the checklist below to make your site accessible to blind and disabled users:

1. Is the text legible? Can it be read easily? Choose text and background colours that contrast well. Avoid patterned backgrounds.

2. Does every image have 'alt-text'? The alternative text attribute of the image tag exists to provide a voiced description of the image for people accessing the site via speech synthesis software. All images must have alt-text (even if the alt-text simply reads '*' to indicate that the image conveys no information).

3. If the site uses frames, is an alternative offered? It's essential that the 'noframes' tag is used to offer links to a frames-free version of the site, as some blind people may be using software that cannot read frames (along with many search engines). Frames must also have titles if they are used.

4. Are navigation links easy to use? Graphical navigational links must be supported by alternative text and the destination of every link must be immediately obvious.

5. Does your site pass the Bobby test? Visit www.cast.org/bobby to run your site through the automated accessibility checker.

Other mandatory inclusions:

◆ Have a privacy policy.
◆ Have a clear returns policy if you sell from your site.
◆ Display clear terms and conditions.
◆ Make sure you abide by Data Protection laws if you are collecting customer information.

STEP 37: HAVE YOUR WEBSITE DESIGNED AND DEVELOPED

Ask potential web designers for quotes based on your brief. They need to understand what you want and who your potential web users are, and if they don't ask for this information, don't let them design your site.

Also, ask to see examples of their work, plus details of languages and future possibilities (should you require a shop or similar in the future, it's best to be able to go back to the same designers to keep consistency throughout), check they can cope with your site's growth and development, no matter how technical it gets. You might need a content management system, or possibly an e-commerce platform with credit card facilities; you might need to add a search engine or some visitor polls, or maybe even member log-in areas and a directory. Also, check out companies' references and testimonials. These will show you the results they've achieved for their clients.

STEP 38: HAVE YOUR WEBSITE HOSTED

Once you have a domain name and a website with as many web pages as you feel is necessary, you will need to host the website, either on a shared server (for lower traffic sites with a lower budget) or on a dedicated server (more expensive, but worth doing if you are expecting thousands of visitors a day/week.) The importance of finding a good host is paramount! Spend time chatting to people you know who have a website and do some research. There's nothing more frustrating than spending time and money on your website and promoting your website, and then finding out that it's gone down. That's down to your hosting company. So spend time finding a good host that won't let you down.

Try www.1and1.co.uk who my sites are hosted with.

STEP 39: MEASURE YOUR WEBSITE RESULTS

To keep improving the performance of your site, you need to get yourself a good statistics package, so you can monitor, test, measure, analyse, tweak, repeat, and find out:

- How many people are visiting your site?
- Where are they coming from?
- Where on the site are they going?
- Where do they spend the most time?
- What pages get the best reponse?
- What are reject rates, especially on contact pages?

Plan – Test – Promote

CHAPTER ELEVEN

Your Website – Launching and Promoting

Having a website doesn't automatically mean anyone will visit it. You need to promote the site. Indeed, having a website without promoting it is like having a dazzling billboard on a disused motorway. Nobody is going to see it. This chapter provides a step-by-step guide to launching and promoting your website, plus practical exercises to help you promote your website cost-effectively. Various online marketing strategies are dissected and evaluated, for you to pick and mix as appropriate for your website objectives; from online networking and e-mail marketing to article writing and online PR.

Successful webmasters and entrepreneurs reveal what web promotion has worked for them and you'll get a chance to create your own online marketing action plan to help you focus on spreading the word about your website to the right people at the right time. We'll look at how to uncover where your target audience goes online and how they find websites, and you'll see how you can implement a link development strategy and use competitor intelligence to improve your presence on the web.

As with all marketing campaigns, you need to figure out the goal of your online campaign. By the end of this chapter you should be able to decide whether the goal of your campaign is:

- To create and establish company identity and brand awareness.
- To encourage readers/users to take action and visit your website and register with you.
- To build a list of prospects and potential subscribers or advertisers.
- To advertise an event.
- To generate repeat traffic and business.
- To provide corporate information and location details.
- To build customer relationships and strategic partnerships.

The nature of your goals will determine which strategies you'll use. Sound familiar? That's because the nuts and bolts of online marketing are no different to regular marketing, in terms of knowing your objectives, your target audience, what they want and where they go to find it. So apply what you've learned in Chapter 7 to your online marketing.

STEP 40: PICK AND MIX YOUR ONLINE MARKETING STRATEGIES

Let's examine those strategies in more detail by reviewing how the great web public source the information and products they are after.

How Do People Find Websites?

1 links from other sites
2 search engines
3 friends: viral marketing; using private network
4 printed media: press releases
5 directories
6 signature files (at the bottom of each e-mail)
7 television
8 books
9 other.

With this data in mind, and knowing what your core online marketing objectives are, you need to decide which strategies to make use of to get people clicking to your site and taking action once they arrive.

You can use:

◆ **Targeted manual site registrations** – to register your web address on relevant sites, directories and search engines, helping to improve your search engine readiness and targeted website traffic.

◆ **Link development** – which entails persuading sites that share a similar audience to yours, but aren't competing, to link to your website. Most will expect you to link to them, so it is important to have a links page and follow the right etiquette in link requesting and reciprocal linking. But more on that later.

◆ **E-newsletters and e-mail marketing** – to build relationships with your website visitors and people who join your mailing list; regular interaction and communication with website visitors is key to repeat business online and e-newsletters are the ideal tool.

◆ **Forums, newsgroups and discussion groups** – to position yourself as an expert in your field, raise credibility, broaden your contact network or source useful information.

◆ **Article writing and posting** – to raise awareness of your website, build credibility, generate inbound links (via your author biography and weblink at the foot of each article) and position yourself as an expert in your chosen subject area.

◆ **Targeted news submissions (snippet press release submission)** – to raise awareness of the brand online.

◆ **Incentives and giveaways** – to encourage e-newsletter subscribers and increase your mailing list sign-up rate, or persuade visitors to purchase.

Let's look at each of these in a bit more detail.

Search engines

Seventy-five per cent of web users don't go beyond the second page of search engine results. That means if your site isn't in the top 20–40 results, you probably won't be noticed. So make your home page indexable. See the previous chapter for details on how to do this.

Why do I need to register my website?

If your site is not registered on search engines or directories, people will have trouble finding it. Also, it is not enough simply to get listed on the search engines, you need to try to get a top ten ranking, so your website comes up on the first page.

For more information on search engines, visit: www.searchenginewatch.com or www.searchengineforums.com

---

◆ EXERCISE ◆

How to register

Brainstorm keywords and key phrases (search terms).

Go back to your customer profile research and feedback results/user focus survey. Based on this, what search terms will people use to find your website? List them here:

_____

_____

_____

There are a variety of 'keyword trackers' available for free use on the net. Go to www.wordtracker.com/report.html. This free service sends you a monthly e-mail containing the top 500 keywords used as search terms, and helps you to choose relevant popular keywords and check how people are spelling search terms.

Write various length descriptions of your website in 25 characters, 25 words, 50 words.

_____

_____

_____

_____

Submit your website address and description to search engines and directories, including Yahoo and Google, AltaVista and Lycos. Submit to Yahoo via this link:

docs.yahoo.com/info/suggest/. You can submit your site to the Open Directory Project (DMOZ) by visiting www.dmoz.org. Once your site is included in either of these directories, Google will often index your site within six to eight weeks, but you can also register your site on Google at www.google.com/addurl.html

The importance of keywords and meta tags

Just as it's foolish to focus on traffic building if you're not getting a good conversion rate from existing site visitors, it's no good submitting your site to search engines and directories if your site isn't optimised for them.

AltaVista look at density of keywords and the ratio of keywords to the rest of the body copy. Don't overdo it though. You don't want to spam the search engines or blur your message. Just tweak your copy to include a few of your primary keywords/search terms.

♦ Write website copy that is keyword rich, especially on your home page (as well as benefit/information rich). Use the words and phrases you've listed: in the opening paragraph of your home page and in your META keyword tag. Brainstorm words that your customers commonly use in searches to find your products and services and brainstorm a list of key benefits and unique selling points. (Your aim is to create keyword rich copy that doesn't detract from your benefit-laden message.)
♦ Write META tags. Meta tags consist of three sections:
  <TITLE>
  < META NAME= "description"
  <META NAME= "keywords"
  Some search engines use them to rank your site, but they are not visible to your visitors. Supply your meta tags to your designer who will include them in the 'source' code of your website.

The Meta Title tag, (5-15 words) the Meta Keywords tag (150 words) and the Meta Description tag (25 words):

♦ In your <TITLE> tag include a description of your page, along with your organisation and/or product name.
♦ The <KEYWORDS> tag is where you put your brainstormed keywords and phrases, separated by commas.
♦ The <DESCRIPTION> tag is where you put the text that will appear when your page comes up in search engines underneath the page title. Your keywords don't appear to site visitors; they are simply to help search engines spider your pages and to direct web users to you when they type in your keywords as search terms.

It can take anything from a few weeks to a few months for your site to appear on the search engines and directories. You can only submit to Yahoo once, others let you resubmit more frequently. Although there is software and companies who will register your site for you, it is widely accepted that it is better to submit your site yourself, manually, to the main search engines and directories.

Link development

Find sites that are complementary to yours and offer mutual links. Many webmasters ignore the importance of linking and think it's a futile exercise to include a web page full of links out to other sites. ('Why drive traffic away from your site?' they protest). Quite the contrary. If you ensure that links out to other sites that you display on a dedicated links page are of interest to your visitors, you add value to your own site (making it somewhere they'll want to return to) and make it easier to persuade other sites to link to you (they are far more likely to link to your website if you are already linking to theirs).

The importance of linking

- Generate high targeted traffic from related sites with good traffic and shared target audience.
- Reciprocal links add value to your own site content.
- Links in to your site from all over the web increases awareness of your brand and web address.
- Links have longevity and often stay active 'indefinitely', unlike message board postings and e-mails that can be deleted. Links generally have more staying power than other methods of online marketing and have more benefits than most strategies. However, implementing a link strategy can be time consuming, so you may wish to employ someone in-house to focus on this on a part-time basis, or outsource to a web marketing business.
- Link popularity is now a central focus to the way some search engines such as Google, AltaVista and Excite rank web pages. The more links in to your site you have, the better your chances will be of receiving a high search engine ranking.

According to the Google Webmaster Help pages:

'If your pages haven't been indexed yet, it's probably because there aren't enough other pages on the web that link to them. Google looks at the link interconnectedness among pages, relying on the vastness and openness of the internet to yield the most relevant search results. If other pages don't link to yours, we can't assign your pages a PageRank (our proprietary measure of a page's importance) in a reasonable way. Once other pages point to them, we'll pick your pages up.'

This is the single biggest factor in determining what sites are indexed by Google, as we find most pages when our robots crawl the web and jump from page to page via hyperlinks.'

So the more quality targeted inbound links you have to your site, the more qualified visitors you'll get, and the more profits you're likely to generate (if you are achieving a good conversion rate, thanks to each variable being fine tuned).

◆ **EXERCISE** ◆

Step one: plan

1. Find sites that attract the same audience as you do, or target the same niche that have high traffic.
2. List the web address and e-mail address for those sites that you actually like (maybe you've bookmarked them) that relate to your business or share a similar target audience.
3. List the most popular sites that share those themes, target audiences, etc. Try to find the sites that get the most traffic.
4. Visit the following sites or use Google's linking tool to find out which websites link in to those sites and those of your competitiors:
   www.link-popularity.com
   www.alexa.com
5. Copy and paste the results (list of who's linking to them) into a text document.
6. Refer to your research. Where have your prospective customers told you they go online? Your aim is to make your presence felt in those places. List them.
7. Spend some time getting e-mail contact information for those sites on the list (from competitor and customer research) that you'd like to link to your own site.

Step two: link

Have your designer add the websites that you intend to request reciprocal links from to your own dedicated 'links' or 'resources' page on your website. Make sure they work and add value to your own site content. For example, UK childcare agency listing site BestBear.co.uk, has a links page with sites of relevance to parents, from baby furniture suppliers to parenting and maternity sites.

Ask your designer to ensure outbound links to other sites open in a new browser window, so visitors will remain on your site, even if clicking the link.

Step three: communication and reciprocation

1. Compile a standard 'link-request' letter telling webmasters of sites you are linking to and how linking to your website is going to benefit their visitors (see example over the page).
2. E-mail the site managers on your list. Make it easy for them to link to you by giving them the exact HTML code (and give them your direct phone number).
3. Alternatively, write a review about a high-traffic related site (a good one) and publish it on your website, then contact the site owner to suggest they link to your review of their site.

◆ **EXERCISE** *(cont)* ◆

Example

```
Hi there,

We've added a link and logo to your website from our links
page, as we found it very useful for our target audience:
www.yourwebaddresshere.com/links

We'd appreciate it if you could reciprocate by adding a link
back to our site.

Search engines now rank pages according to the number of links
in, so linking to each other is a win-win situation.

Here are our site details to add to your site. Many thanks for
your time.

Website: *www.bestbear.co.uk
Title: *Best Bear UK Directory of Childcare Agencies and
Parenting Information

Description: *Best Bear Childcare is a unique and independent
service listing recommended childcare agencies and nurseries
throughout the UK, offering researched information on all
areas of childcare and a comprehensive database of nurseries.

Many thanks. Logo is available on request. Please let me know
if you require one.

Keep up the good work
Best regards
Your Name

*************************************************************

your-email@yourwebaddress.com
www.yourwebaddress.com - Your strapline

*************************************************************

*replace website, title and description with your own.
```

Online networking: newsgroups, forums, chat and discussion boards

Another way to build your prospect list is to establish your credibility and get involved in relevant online discussions. You can position yourself as an expert in your field by visiting forums and discussion boards and answering questions on hot topics. By advising and offering help you can build trust, confidence and loyalty, and attract people to your site, therefore building your prospect list, attracting potential partners, customers and referred business.

However, e-networking is not just another marketing strategy. It involves getting connected, getting fresh ideas, and sharing and solving problems quicker, connecting with people you'd never ordinarily meet and then building new and productive relationships.

This is one of my articles originally published in *Internet Works* magazine, issue 86, republished with kind permission from *Internet Works*.

Ten ways to get more from e-networking

1. **Read and learn.** Sign up and start reading what others are saying. What topics generate the most interest and response? What types of people interest you? Learn about people who are frequent posters or 'top networkers', and read as much relevant advice as you can. Soak up the atmosphere. Now you're ready to introduce yourself.

2. **Be yourself.** Capture your identity in an e-networking profile, signature file or website directory listing, if provided by the e-network. This is your 'bait'. However, avoid the 'about us' page approach to profile creation. This is your chance to get people's attention and inspire them to get in touch, so focus on you. By connecting on a personal level and developing conversations about shared interests (wine, books, dogs) your relationships and 'connections' can advance quicker. As Mike Southon says in his guide to networking, 'people buy from people, not companies.' So be nice, be liked, respect opinions, but above all, be yourself and relax!

3. **Be prepared.** Think about experiences you've had that may be of use to others. Who is already in your personal and business network and what do they do? If new to online networking, post a message to the group or the owners/top networkers telling them so. They will be happy to give you advice on getting the most from the network. A problem shared is a problem halved and how people love to give advice. So ask for it and give it.

4. **Collect people and connect with them.** A good place to start on any e-network is by introducing yourself to the newest members and the most enthusiastic networkers, those like you and those unlike you. Introduce yourself. Consider any synergies. Make friends. Large e-networks, like Ryze.com, Linkedin.com and ecademy.com enable you to invite contacts from your Microsoft Outlook Address Book or e-mail multiple invites. Grow your e-network, because you never know who might be the missing link in the chain.

5. **Give and share.** Do not see e-networking purely as a marketing strategy with a focus on short-term results and business transactions. Successful e-networking is about mutual gain, collaboration, community and sharing. What you give is what you get with e-networking, so it should not be used as a primary lead-generator. CEO of ecademy, Thomas Power says, 'it's not just about transactions, it's about connections.' So refer and match-make within your networks. What are people looking for? What are their goals? Do you know anyone who can help them? Pay attention to words and create matches. Don't ask for something in return. To paraphrase JFK, 'ask not what e-networking can do for you, but rather what you can do for e-networking.' Good e-networking can create many thousands of pounds worth of new business from the best source of all – referral – but not without effort, integrity and a lot of work. Bottom line? Karma is alive and well within e-networks.

6. **Participate and contribute.** Work hard and invest time in e-networking. Start new conversations, change topics, make comments. Remember people. In the words of Ivan Misner, 'it's *network* not net-sit or net-eat, you have to work at it.' Julian Guppy of hki-systems.co.uk agrees, 'it is more important that you contribute with online networking than face-to-face networking, where you can promise a name and number and maybe never get round to doing it. Contribution is the key.' Julian has done £10,000 of new business via ecademy, but has given as much business through referral to other members. 'If you don't help others, you will not last in e-networking.' Thomas Power agrees, 'Community comes first, commerce comes second, relationships first, transactions second.'

7. **Raise your profile and credibility.** Meet people and build your reputation. The more connected you are the more credible you become. Have regular small conversations, post regular helpful messages, and attend events where possible.

8. **Grow your network.** Set yourself targets, such as meeting all local members of your network by the end of the year. Springboard your e-networking to harness the network on your doorstep, and the global village beyond.

9. **Create your own luck.** Get actively involved in your e-community. Recent studies have proved that the more people you actively network with, the luckier you are likely to be. Community and connection are the life-blood of e-networking; they are what motivated 30,000 members from 172 countries to join ecademy. Kerry Santo of As And When is now top networker on ecademy, above founder Thomas (with her 2,691 connections). She says 'I wanted to see if it could be done and it can. I have got a lot of connections in a short time and am now taking time to know them all properly. It just reinforces that nothing is impossible.'

10. **Create your own e-network.** Represent yourself online, your business objectives, your hobbies. Make friends, nurture relationships, have fun and watch your e-family grow.

E-networking: what to avoid

1. Do not see e-networking as a substitute for sales and try to sell your product or service at every opportunity. In order to connect properly and gain tangible results from e-networking you need to listen to people, and give them what you can, rather then taking what you can and ramming your sales message down your network's collective throats.

2. Never spam the network as a whole or individually. Nobody likes a spammer. The way to harm your chances of success in e-networking communities is to annoy people. Use your signature file or profile link as your marketing tool. Connect before you sell. Give before you take.

3. Be a taker. You should contribute to your network, in the shape of messages, blogs, articles, useful news snippets or web links, advice or tips. Contribution and giving is the key to success in e-networking. The more people you help in a positive way, by

referring business to them, matching them with someone you know who can help them, or simply offering kind words or support, the better long-term rewards you'll receive. Never contributing means never getting anything in return, a pointless exercise in e-networking.

There is a veritable plethora of places where people go to chat and interact, express their opinions or seek advice online. Many website have their own communities, discussion groups, message boards or chat rooms. People discuss everything from the election and state of the world to Big Brother gossip and fishing bait. So in some of those hubs of online chatter people will be discussing your area of expertise.

Select forums and discussion boards to join and see what people are talking about. Take note of the kinds of headings that attract the most readers/postings. Apply similarly engaging subject headings to your own postings. Try to offer free snippets of advice or useful weblinks other than your own at first. Answer questions, solve problems, help people out and be friendly and polite. Make sure you always include a 'signature file' on each posting that includes your website address/link, plus your snappy site description. This can be an effective website traffic-generating method, and a great way to network and build credibility.

◆ EXERCISE ◆

Find some relevant networks and forums to join. Here are a few business forums to consider, but also think about which subjects your target audience would discuss and find forums in that area, and local networks too.

www.ecademy.com
www.ryze.com
www.linkedin.com
www.skype.com
www.orkut.com
www.newbusinessvoice.com
www.onlinebusinessnetworks.com
www.digitaleve.org.uk
www.busygirl.com
www.chinwag.com

E-newsletters/zines, opt-in and e-mail marketing

Always remember, marketing is not just about getting an order, it's about getting a customer and keeping them. Nurture your customer relationships with regular e-mails.

E-mail marketing

Of course, your e-mail is jostling for position in cluttered inboxes:

◆ The average UK office worker spends 49 minutes a day working through their e-mail (BBC, 2002).
◆ Many business people now receive over 100 e-mails a day.
◆ Spam accounts for between 36-64 per cent of all e-mails worldwide.
◆ One out of every 2.8 e-mail messages tracked worldwide was a spam message.
◆ Over 50 per cent of spam messages in 2003 came from the US.

So today's challenge is to get e-newsletters and e-mails opened, let alone actioned. These figures illustrate that you need to make your subject line and opening paragraph scream read me rather than delete me. How do you make your e-communications stand out from the rest? By sticking to a few roles. For example,

A key e-mail marketing campaign message should:

◆ have a single, clear, immediate message
◆ have a compelling headline or e-mail subject line to attract interest
◆ provide value and stimulate interest
◆ reveal benefits and end-results
◆ call prospects to take action
◆ act only as a teaser.

But make sure your emails are:

◆ timely
◆ relevant
◆ solicited
◆ quick and snappy to read
◆ precise, clear and simple
◆ personal
◆ containing information of value to the recipient
◆ well targeted
◆ customer-focused
◆ urgent
◆ selling only the web page and not the whole kit and kaboodle
◆ fully integrated.

Why e-mail?

◆ It's quick, cheap and cost-effective.
◆ It gets better response rates than direct mail and other media.
◆ It allows for good customer retention and prospect list building.

- It's a great tool for viral marketing (including something in your e-mail that is compelling enough for the recipient to pass it on to their contact network by e-mail, spreading the e-mail like a virus across the globe).
- It allows customised, immediate, automated responses.
- It offers a quick method of distributing customer surveys and tracking message results.

E-mail also puts you on an even footing with the big boys. Posh stationery and logos, large corporations and smart offices are irrelevant in the realm of e-marketing. With regular e-mails you can build relationships and gather market intelligence. Send regular e-mails to your online prospect list containing special offers, useful information, resources and links, product or service updates, new offers or free reports and surveys. You can also establish yourself as an expert, as a resource for invaluable information by sending out useful e-newsletters or e-zines. At the same time, you can find out what offers your audience responds to best, and what they want to gain or achieve, by e-mailing surveys. You can also respond fast to enquiries from your site.

However, with new laws on unsolicited e-mail (SPAM), you can only build your list of people to e-mail regularly by giving them the chance to **opt-in** and subscribe to your list. They must be able to request removal from your list at any time, and you mustn't share or pass on their details.

Encourage website visitors to subscribe/opt-in by having an opt-in box on your website.

Build your own prospect list
Opt-in e-mail allows you to qualify your online prospects, and ensure they are interested in the topic your site covers, your products and your services. Only those interested will opt-in or register. And, once they've permitted you to send them regular e-mails, you can use e-mail as a tool for getting your message across, gaining credibility and building your relationships with them.

An opt-in box is a simple form on your site, where a visitor can leave their name and e-mail address in exchange for:

1. Some information that relates to your website theme and target audience's interests, such as articles, industry news, updates, reports, e-books or white papers.
2. A free subscription to an e-zine or e-course, which can build trust and put you in regular contact with your prospects, as long as the information is good, timely and useful. They also allow you to create a family of subscribers to whom you can offer special discounts, and 'privileged information'.
3. Regular updates on special offers, new services or products.

For example, your opt-in box text might say: 'Enter your name and e-mail address below and we'll keep you posted about the latest ideas on training your team.' The website visitor simply enters his or her details and clicks a button. They've then opted-in to receive further information from you.

What to send your opt-in-ers

First send an e-mail saying that they've subscribed and this e-mail is solicited. Redefine the benefits of subscribing and tell them how often they'll receive the e-newsletter. Tell them how they can unsubscribe and about your privacy policy. Keep a record of each opt-in. Contact your Internet Service Provider (ISP) and notify them that you may be sending bulk e-mail to your solicited list.

The purpose of this opt-in strategy is to build a prospect list of people who are interested in what you offer, and in subjects relating to that offer. These people are giving you permission to e-mail them and may buy from you at a later date. You can offer incentives to your prospect list/subscriber base, to encourage them to buy.

As long as the information you supply to your prospects is useful and good quality, you will build credibility and a loyal customer base, to whom to sell related products/services.

◆ TOP TIP ◆

Go viral! If you create and use a signature file to go at the end of every e-mail you send, you can spread the word when people forward your e-mail messages. Always include a signature file on your postings to discussion boards and forums. It should always include your URL (web address) and be six lines or less.

When to e-mail:

- ◆ Most worldwide net traffic occurs on Mondays (15.31%).
- ◆ Net traffic is at its lowest on Saturdays and Sundays.
- ◆ Use your own web metrics to see which day your site is the most popular. Send e-mails on the morning of your site's most popular day.

E-newsletters

By creating a regular e-newsletter for those who sign up to your mailing list, you will raise awareness, credibility and keep communication channels open with those who want to hear from you. Ideal!

What should you include in your e-newsletter? First of all, your e-newsletter should be presented in digestible bites, offer food for thought and prompt readers to open your publication issue after issue. The main thing subscribers will be looking for is **value**.

Include a selection of the following:

- ◆ clear branding/logo
- ◆ an opening editorial statement
- ◆ a table of contents

- a section of bulleted tips
- a short and snappy guest article
- links to relevant useful sites
- industry and company news and updates
- an invitation for subscribers to forward the newsletter
- a privacy policy and copyright notice
- valid 'from' and 'subject' lines
- an unsubscribe link and instructions on how to unsubscribe and subscribe
- your contact information.

Also consider including extra content in your newsletter, such as:

- recommended reading
- director's note or personal comment
- featured products or services
- a search function that searches your website from the newsletter
- a log-in box
- task led links to your website and others
- short case studies
- snippets of news
- motivational quotes
- a short cartoon strip
- giveaway details; chance to enter a competition via your site.

Use your web stats software (such as Urchin, Webalizer or Webtrends) to analyse which day of the week your website gets most traffic and/or most conversions. This is the day you should send your e-newsletter.

- Test different versions of e-newsletters to maximise response.
- Test which subject line pulled the best response.
- Which body copy worked best?
- Which offers did people respond to the best?
- Which niche market responded the best?
- Which call to action generated the best response?

You can then use this information to make each e-newsletter more effective than the last.

E-mail marketing checklist

- Think about what you want to say before you write anything and then organise your ideas into bullet points and short summaries.
- Think about your e-mail recipient as an individual. Where will they be when they read your message, who are they and what do they want or need from you? How would you respond best if you were them? Get that imagination working.

- Write notes about the key points you want to get across, their priority and the e-mail's purpose. Think about any questions your e-mail recipient may have about your offer. Try to answer these briefly.
- Only write one point per paragraph and keep sentences and paragraphs short (four to six line paragraphs and the entire message a maximum of 300 words in length).
- Highlight keywords, use bulleted lists and keep it short. These techniques improve the readability of online messages. According to usability expert Jakob Nielsen (www.useit.com) and a recent eye-tracking study by the Poynter Institute, 79 per cent of readers scan online text, picking out parts that interest them.
- Simply recycling traditional marketing materials won't do. This doesn't translate to the net easily. Nielsen advises marketers and webmasters to use 50 per cent less text in their online messages as the reading process online is 20-25 per cent slower than print.
- Incentivise your readers to act with a time-sensitive compelling offer.
- Always include a call to action.
- Always use a signature file and encourage readers to pass the message on to friends or associates who might find it useful. Viral marketing can harness the power and simplicity of e-mail for maximum effectiveness. A signature file is crucial to this end.
- Send out online questionnaires to your e-mail list to find out how they learn and what they read. Find out what magazines and e-zines they read or subscribe to; what their favourite websites are; which sites they have bookmarked. Use the information to amend your promotional campaign.
- Keep the text upper and lower case and don't shout by using capitals.
- Format your e-mails so they are easy to read in any browser. If your e-mail program doesn't include word-wrapping facilities, make your line length a maximum of 60 characters and press return at the end of each line. When printed, it will be neatly laid out.

E-mail is one of the best online marketing tools at your disposal. Use it wisely and make your messages stand out from the rest; find out what works and what doesn't, and come up with your own winning formula.

Article writing and positioning
If you can write and spell and are knowledgeable about any topic relating to your website, products and services:

1. Write a short article or series of informative articles about the topic.
2. Include a good signature line at the end of your article, e.g. 'Written by Cheryl Rickman of www.webcopywriter.co.uk. For more tips on writing for the web e-mail info@webcopywriter.co.uk'.
3. Submit your article to relevant offline and online publications with permission granted to reprint the entire article, including the contact details, copyright notice and signature line.

> ◆ **TOP TIP** ◆
>
> By using articles to promote your website you can establish yourself as an expert in your field and build your credibility continually, as articles can be passed on and used over and over again for many years.

And it **costs you nothing** but a little time (unless you hire a professional writer to write them).

You've examined each online marketing strategy and know what you want to achieve from your online campaign. It's time to pick up a few pointers from the pros before launching your website to the world.

STEP 41: LAUNCH YOUR WEBSITE

What Works? Tips from the Top

Harry Ganz of The Garden Pharmacy has made some smart decisions when it comes to promoting his website:

◆ No print advertising.
◆ No paying for space (eg banners, pop-ups) on other sites except on a pay-per-click or commission basis. (Pay-per-click advertising by sites such as Overture and Google involves setting a budget to pay them for certain keywords. You pay only for visitors who click through to your site.)

Tim of iwantoneofthose.com agrees, with his tips including:

◆ Don't advertise.
◆ Hire a PR company for launch or relaunch if you want instant sales.

Affiliate resellers

One of Harry and Tim's secrets to attracting visitors is affiliations. Garden.co.uk currently has a network of 900 affiliates through AffiliateWindow.com that generate 12-14 per cent of traffic.

Of course, affiliates are paid commission and Harry has opted for a generous ten per cent, double that of the majority of beauty sites, but he is more than pleased with the results:

'With affiliate marketing you're giving a percentage of your sales, but you're only going to pay if the sale is made and it's sales you wouldn't have seen ordinarily. Also, you hope that once you've hooked the customer, they'll come back to you directly without going through the affiliate and it won't cost you for their future business.'

So if you will be selling products from your website, consider joining one of these affiliate marketing companies as a merchant and you could soon have lots of sites all over the web affiliated with you, that link to your site with a unique trackable link. Commission can then be tracked by the affiliate marketing company and paid by you on sales you would never have had.

Relying on traffic and sales from affiliate and strategic partners can be a great way of getting the most from the web: hundreds of other sites all reselling your products on your behalf.

Sharpcards' Will Walsh also made good use of this online strategy, which offline would be comparable to having lots of instant distributors who earn commission from each sale they make. You balance out the cost of acquisition of customers (which is now their cost) with having to pay commission.

'One of the first things we did was to sign up with TradeDoubler, and they're very useful for getting in the traffic and links. We also had a person totally dedicated to setting up these online partnerships, which range from quite small ones to BT and Lastminute.com.' Will Walsh

Sharpcards other marketing strategies include:

◆ stickers on all envelopes with web address
◆ word of mouth
◆ a referral programme offering free cards to people who refer a friend.

'It's all been online marketing except for freelance PR – which is important as none of us have any PR knowledge. We've also got involved with partners to keep the momentum going.' Will Walsh

Keep it targeted

You might jump with glee if you suddenly get 1,000 visitors one day, but not if none of them take action by signing up to your mailing list or buying something. You can improve the chance of them making a purchase by aiming to drive targeted traffic to your site – those most likely to buy from you.

'*Our conversion rate is actually about four per cent overall from front-end unique visitors to orders,*' says Keith Milsom of AnythingLeft-Handed.co.uk. But Keith's expertise on the subject of conversion rates has taught him that very much depend on the type of traffic you get to the site.

For example, when left-hander Eminem won a global music award for his album, Keith put up a page about Eminem. '*This brought in thousands of people looking for information about Eminem,*' explains Keith. '*None of them were interested in buying left-handed products, so lots of traffic, with very low conversions.*'

The opposite method is to do pay-per-click advertising for individual product key-words, so the visitor has already made the decision that they want a left-handed product, and is visiting the site with the specific intention of comparing it or buying it. '*That would increase the conversion rate up to 40 per cent, but neither of those routes would do us much good,*' Keith adds.

'*In practice you need the right balance, so we try to bring in as much untargeted traffic as we can, because some of it will skim off and buy things, and we do targeted marketing as well.*'

Anything Left-Handed's traffic comes from three main sources, roughly a third each: through offline and online editorial and e-marketing; through search engines; and through the 1,200 incoming links to the site, some of which are affiliate links.

Keith has tried and tested and done the sums:

'*Our general pay-per-click advertising has a return of about 500 per cent – so I know for every dollar I spend on Overture I get $5 profit. It's critical to know your conversion rates on your pay-per-click advertising for it to work effectively.*'

◆ EXERCISE ◆

- ◆ Set yourself a target of doing three things to promote your website every day. Make a phone call; send targeted e-mails; write an e-zine or press release; contact one publisher or potential advertiser/link partner; post one message on a forum…
- ◆ What will you do on launch day? Submit your site to ten search engines? Submit a media release to your list? Send out your first batch of link request e-mails?
- ◆ How much will you need to include in your budget for online marketing, including paying a PR expert, paying-per-click or registering on targeted directories that charge one-off fees?

_____

_____

_____

_____

_____

_____

_____

Prepare to promote.

CHAPTER TWELVE

How to Manage and Grow – Tips from the Top

Effective Management, Leadership, Time Management and Coping with Stress

You're nearly there. But once you've launched and are up and running, don't go thinking you can rest on those laurels. Things change. Be anticipatory.

So you've learnt the individual elements of starting up and running an effective small business. By the end of this chapter, you should be able to answer the following questions:

- How do you put it all into practice, start up and manage the business?
- How do you grow the business?
- How do you meet your objectives that you've carefully prepared?

This chapter provides accounts from small business owners and highly successful entrepreneurs on how they've managed their small business and overcome obstacles and challenges. Time management, general business management and strategic planning are reviewed with ways to manage all of these factors effectively.

Learning from those who have been there and done that is one of the best things to do as a small business owner. So let's learn from the best and uncover some secrets of success.

Britain's Best Bosses

The greatest asset of any business, no matter what its size, is the people who work for it. But how those people perform depends largely upon the skill of their boss – and sadly not all measure up. There is the dictatorial boss with the 'us and them' attitude who docks wages for being five minutes late and breathes down your neck, constantly asking what you're doing, the 'unapproachable' boss who appears continuously stressed and grumpy, and the uninspiring boss who fails to praise staff for their accomplishments.

None of these people are getting the most out of a valuable – and expensive – asset: their people.

◆ **EXERCISE** ◆

Reflect on your life since leaving school and remember your good bosses, the ones you enjoyed working for, the ones you worked productively for. Consider why that was. Were they approachable, inspirational, flexible, firm, fair, fun?

Write down what kind of boss you'd like to be. Motivational? Understanding? Appreciative?

_____

_____

Good management is about valuing people and getting the most from them, so how do you do this in practice, now that it's your turn?

1. Be flexible.
2. Get to know staff as individuals.
3. Praise and encourage.
4. Communicate your vision.

'You praise, you praise, you praise. You can do lots of good things, you can give good pay, but what young people want is something to believe in. So make sure you're a company that has certain standards whereby you care about your employees and communicate with them. Communication is major on this issue. As long as you're transparent about your ideas and have a sense of integrity, I think if staff are proud and thrilled with the company it bleeds down into the consumers. So finding a way to have a sense of protecting the family is what companies should be doing.' Dame Anita Roddick

Sir Richard Branson agrees:

'I will praise, praise, praise and only criticise if they are going to kill themselves crossing the road. People know when they've done things wrong; they don't need to be told. When I write my letters to employees, you'll never see a line of criticism.'

Best Boss Kevin

The following is extracted from my article in *Better Business* magazine (www.better-business.co.uk) reprinted with kind permission from Active Information:

Kevin Coleman, Britain's Best Boss for 2001 is an approachable and family-friendly boss who embraces work-life balance and aims to create a happy working environment for his employees.

He also takes this attitude and it reflects in his staff's loyalty.

'I enjoy being at work,' says Debbie Hodge who nominated her boss Kevin for the accolade. 'And when you're genuinely interested in your work, you find yourself coming up with ideas outside of work, all of which benefits the company.'

Achieve balance – be flexible

'*All of my full-time staff have children, so if they need to pick them up, take them to the doctor or attend their sports day, that's fine – as long as I have notice,*' says Kevin.

'*Staff are also free to bring their children in here if they need to – no problem. Flexibility is crucial. If people want to start later and finish later, that's fine, too. I'm all for getting a job done well with a happy team, because this means there are ultimately less problems and the client is happy. In my experience a happy and well-informed staff is a productive one, and this, in turn, leads to a happy client base and plenty of referrals.*'

'*Apart from creating a more productive and happier workforce, good communication and flexibility saves time and confusion,*' says Kevin.

A family approach to business

Written policies are unusual in a small firm, but Kevin decided to formalise his policy because all of his staff are parents. His associate director has a family, and Kevin himself recently became a father to baby daughter Annie. At Swift, jobsharing is formalised and flexibility encouraged.

Kevin's mum was a key influence in the formalisation of his family-friendly policy.

'*When I was four years old my mum used to take me to work with her,*' says Kevin. '*This had a beneficial effect on how I run my own business. I saw my mother relaxed and fulfilled in her own workplace, so now I'm at the other end of the spectrum I'm doing the same.*'

Be open and united

Other past experiences have also shaped Kevin's outlook on business management, including those from his early working life.

'*My early working experiences also had a profound effect on my management methods,*' says Kevin. '*My first job was as a trainee manager for a large retail chain. I had to leave home and live in a bedsit at the age of 18, and the only other young guy worked in the warehouse. We got on famously, and he became my best friend.*'

'*One day the assistant manager pulled me to one side and said I shouldn't socialise with the warehouse staff. I resigned two days later. I couldn't work for a company that had such an "us and them" approach to the workforce. This stuck with me and shaped how I run my business and treat my workforce today.*'

Kevin has an approachable attitude, much like Napoleon, who had an open door policy whereby his officers could enter his tent freely with any problem they might have, on the basis that they could offer a solution to the problem themselves first. This encouraged his officers to consider solutions to their own problems first (thereby not relying on their boss to fix things all the time) but also reassured them of his support.

Kevin's tips on effective management are to:

- Set a level for people to work to, and once they're at that level they can get on with the job and show a natural progression towards higher achievements.
- Be relaxed with new staff and become friends, but set a level so the line isn't crossed. 'I'm still the boss. With all my staff I aim for that level of mutual respect and equal trust.'
- Have a non-dictatorial approach by proactively engaging your team, keeping them involved and establishing mutual trust and respect.
- Communicate and involve all staff so everyone knows exactly what is going on, where, why, how and when.
- Be open and frank with staff and share responsibilities.
- Always remain positive and avoid being grumpy. A smile goes a long way in keeping staff productive.
- Try ideas your staff suggest. Create an open culture. Have staff send in suggestions and reward the best ones.

Best Boss Lin

Another winner of Lloyds TSB Britain's Best Boss accolade is Lin Arigho, whose commitment to encouraging a healthy work-life balance has made her an inspirational boss to work for.

Lin set up Aricot Vert Design when she was just 21, working from a bedroom at her parents' house. Now Aricot Vert has developed into a successful graphic design company that employs 17 staff at premises in Fleet, Hampshire and has an annual turnover of over £1 million. The staff are productive and enjoy their work – as do Lin and her co-director, Ed.

Flexible attitude

'*Lin has a flexible attitude and a very open character,*' says office manager Catherine McCulloch. '*You feel that you can ask her anything because of her caring and considerate nature.*'

A flexible and holistic philosophy is the lynchpin of working life at Aricot Vert, allowing the staff to remain focused on their jobs while in the office, but free to take care of family issues and appointments if need be.

The end result of this philosophy is a happy working environment in which staff are focused and perform well.

'*It's hard work to sustain,*' says Lin. '*If I ran a firm with nine to five hours I'd do the same amount of work, but would be less involved with my family. We wouldn't eat dinner together or have so much quality time. It's my choice to work this way because I feel these family times are important. When the kids are home, I'm home, so my working has no effect on their lives whatsoever.*'

Flexibility is the key to this approach to work and life. If the children stay late at school, Lin will stay at the office and work; when they need collecting early, she'll leave early and finish her work when the children are tucked up in bed.

Finding balance

Happiness in life comes from balance. Sometimes trying to juggle and balance your family, friends, learning, business, health, money and love can make you feel unhappy and stressed, but, if you are able to find balance within the mayhem you'll find the key to being happy and appreciating each area of your life and your business. So you need to make every second count.

'If you've got a family, you've got to structure. You can't leave the family. You have such a responsibility to balance life with employment.' Dame Anita Roddick

Get to know your staff

'You need to know your staff as individuals. By knowing their lives and schedules, you can adapt working practices and adopt a flexible, yet productive, work ethic'. says Lin Arigho

The Aricot Vert team go on monthly outings and have even had an Indian head masseur visit the office – further evidence of Lin's holistic approach to life and work. *'We go to pottery and the theatre and we've been snowboarding and sailing,'* says Lin. *'It's good to form a social community and give the staff a chance to wind down.'*

'We would do bring your daughter to work day or your partner to work, so everybody got to know each other,' adds Dame Roddick.

◆ EXERCISE ◆

- ◆ Brainstorm ways you can create a balanced and flexible work ethic.
- ◆ Write down ways to get to know staff on a personal level.

_____

_____

_____

_____

Communicate

Communicate with all staff, but also with everyone in the loop, including suppliers and investors.

'Keep investors informed and communication clean,' advises Sharpcards's Will Walsh. Will sends his investors a five-minute e-mail once a month to keep them posted.

'They're all really appreciative of that and tell us how good we are in keeping in contact with them, in comparison to other companies they've invested in and then never heard a word from until they've either gone bust or done well. So it's important to keep investors in the loop.'

'You should never lose sight of your vision and should communicate well. Communication is the most important tool of leadership. I used to use newsletters and videos to get through to everyone in the company – when you're exhausted from saying something, this is about the time that people are getting it!' Dame Anita Roddick

Perween Aarsi, founder of £100 million turnover company S&A Foods, believes focusing on creating a strong family culture among staff is critical to success, along with being able to communicate effectively with that family:

'A business is built by people, not bricks and mortar. Communicating with passion inspires employees and instills a real sense of ownership in the business.'

Consider methods and policies for communicating with your staff, your customers and your investors effectively.

Listen and learn

Listen, communicate, listen some more. Listening should be thought of as a whole new skill to be developed and nurtured as a small business owner. In fact it should be taught at school – listening classes. We are born listening and learning but somewhere along the line (possibly around adolescence) we begin to think we know it all. We make mistakes and can't know everything, so communicate properly by listening more than you talk. Gain more respect and more knowledge, then get out there and use it. Be a lifelong learner.

Most small businesses find it difficult to listen because they're so darn busy, but listen they must. Work at listening – it's a great skill and is less easy to master than talking. Of course, not everyone talks wisdom. Sometimes you will know more than others, but you can still learn from them. You can even learn from people what *not* to do.

Understand you won't often get it right first time. Sure, if a job is worth doing it is worth doing well but don't sweat the small stuff. Learn and reapply yourself so you get things right eventually. Embrace your learning curve, don't fight against it and bounce off. Sometimes you'll have to take risks. These may work or may backfire, but you must make mistakes in order to learn from them.

Mistakes are good. If you never made any mistakes you would not learn. You do learn from your mistakes (mum was right) and this is particularly true in business as much as it is in life. As you grow in business and in life you learn important lessons, and the more you make, the less likely you are to make that mistake when it *really* matters. So if you, your skills, your staff or something else is getting in the way of progress, you need to address that – address and learn from mistakes, listen to suggestions, make changes where necessary, but above all *never* stop learning. Be open to it, always!

'As soon as you think you know it all you're history. You've got to keep your mind open and ask questions constantly.' Will Walsh

Stay open. Stay fresh. Stay in tune with your staff and customers.

'Be tenacious and continually creative and continually ask for help. Never stop asking for help and never stop learning. You need to be learning all the time. All the time.' Dame Anita Roddick

'The best piece of advice my father gave me was to ask people for advice and not for things. People like to give advice, so I've always been a listener and always ask for advice. I'll listen to people and assimilate it, not assume they're right, but in terms of professional advisors, if there's a very specific thing you want advice on, I'm very pro paying for professional advice.' Simon Woodroffe

'But I never ask for advice on whether anyone thinks it's a good idea or not. They'll never know, they don't know that incredibly complex conundrum that's brought you to that point, and someone picking up a drawing of my new hotel or something might say it's not a good idea, but it's taken me 20 drawings to get to that point, so it doesn't really matter.'

You need to be able to select the great advice from the questionable stuff. For example, many bank or government-funded business advisors have no real experience of running their own small business, but have experience working for large corporations. So their advice sometimes may not translate well in the form of consultancy. In my experience, such agencies are worth using for gathering reading material, business plan templates and funding advice, but aren't always up to delivering real-life business advice that actually works.

An E-Business Advisor for a government-backed Business Advisory Service once sent me an e-mail that displayed all the other recipients' e-mail addresses in the 'carbon copy' field. This is one of the cardinal sins of sending e-mail as all recipients can see the distribution list and can use it for their own uses, increasing spam and sharing recipients' details they may not have wanted me to see. This alone didn't give me confidence that this supposed e-business expert knew more than me. As an E-Business Advisor he should have known to use the BCC 'blind carbon copy' field. So I won't be taking advice from him on my e-business. By contrast, another E-Business Advisor for the same service has been fantastic – sending referrals my way, telling me about grants my clients or I could apply for, and keeping it to a one-on-one communication. His advice I appreciate and respect and listen to.

Assimilate advice you receive and use it to make informed choices based on your heightened understanding.

*Consider this a business version of The Green Cross Code: **ask, listen, learn** your code of doing business.*

Get a mentor
We all need guidance, someone to bounce ideas off, someone who can play devil's advocate sometimes and encourage us too.

'A mentor can be worth their weight in gold. They can be the difference between an idea's success and failure.' Mike Southon and Chris West, authors of *The Beermat Entrepreneur*

They suggest that you choose a well-respected person within your industry or someone who knows about business and approach their gatekeeper (assistant) rather than try to approach them directly. You should then explain, either on the phone or in a letter, that you'd like a brief appointment with the gatekeeper (not your proposed mentor) so you can tell them that you want to speak to their boss because you have a business idea of interest. Explain what that idea is (in brief) and why you've chosen their boss as your potential mentor.

Will Walsh says his most useful help and advice has come from Sharpcards's non executive, his mentor, Andy Ripley. '*He was an international rugby player, now he's chairman of Earthcore plc, and he's very down to earth and just looks at you and what you're going through. He has faith in me, tries to boost me and he has given me total encouragement the whole way through. It's important to have that mentor and someone to talk things through with.*'

◆ EXERCISE ◆

Who do you trust and respect who has had experience of running their own business? Speak to them and arrange visits and reviews. Listen to their guidance, take heed and make informed choices based on good advice.

List possible mentors here:

_____

_____

_____

Be organised

Good bosses know who owes them money, who they owe money to, where such and such a product is, and are aware of all the details. Furthermore, good bosses measure results of marketing activities, staff productivity and operations procedures to see where strengths and weaknesses are.

Implement your plans and check to see which plans haven't been implemented and why on a regular basis. Make sure your well-crafted plans don't go to waste.

1. Understand the detail, you can't skim it. You need to know how everything works. Understand supply, distribution, purchasing, costs, staff issues, product development problems, internet usage, cashflow. Don't think this means you can't delegate. Just make sure processes are in place so you are kept informed and can measure and test necessary areas of the business. Stay in control. Stay organised. Stay knowledgeable.

2. Know where you're going and have a clear plan and clear objectives with times and measurable outcomes, and have a clear business plan that tells you how you're going to get from where you are to where you want to be, plus some financial forecasts of what's going to happen on the way. Remember, planning reinforces your passion too, because it's easier to be passionate about the future if you can see where you're going and how you're going to get there.

3. Review plans, attitudes, thinking and adapt where necessary. Don't fear change. You are still in control. What you can measure you can test, and what you can test you can improve.

'You plan by writing lists. I write lists and notes a lot of the time and they're part of my archive, so that's the way I plan things in advance. It's about creative ideas for me. I have a creative ideas book and I'm a list maker.' Dame Anita Roddick

'I'm a big list maker too. I've got an ongoing to do list that gets updated. And I find it very satisfying when I can take things off my to do list. So it's a case of ok, I have 279 things to do, but I did get through six of them, which keeps me going that I'm making progress.' Julie Meyer

Stay Focused

Understand what might be going in the wrong direction, and understand when to ask for help. What is most important to you at any given time? Keeping costs down, improving turnover, retaining staff? To keep on top of the bigger picture despite all the distractions, keep a notepad with five to ten bullet points listing what you currently want to achieve, on your desk, and take it wherever you go.

◆ EXERCISE ◆

1. Declutter to improve planning and action. Clear your desk, your bag and your car.
2. Write down five key 'to do' bullet points that summarise what is important right now. For example, you might need to focus on writing a business plan, researching the market, finding finance or cost effective suppliers who supply credit, which may be part of the bigger picture (ie starting up your business). Now give yourself a realistic time frame.

After each bullet point – write this as if it has already happened. For example 'fully understand the direction I want my business to go' or 'I have completed my market research and understand the market to make the most of opportunities within it,' or 'I have raised the cash I need, I'm ready to go.'

By writing the tasks as if they've already been successfully completed even though they haven't yet, you are affirming them (see Chapter 1) which makes them more likely to happen. Writing down your goals as if they've already happened makes them more likely to. Remember the university student experiment and my own story? Make it work for you.

Finally, ask yourself if every bullet point relates to your 'bigger picture' in some way. For example, does raising cash for your business venture relate to you being closer to your even bigger picture dream, of living in a house in the country and having a family/buying a second home abroad, etc? If each bullet point does relate to that bigger dream, draw a sketch of that bigger dream on the back of the piece of paper.

Keep this piece of paper with you in a safe place and/or pin to your pin board or leave on your desk at all times. This will help you focus on your goals and remind you to enjoy the journey.

◆ TOP TIP ◆

You will cope better with the whole rigmarole of business management if you plan, schedule, action and review. Just don't over-schedule your life. Be realistic.

Daily planning

Once your business 'is go' use this list of questions to plan your day effectively:

◆ What do you want to achieve today? List one or two things only.
◆ What do you want to do today that will inspire and motivate you?
◆ Which tasks are you willing to delegate today or say no to doing?

Lists will help you to stay on track, keep motivated and feel a sense of achievement each time you tick something off. Having a timetable for each day can provide focus to an eclectic working day, and give you an essence of routine. For example, you will already know your own creative peaks and troughs, when you feel most focused or energetic and when you feel most lethargic. Plan tasks according to your own biological ebb and flow.

Monday – ADMIN. Plan the week, send e-mails, work on projects/product development/ distribution, CLIENTS/PROJECTS

Tuesday – WRITING, MARKETING. Send out e-marketing/newsletter, contact editors, general marketing and getting clients, post on message boards, network, meet new clients

Wednesday – CLIENTS/PRODUCTS/PROJECTS. Work on projects (services) or on product development/distribution

Thursday – NETWORK AND FOLLOW UP. Make phone calls, meet suppliers, admin, accounting, work on projects or product development/distribution

Friday – ADMIN/FOLLOW UP answer e-mails, update website, writing, CLIENTS/PRODUCTS/PROJECTS

Saturday – Tasks held over from the week and reading/research/learning, CLIENTS/PROJECTS

Manage your time effectively

Overworking can be counter-productive. Believe me, I've done it, a lot!

Your time is *valuable* – more than ever before. Spend time on tasks and areas of the business that will add value to it. Cost your time properly and focus on what is most important rather than the most urgent.

- Start your day with a plan of action. Don't spend your day responding to other people's demands. Don't respond to the 'he who shouts loudest' syndrome.
- Keep tidy and have a clear desk area. Studies reveal that messy desk people (myself included I'm afraid, but I do try) spend, on average, one and a half hours per day looking for things or being distracted. That's seven and a half hours per week.
- Get enough sleep. Plan your day, and you'll achieve more, thus going to bed without feeling stressed to enjoy a restful sleep.
- Take a lunch break. Don't 'dull out' halfway through the afternoon.
- Get caller ID to screen unnecessary phone calls and restrict your time on calls.

'Time management is not doing the wrong things quicker. That just gets us nowhere faster. Time management is doing the right things.' Management consultant Dr Donald E Wetmore

---

Make The Most of Your Time

Seven lean marketing laws for the inspired entrepreneur who wants more by doing and spending less

by 'Dangerous' Debbie Jenkins www.marketing.co.uk

The following laws will provide guidance on how to act, think and work in a lean way. You can apply these laws to all areas of your life, work and business to get bigger results from the time you invest.

1. **Multiple rewards**
Aim to be rewarded multiple times for a single effort. Money can be recovered but time cannot. Time gets spent. You can't put it in a bank and you can't earn more of it. Wherever possible, you should look for ways to get paid/rewarded multiple times for each hour you invest. You will never be truly independent if your income comes from your own time and labour so package your knowledge as a product. Once you have a product you can sell you're packaged time again and again.

2. **Mistakes are gifts**
Mistakes are nothing more than learning opportunities. The best way to learn more and grow more is to make more mistakes. Mistakes are unavoidable when you're learning so adopt a ready, fire, aim approach to decisions and learn as you take action. If it doesn't work you can easily make another decision to put things right again.

3. **Know when to stop**
Be prepared to stop what you're doing. Take stock and try something different. Don't let pride, fear of ridicule or ego get in the way of good judgement. When a mission is over, learn from it and move on.

4. **Use your levers**
Do the little things that make the biggest difference. Aim for maximum impact with minimum effort. Focus will help but there are other forms of leverage too. Here are just two.

OPT – other people's time. Don't be afraid to ask for help. You don't have to do it all yourself. Use your network. Ask and you shall receive. Give and you shall get.

Recycle – learn to recognise value in everything you do. Turn your e-zine into a book and sell it. Write your words of wisdom down and share them.

5. **Don't be busy – be effective**
Don't waste your hours simply being 'busy'. Being busy does not cause you to be wealthy. So don't be busy – be effective. Remember the 80:20 rule. Typically 20 per cent of the things you do will be responsible for 80 per cent of the results you get. So focus on the 20 per cent that gets the result.

6. **Always look for the easy route**
If there's an easy way to do something and a hard way – take the easy way first. I call this 'inspired laziness'.

7. **Measure progress by what you reap**
The only truth is the result. Doing lots of things is not the same as achieving lots of things. Measure progress by your outcomes not your inputs.

4 Out Of 5 Small Businesses Go Bust Inside 5 Years! Finally – A Guaranteed Way To Make Sure You're Not One Of Them! Learn More Here. http://www.leanmarketing.co.uk/toolbooks

Coping with it all

Running and managing a successful business can be an uphill struggle, trying to juggle everything while planning and managing to cope. So the best advice is to give yourself a break. Don't make it harder than it need be.

Get refreshed

Give yourself a proper lunch break and have a decent breakfast. I skipped breakfast for many years, starting the day with a coffee and cigarette, and wondered why I'd be flagging before noon with my concentration waning. Or I'd find myself so busy I'd practically 'forget' to eat, ignoring the stomach rumblings to crack on with a deadline-ridden article or project. Then I started to eat a small breakfast, break from 1-2pm for lunch involving nothing to do with the business (a spot of *Loose Women* on ITV or reading a glossy magazine, walking the dog or going for a swim) – the result was, quite obviously, more energy, focus and a more productive me. Sometimes you can get so bogged down in everything you forget to look after little old you. Try not to forget, and don't overdo it!

Never promise what you can't deliver. Rushing to win new contracts and grow your business at super speed runs the risk of over-stretching resources and disappointing vital new customers.

Have some quiet time, some space. Breathe! Play, exercise, clear your head. Take up yoga. Walk the dog. Go swimming. Schedule this into your week. You need a balance and to take breaks from work, work, work. You need to refresh yourself, body and mind, in order to function properly.

So book yourself a massage, take the scenic route to the office or to see your next client, read an invigorating novel, switch off. Relax and you'll avoid the burn out.

Stay motivated

It has been said that **motivation is the bridge between passion and action.** So reward and motivate yourself. Give yourself something to look forward to for keeping up with your work. You need to treat yourself, to create a positive outlook and stay motivated.

So inspire yourself. Each time you find an inspirational quote, cutting, story or image on the web or in a magazine, print, cut it out and stick it up or add it to your Ideas and Inspiration book. When things get too much read them and remind yourself why you are doing what you're doing. Revisit your notes in Chapter 1.

Delegate and share

'Don't try and do everything yourself – entrepreneurs are generally crazy people and they can vision things that others can't but they need brilliant people around them to expedite that. Entrepreneurs have an energy. Because actually what they're doing is putting their thumb print on a blank canvas and trying to create a livelihood, so it becomes obsessional. Entrepreneurs don't worry about not being an organisational genius. Somebody else can do that for you.

What you've got to have is this vision. If the idea is there, and you can find somebody to expedite the idea for you, like I had my husband Gordon, who could plan and organise. Don't do everything, don't control everything. Give everything away that you can and just stay with what you want to do.' Dame Anita Roddick

Sir Richard Branson echoes this advice, saying that entrepreneurs should give responsibility to others and let them run with it. Indeed, when extremely successful entrepreneurs are asked what their best decision has been, many come back with 'sharing responsibility' or 'hiring a managing director to run the show'.

'My best decision was hiring my MD,' says Simon Woodroffe. As was Martyn Dawes's of Coffee Nation.

'I'm good at marketing but I'm not a great organiser. Detail isn't my forte,' says James Coakes who has grown his one-man band to a multi-million pound turnover company:

'When I was a one-man band and had to do everything the delivery end of the events used to really stress me. As I have grown I have taken on staff who are good at the things I am not so good at. Now I can focus on the areas that I am best at and relax knowing that good, well chosen people are dealing with other areas.'

This goes back to not thinking you know everything. You don't. Dame Roddick doesn't, Simon Woodroffe doesn't and neither does Sir Richard Branson. So take on people who are better than you, so your strengths and weaknesses complement each other.

This is how I myself have created successful businesses, by surrounding myself with people who are better than me. My partner James is the ideas person. Proactive, always considering alternative solutions, pushing things forward. Whereas I'm a grafter and organiser, putting those ideas into action. He's fabulously creative. I'm the wordy one, and it works very well.

Don't sweat the small stuff

'Channel your priorities. It's easy to get dragged into what seems to be urgent, rather than what's important. Sir Richard Branson said, 'Don't sweat the small stuff' because you've got to keep on the big stuff that takes you towards your objectives.' Keith Milsom of Anything Left-Handed

Remember – s**t happens, both in life and in business. You can't always control situations or circumstances, because you frequently rely on others to do a good job. But you can prevent things from getting you down by controlling your attitude. If you feel positive, energetic and passionate, the unavoidable nuances will sort themselves out. It's like your business is a garden. You plant the seeds, some grow, some don't and you tend the ones that do.

'The best advice I ever received was that everything takes a lot longer and costs a lot more than you expect it to. I think it's because I'm aware of that and prepared for it that I don't really get stressed.' Richard Davies of Wild West Foods

Know what to expect, delegate and don't panic. Things have a way of smoothing out if you step back and take a deep breath. And in business there is both good and bad 'stress'.

As James Coakes points out:

'Harmful stress comes from having to do something you're not good at or from not being in control. Good stress comes from running whilst everyone else is walking, from big plans, from taking risks but knowing you've a fair chance. Good stress is the spark of evolution, there would be no change in the world without it.'

Reward and treat yourself for managing a problem, getting out of a hole, making that difficult sale or working extra hard. You deserve that new bag, pair of shoes, holiday, mini-break with the kids. Remember milestones and celebrate them. Have some fun, let off some steam, free yourself.

STEP 42: HIRE STAFF

Getting the Right Team

The product has to be right, but it's ultimately your team who will drive your business towards success. Review your personal assessment to reveal in which areas you are short of skills. Hire in this area.

'Remember that a team effort is going to make your business successful.' Coffee Nation's Martyn Dawes

A happy team is a good and productive workforce. It is one of the biggest challenges that business owners face – employing the right staff and keeping them. Recruiting and retraining are costly, as can be employing the wrong people. So what advice do successful business owners have?

Sir Richard Branson believes that the correct pecking order is employees first, customers next and then shareholders, and he goes to extraordinary lengths to walk the talk.

He regularly takes out entire flight crews for dinner, gives every Virgin employee a Virgin card, which provides big discounts, and takes employees from various Virgin companies to his private Caribbean island, Necker. Not senior executives, but a house-keeper from Johannesburg, a switchboard operator, a reservations clerk, a pilot, all invited to join Branson having done a good job. He likes to praise and show he values his staff and what better way than an exotic holiday?

Creating a happy workforce

Sadly, we don't all own billion pound conglomerates or have our own islands. So what can you do to create a happy and loyal workforce?

Provide loyalty and receive loyalty

You reap what you sow. Farrelly Facilities & Engineering forbids overtime and working on birthdays, and plays soothing music to its 50 employees. This has had astounding results – a 200 per cent increase in profits since introducing this new considerate ethos.

How can you give your staff extra perks? How can you provide loyalty? List ideas.

Cultivate happiness in the workplace

Dave Wallwork of The Feel Good Drinks Company takes that part very seriously, even declaring the occasional day as a Feel Good Day.

'We celebrate every success and will spontaneously declare a day a Feel Good Day and tell the team to drop everything, then we'll go out and do something fun for a couple of hours, such as going to a spa and having massages, or going to lunch or for cocktails after work. It's about keeping the guys positive and buzzing in the team, and making sure they're passing on that feeling to customers. It's a nice environment to work in, but it's extremely hard work.'

Dave also ensures that each member of staff, including administrative staff, have their own customers.

'It keeps everyone focused on staying commercial and keeps us focused on making our commercial proposition simple.'

Google has a similar philosophy. Their moto is 'do no evil'.

'We still believe that it is important to have a work environment that is fun. That is still true, just as much now as it was when we started, even though instead of having one massage therapist come in, a few times a day, we have a whole crew going in, making sure that everyone can get a massage who wants or needs it.' Google's Craig Silverstein (Technology Director)

The Googleplex is an employee paradise with free food, unlimited ice cream, pool and ping-pong tables and complimentary massages, plus the ability to spend 20 per cent of work time on any outside activity. Bikes and hammocks line the hallways and the Grateful Dead's former chef oversees the 24-hour food operation. '*We've made a tremendous amount of progress, but we have so much more we can do*,' says Larry, co-founder of the mighty Google.

Get to know people as individuals first

Find out what motivates them. Staff at Pret A Manger are carefully screened before they join the company. MD Andrew Rolfe believes that sharing the company's values is essential to wanting to work for Pret.

'There is a rigorous assessment for each potential employee. We make them work in a shop for a few days, they have several interviews and, in each case, we try to get to know them as individuals.'

Similarly, the personnel interview at IT Consultancy, SSS Ltd is called the 'fit' interview.

'It's all about whether or not the person is likely to fit well in our organisation and whether they think they'll fit. We always start the interview by asking them what gets them motivated in the morning, and it's often the motivational aspects that sell people to us.' Owen Weeks

Go with your gut feeling

'Go with first impressions and your gut feeling when employing staff, as well as what's on paper and their references.' Harry Ganz of The Garden Pharmacy

'You're looking for honesty. And you need to get to know people over time and ask them to tell you how they dealt with mistakes they've made in the past, then walk away if they don't fit. Follow your gut about people you should or should not be doing business with. Always have a three month trial period in place.' Julie Meyer

Involve existing staff in the decision

This is preferable to using an agency or HR department.

'Get everyone in the organisation involved in recruitment. Hire via contacts internally (someone in accounts may know someone who'd possibly be ideal) and by interview. Don't use a human resources department, instead make the department head in charge of recruiting members for their own departments. Introduce potential new staff to each member of the department or team, and if anyone has any misgivings, rethink hiring that person.' Beermat Entrepreneur authors, Mike Southon and Chris West

Provide opportunities and something to believe in

'Our staff turnover rate is extremely low. We've given a lot of people a lot of opportunities that they wouldn't see anywhere else. They appreciate that and we get loyalty in return.' Owen Weeks of SSS Ltd

'If you are doing the right thing, employees really want to stay. That showed in our staff turnover rate at The Body Shop. They understood what we were trying to do.' Dame Anita Roddick

Create nice surroundings to work in

Provide an environment where the hearts and minds of your employees can grow.

'Understand the aesthetics of the workplace. That has shaped the joy of the workplace – people love coming to our international headquarters because it looks so damn cool, there are babies everywhere and music playing.' Dame Anita Roddick

Support families

Make the workplace somewhere where parents are served, children's needs are supported and families are welcomed, valued and protected. If you have a lot of parents working for you, install a crèche or child development centre and watch productivity grow.

Offer good work-life balance through flexible working opportunities. Run family days, where staff and their families get together, and company days, where different departments mix with each other, debate issues and ideas, then let their hair down.

Don't Fear Change

'You can't outsource your problems,' says Julie Meyer. *'So you need to deal with problems promptly and calmly.'*

Not realising this or not being flexible enough to change or work on areas of weakness could get in the way of your business's progress.

Stay aware and embrace necessary changes.

'Here is Edward Bear coming downstairs now, bump, bump, bump on the back of his head behind Christopher Robin. It is, as far as he knows, the only way of coming down stairs, but sometimes he feels that there really is another way, if only he could stop bumping for a moment and think of it.'
A. A. Milne, *Winnie The Pooh*

CHAPTER THIRTEEN

Lessons from Leaders in Business

Success Stories, Mistakes and Top Tips

This chapter provides a summary of case studies that will give you an insight into business success stories from the owner's point of view. What have they achieved and how did they do it? Successful entrepreneurs featured also provide useful tips and advice, including what they'd have done differently with hindsight, and spill the beans about their biggest mistakes.

So let's get down to business. What does success look like to you and for you? How would you define success and the kind you want? Write it down, draw it, colour it in, dream a little, visualise it.

You need to know what success looks like for you before you can strive to achieve it. Revisit Chapter 1 to see your vision on paper.

◆ **EXERCISE** ◆

Write yourself a letter every year. Tell yourself in the letter what your plans are, what you intend to do with your life and business, what your goals and dreams are and how you plan to materialise them. This might sound slightly 'out there' but it works.

How We Made It

The following is my article reprinted with kind permission from *Better Business* magazine.

ROCk-solid growth and success for ROC Recruitment

Former secretary Debbie Burke, who started her recruitment business alone in a room with a borrowed manual typewriter, a Barclaycard and a £10,000 overdraft, has turned ROC Recruitment into one of London's leading and largest independent recruitment companies, with over £13 million turnover, offices in London and Manchester and a staff of 50.

Debbie has been rewarded as runner-up in a Women Entrepreneurs of the World life-time achievement award. And her company, ROC Recruitment, has been recognised in the *Sunday Times* and by Deloitte & Touche as one of the UK's fastest growing companies. So what does Debbie consider to be her secrets of success?

1. Being resourceful

'Within four hours I had negotiated a deal for a room in serviced offices, which I paid for with my credit card, and had persuaded my female bank manager to give me a £10,000 overdraft facility, by putting my house up as a guarantee.

I started with three desks, three telephones and a manual typewriter that I'd borrowed. I then got a photocopier and made extra money by renting it out for 10p a copy to other tenants in the building. Thanks to loyal clients, most of whom I am proud to say are still with us today, ROC Recruitment got off the ground.' Debbie Burke

2. Over-deliver and build relationships with both customers and staff

The most evident ingredient of Debbie's success is by far her commitment to over-delivering in terms of customer satisfaction and valuing her people. Ultimately, Debbie's success has been founded on her client retention – the lasting relationships that are built and maintained by working to quality measurement and core values.

'We've achieved this rate of growth primarily because we believe our staff, our clients and our candidates are special, and it is our aim to always make them feel special.'

A great testament to the success of ROC is that most organisations who retained their services in 1991 are still using ROC today.

Debbie considers her staff equally important and 'special'. In most marketplaces today the average employee stay in a company is four years. As a result, some businesses place less importance on the welfare, training and motivation of their staff – but to encourage loyalty and productivity, staff should be invested in and made to feel appreciated.

'We have monthly and annual meetings to share the company's vision, motivate staff and congratulate top performers.

When you've got good staff you have to value them, even with small things: acknowledge that they've done well, remember people's birthdays. You have to make people feel special and a part of something. You can give people incentives or put them on training courses, but at the end of the day, the workplace has to be fun and enjoyable in order to motivate people to come in each morning.'

Through links with the charity ROC supports – Children with Leukemia – the company has had celebrities such as Paul Young and Jeremy Beadle attending their Christmas parties, making them really memorable occasions for members of staff and further boosting morale.

'Our future success will continue to be built on maintaining lasting relationships and focusing on every contact with clients and candidates to see profitable growth. We're able to nurture these relationships by embracing a strong set of beliefs as a company.'

Those beliefs are posted around the ROC recruitment offices and are a mantra for staff and candidates to apply themselves to:

- be open in communication
- treat other people as you would want to be treated
- promote a positive working environment
- take responsibility to provide solutions
- act in the wider interests of our business
- embrace equal opportunities legislation.

And it's all of these elements together that have been instrumental in helping ROC and Debbie to win so many accolades. Sir Richard Branson himself has even said of ROC, '*one of an elite group of companies who are the definitive barometer of the future of business in Britain.*' Not bad for a business that began life with little more than a typewriter.

◆ TOP TIP ◆

Be different, be honest, be interesting

With half a million small businesses starting up in the UK each year, you want yours to be a pleasure to work for and buy from. The best way to do this is to create a transparent, innovative and proactive business – one that your team, customers and self can believe in. So be honest and interesting. Remember, trust is efficient.

'My secrets of success are probably not going to business school, having a huge social agenda that, at that time, put me on such a different platform to everybody else in the beauty business. I was a different type – I was an activist rather than a beauty diva, so I think that helped shape a lot of the editorial. We were just interesting. We were much more interesting than just making bubble bath. That really helped us. We had so much editorial coverage, not for our beauty stuff, because we never paid for an advert so they didn't want to honour us. But my God we were so interesting and our customers trust us. If we say anti-aging creams don't work, our customers trust us. There's that honesty thing.' Dame Anita Roddick

Believe in Yourself

Be committed. '*Regardless of the "do you realize that…" and "that won't work because…"* comments. '*It's how not if*,' says Sahar Hashemi of Coffee Republic.

Bobby Hashemi could and nearly did go back to his six figure salary after having little to show for his efforts after his first coffee shop launched. But soon after that Coffee Republic appeared in some in-flight magazines and *The Independent on Sunday*, then

Vogue and *Tatler*. Their cinnamon latte sales soared after **Vogue** recommended it. Fortunately Bobby decided to stick with it and it paid off handsomely.

Myself, each time I've felt like running back to the comfort zone of a job, something has come up and I've turned the corner. So persist!

'Keep on going. It's easy to give up and get low, but time is the critical thing and if you can persevere it's the best decision you can make.' Will Walsh of Sharpcards

And he should know having survived the dotcom crash a few weeks after he'd secured hefty investment. Three years in and Sharpcards has weathered the storm and laid solid foundations to expand.

'Companies now start to approach you, rather than the other way round, so it's getting better and better and we are now in profit.

The future's very bright, and we're on a sea of change, moving into new areas. The internet is back on the map from a perception point of view, and realistically things are starting to happen. Broadband is helping too, so for me this is the most exciting time.'

Lucky he didn't quit. Persistence is the key.

'Much of being an entrepreneur is about risk and learning from the past. Perseverance has been an advantage while launching 12 companies in as many years and having them all still growing. The business plan has to be worked on and amended in the early years and I've seen a couple of my companies come good after some difficulties in starting. So hang in there!' Stelios, founder of easygroup told me.

Dame Roddick's advice echoes this requirement for entrepreneurs to be persistent:

'You will never understand how you will have found so much amazing energy. When you have an idea that overtakes your entire system, body and mind, it is so thrilling if you can see a light at the end of the tunnel. So stay with it because it's your identity. If you're starting out, it's your route to freedom. Stay with it as long as you can and surround yourself with people that support you. It's so thrilling when you can see it working for you.'

It's all about persevering and putting in the effort to generate results.

'Put in the effort. My old boss gave me a good piece of advice. You reap what you sow. Very true that you can get out what you put in. If you believe that and put in the effort, you will be successful. You keep going until you see the shoots of success and then keep going to the next level, and the next.' Debbie Burke

Be persistent

Equally, when times are difficult, belief in yourself and your business idea will be all you have, so use that belief to carry you through.

Have the courage of your convictions, show leadership and inspire people to follow. You'll find it much easier to deal with challenges and obstacles as they arrive.

'Go round stone walls and believe in yourself. I was speaking to two girls who are trying to do a tea business. They are really enthusiastic about it and are thinking big, but someone has said to them, 'well, what's the point in doing it, because as soon as it catches on, Starbucks will just do it and wipe you out.

When you come up against those things, which are like stone walls, it's so demoralising and leads to doubts. But of course, none of the objections matter, as long as you're passionate enough to carry it through. Sometimes you go up the wrong track and you have to come all the way back down the track to the fork and go up another track, and that's the test of the person who doesn't or does do it, of being prepared to carry it through. It takes a lot of resilience and a lot of energy this entrepreneur business.'
Yo Sushi's Simon Woodroffe

You have to have utmost determination to take your business forward, regardless of what others say.

Even JK Rowling was turned down by three publishers before having her Harry Potter books snapped up. If she'd fallen at the first or even third hurdle, she'd not have brought Harry to the world and riches to her pockets.

Don't give up.

Most successful people have at least one failed business behind them. The difference between successful people and others is that successful people persist.

In his early twenties, Peter Jones, multi-millionaire and star of BBC's Dragons' Den and ITV's Tycoon was a millionaire. However, through a combination of circumstances and personal mistakes, when a few major customers went out of business, Peter lost his business too and was left with nothing.

Says Peter, 'I needed to get back on my feet and earn money straight away. The quickest way for me to do that was to get a job where there were prospects. So, I did that for two years and earned enough money to start my own business again.'

That business was Phonos International Group, a company that turned over £13.9 million in its first year and now brings in £200 million. Evidently, it's persistency and how you view failure that makes all the difference. For example, Peter says, 'there's no such thing as failure, only feedback.'

'When Thomas Eddison, who invented the light bulb, was asked what it was like to have failed 1000 times in trying to invent it, he replied that he didn't fail, he just found 1000 different ways not to invent the light bulb. That's what it's about, that's the way we should view life.'

Patience is a virtue

Some business owners have so much dogged determination to their business idea, they'll wait and wait for their objectives to come to fruition.

For example, Figleaves.com, an online supplier of lingerie, were very patient and persistent in order to get the suppliers they wanted.

'When suppliers said 'no, but come back in six months', that's what we did, and eventually it paid off. The day La Perla called and said yes, we're going to supply you, we were all jumping around the office – it was a very exciting day. A lot of people who said no for a long time are now major partners.' Chief Executive, Michael Ross

Persistency paid off in that instance. But possibly one of the most persistent and unrelenting entrepreneurs is the hero-to-zero and back to hero, Gerald Ratner, whose jewellery business faltered after he said one of his products was 'total crap'. (The moral of that story, by the way, is not that you shouldn't be honest with your customers, but that you musn't make crap products.)

At the Small Business Show in London, 2004, Gerald recounted how he felt when it all collapsed:

'I had reached the age of 37 and had an empire of 2,500 shops and 25,000 staff that I had built from nothing. I had to pinch myself. It was fantastic. Then to have it all taken away overnight was one of the most traumatic and diabolical experiences. It was life-changing — a terrible, terrible shock.'

However, he wasn't about to be beaten and came back fighting.

'I was told I was unemployable even after building the world's largest jewellery business in seven years. I wouldn't be offered any job because of the stigma that went with my speech. When people lose their jobs they either take Prozac or go to the gym. I went to the gym. Then I noticed that, although there were lots of gyms in London, there weren't any where I lived.'

So Ratner seized on the gap in the market and set up his own club in Henley. The banks and private investors refused to back him, so, under pressure to come up with the cash or lose the building, Ratner took out an advertisement in the local press.

'*It cost me £250,*' he said. '*It said there was a new club opening in Henley and if people joined now it would cost nothing, otherwise the joining fee would be £250. More than 600 people signed up. I didn't have a club or a building but I had 600 people.*' Ratner returned to the bank for money but was again refused. So he remortgaged his house and took out loans, effectively risking everything he had once more. In April 2001 he sold the club for £4.7 million and is well and truly back on his feet. Ratner has now re-entered the jewellery trade with an internet business. Now that's what I call persistent.

If Only I'd Known ... Mistakes

With your personal radar tuned to **ask, listen and learn,** you should now be fully aware that mistakes are fantastic learning tools. So what better way to learn than from the mistakes of successful business leaders?

CASE STUDY

'Tackle problems early and learn from your mistakes,' says Simon Woodroffe. *'Yo Sushi is five years old, and we would be a year further ahead if I'd done two things. First if I'd had the courage to hire more expensive and experienced people earlier, rather than getting the cheapest people and do it myself and, second, if all the people who came three to four years ago to me and said, 'we'd like to open one in Abu Dhabi or Moose Droppings in Iowa, could we have a franchise,' if I'd said to them, please come back in three years when we've grown up, instead of saying come on in, I'll get the lawyers onto it, which wasted a lot of time and money. We all know that the only thing you learn from is mistakes and experience, and they are my two worst business mistakes.'*

Lesson – Don't run before you can walk (and go for quality in staff from the outset).

CASE STUDY

'Going into the malls of America was a mistake for us,' admits Dame Anita Roddick about The Body Shop. *'We should have kept to the urban areas, because we're an urban cool company, but going into the malls of America made you ubiquitous – the same as everything else, every mall, every shop, all the same.'*

Lesson – Keep it real. Stay true to your brand.

CASE STUDY

'We made rushed decisions, tried to get involved in everything, tried to target and market to everyone, and you can't do that,' says Will Walsh of his early errors.

Now Will is a lot choosier about whom he partners with. *'I look back and there was so much time wasted, so we've got more focus now. But in any business that is a natural cycle. You never know quite where you're heading until it becomes obvious, so you've got to be flexible, and maybe go a route you weren't planning to,'* adds Will.

Lesson – Stay focused. Don't try to do everything at once or be all things to all people.

CASE STUDIES

'*I've made loads of big mistakes, one of the biggest is being seduced into thinking that other people knew better than what we ourselves would have known, ie going on the stock market,*' says Dame Roddick.

This is difficult, because with professional advisors or specialists, you expect them to know better than you. You need to follow your gut instinct and ask questions.

'*The biggest mistake I made as a manager was going public. We should never ever have gone public; it's just too bloody boring.*'

'*Going public was a major step towards respectability, and for that I am thankful. It gave us freedom, it gave us the chance to invest in our huge manufacturing plant. However, although the constraints of going public are not that bad, they're constant. You never had time to reflect and pause and say, "Are we having fun? Do we want to grow this year? Why don't we just have more fun with our employees? Why don't we do more social activism?" So you never have that real freedom to be able to take the identity of your company – which is, in essence, your own identity – and form it into something else. You're structured by the profit-and-loss sheet.*'

We ourselves at WebCritique.co.uk made the business mistake of being seduced by a company who I wrongly assumed knew more than me about search engine ready websites. With hindsight, when that design company offered to redesign my website rather than pay commission for work I'd sent their way, I shouldn't have been so fast to accept the offer. Similarly, when I noticed they'd used quite appalling techniques and wasn't overkeen on the new look, I should have spoken up, rather than being democratic and silent. But I was too sheepish to question their authority. They had convinced me they were top of the range web developers. It appears that this development firm are great at building software solutions, but not always so great at building commercially viable indexable websites and truly appalling at understanding their customers' needs.

I've learnt my lesson there, and will always speak up if I have issues and avoid having anything done that is perceived by either party as 'free', as this can move you down a company's list in terms of priorities.

From letting someone persuade you to buy advertising space, taking the wrong advice, or choosing the wrong people to partner with, avoid being seduced at all costs. It can be expensive, messy and regretful.

Lesson – Avoid being seduced by advisors, designers and the Stock Market. Speak out and follow your gut instinct.

CASE STUDIES

'*Another worst business mistake I've made is employing the wrong people,*' recalls Dame Roddick. '*Just an appalling litany – I mean Harvard Business Review ought to do a case study of how many crap individuals we employed thinking they would shepherd the company in the right way, and they were absolutely wrong for the company. Leaving the future of my company, in terms of people employed, to head hunters was a huge mistake. We didn't spend enough time with the head hunters saying "these are the kinds of people we want." In a way we gave up to their intelligence how to find the right people.*'

'*I don't think I had due diligence – we had one guy in who I thought would be brilliant, and it turned out he was the biggest bully you could imagine.*'

Dame Roddick was able to turn some of these problems around and the vision was not entirely lost.

'*When The Body Shop was at its most profitable and strongest in the mid 1990s, it was incredible how we transferred the profits into the social institutions,*' says Anita.

However, having realised in her fifties that she was getting more radical, she decided the board was getting further from her outlook and wavelength. The board room became the inevitable bored room. So Dame Roddick stepped down as Chief Executive of The Body Shop in 1998, but remains a non-executive Director of the company, and now has more of a consultancy role; sourcing community trade products, spearheading campaigns, attending Body Shop At Home conferences and speaking engagements, alongside running her publishing firm – AnitaRoddick.com.

Many companies have made the mistake of hiring the wrong people or creating the wrong job. SSS Ltd's worst decision so far has been to hire in sales experience. '*That didn't work at all, so that was a bad decision,*' says Owen Weekes. '*I wasn't sure if it would work before I went ahead and I was proven correct. So there's a lesson in that to follow your gut feeling.*'

Remember, it's OK to ask questions, you're the boss. You can be too trusting, as Amanda Strowbridge from Heaven@Home discovered.

'*I employed some therapists who worked in my Kensington salon and they left and set up something very similar down the road and poached my ideas. Sometimes you have to not be too friendly and make sure people know you're the boss, otherwise people can take advantage of you.*'

James of Finishing Touches, a painter and decorator from London, also had the advantage taken:

'*My worst decision was to use friends. Never mix business with pleasure,*' says James. '*I asked my mate to come in as a plumber and he ripped someone's bathroom out then went on the razzle for a week and didn't come back. I lost that job. But I've learnt from that mistake.*'

The girls at Squeaky Records admit that their worst decision was to take a chance on students to make their first video.

'We paid them and got the best students. And it was good enough for cable TV, but it wasn't good enough for anything else,' says Alice. *'It wasn't because the concept was bad or it was made badly, it just wasn't quality enough.'*

Quality when outsourcing or hiring in talent is crucial. And if you do hire an HR company to recruit, make sure you brief them and work with them. Leaving the recruitment of your staff to others can create issues unless fully planned, something that's not always possible when growing at top speed.

Lesson: Hire your own staff and focus on quality recruitment policies and checks.

CASE STUDY

After starting her working life as an office junior, Rachel Elnaugh founded her first business Red Letter Days in 1989 at the age of just 24, and grew it into a market leading company with an 18 million turnover. She took something from nothing to being a brand leader and pioneer in the experiences industry. By 2002 Rachel was being feted by the Press and won an Ernst & Young Entrepreneur of the Year Award as well as being shortlisted for numerous other accolades including the Veuve Clicquot Businesswoman of the Year.

Her appearance on BBCs cult business show Dragons' Den shot her into the public eye in early 2005, the only woman on the panel of five Dragons. But business life is fickle, and following her decision to appoint a new CEO and step back from the company in 2002, Red Letter Days plunged into losses of £4.7 million. Despite Rachel's attempts to save the company, a series of betrayals and misplaced trust led to Red Letter Days falling into administration on 1 August 2005. The ensuing publicity was perhaps the most generated by any unlisted SME in British Business history.

Rachel has since been appointed as Chief Executive of the UK's leading online art retailer easyart.com, with the brief to grow the business and float it on AIM in 2007. Rachel is acquiring a 20% stake in the company through a combination of personal investment and share options.

Undefeated by the setback of seeing RLD fall by the wayside, I spoke to Rachel in December 2005 and she revealed the story of what went wrong with Red Letter Days and what she'd have done differently with the benefit of hindsight.

'There were stages – pits of depression – when I just felt like throwing in the towel,' admits Rachel. *'But I realized, thanks to the support of my family, that I had to keep going and fight; to try everything. Because, if I'd just given up, I'd always wonder 'what if I'd given it one last shot?' And I know, having gone right to the bitter death and still fighting for the business on that final day, that there's nothing more I could have done.'*

Once the business had collapsed and was bought out by two of Rachel's fellow dragons, Rachel dusted herself down, held her head high and launched forth into her next project.

'I was feeling like a plane pilot knowing it was about to crash, so my attitude was like a pilot in that situation, trying to save as many people as possible.' Jobs were saved and customer purchases honoured, but now it was time to move on.

'Of course, there is a temptation to hide under the bed covers and say I'm not getting out again, but you can't just sit there feeling sorry for yourself,' smiles Rachel. *'In fact, because it was so high profile, so much opportunity flooded in, asking me to look at various business opportunities.'*

Rachel took the decision to step back and not take *anything on immediately, but when the EasyArt.com opportunity came up, she jumped at it. 'It felt so right, and just felt like the right move.'*

'It's bizarre because art was the thing I wanted to do when I left school and I couldn't. I didn't get into university and ended up working as an office junior, but it was always my first passion, so it's bizarre how sometimes in life things can come full circle.'

So what were the key mistakes that created the problems faced by Red Letter Days?

Mistake 1: Not enough controls and a poor choice in delegated authority
'The big mistake is allowing yourself to go down the well in the first place, as once you're at the bottom of the well it's very difficult to climb out. It happened for me with a combination factors: I had bad financial information and I didn't have enough controls in place. I had also delegated too much authority to people who didn't have enough of vested interest in not spending all the money.'

Mistake 2: Handing over the reigns to someone else
'It was a big mistake hiring a new CEO,' admits Rachel. *'It's very difficult for entrepreneurs, because there is a big wave of opinion that entrepreneurs are only good for a start-up, and that there comes a time when you've got to hand over the reigns to a 'proper' CEO, but so many stories you hear of entrepreneurs who've had to go back in to recover the business from the mess.'*

'Quite often, the entrepreneur who gave birth to the company really understands the brand; they live it, they breathe it, they totally understand it, and if someone new comes in they can totally miss it.'

'Going into Tescos and Sainsburys was not the right move but, when we reversed out of that in 2002, the mistake I made really was stepping back from the business and allowing someone else to come in and drive this step change without proper controls. So much money was spent in that year its outrageous.'

Mistake 3: Misplaced trust beware the vultures
Rachel returned to Red Letter Days in January 2003, seven months pregnant, not knowing who to trust. The company went through a series of refinancing and, in early 2005, announced they would be taking the business to AIM to float on the stock market.

'All the advisors just said take it straight to AIM, it's big enough, its high enough profile, it's a great story, you'll have a huge interest. But the advisory couldn't do that until 2006,' Rachel explains. *'So, off the back of making that announcement, we went out to get pre-IPO funding. When we announced that we'd appointed Sir Rodney Walker, the chairman of Donnington Park racing circuit, it got into all the papers that we were going to AIM and immediately people start phoning to invite us into partnership with them.*

'We had a meeting with a trade partner who said, 'forget the pre-IPO funding, forget the AIM thing, come into partnership with us, everything will be wonderful.' I said 'I cannot go into exclusivity with you unless you are absolutely serious about doing this deal, because I can only focus on one deal as we don't have time or the resources. We must choose one horse and back it. So we trusted them and we gave them every piece of information they needed up front, laid it on the table right at the outset, and we were due to complete on the 5th July. I got married on 2nd July and on 3rd July in the evening, after we'd had one day's honeymoon, we received the call to say they'd had a dramatic change in deal terms which would have completely shafted us. We were due to complete on the Wednesday and then they suddenly pulled out. And that's what can happen in business, particularly when you get to the size that we were; you are open to the vultures. But I consider that a betrayal.'

'Their parting shot to us was 'talk to the administrators'. So clearly, they'd lured us to a point of no return where they'd be able to do a deal and acquire us for next to nothing.'

Mistake 4: Running out of time

Poor cash flow is the biggest killer of business and, once the creditors start chasing you, you can find the money but just a little too late. Some creditors can be short-sighted while some are more flexible. The trick is to build good relationships with them and try to work with partners you can trust. This isn't so easy when your business is growing fast.

Despite being eight months pregnant, Rachel was undeterred, determined to keep fighting. *'I had to resurrect all these old deals that I'd parked six weeks before, knowing that I had literally weeks to do them, which is not enough time in corporate finance terms.'* But Rachel traipsed from meeting to meeting, heavily pregnant and desperate. *'It's a very difficult position to be in. Ultimately though, we DID find a deal, but we just didn't have enough time to complete the due diligence, and actually, if I'd just had a few more weeks, I could have completed it and done the deal.'* Sadly, the creditors, despite potentially losing everything, were hounding Rachel and wanted to put the business into receivership.

'It was very short sighted, as they'd have got more of their money back if they'd been more flexible, and I actually said to one of the key creditors who was rattling his saber, 'work with me, I will sort this,' but the next day he went to the press, and once its in the press, creditor confidence collapses. That's what happened at the end.'

Mistake 5: Manic rather than organic growth

'In business, so many people I speak to say the same thing, 'if only I'd allowed it to grow organically and steadily rather than going for gold or over-leveraging the business and getting VCs on board who are relentlessly driving it, which in itself is a golden cage. Sometimes in business it's much better to grow slower. The best equity is profit, so finance future expansion from hard earned profit, rather than over-leveraging the business and putting so much strain on it. It's not very pleasant having to dance to other people's tunes all the time, because most Venture Capitalists want short-term results, whereas an entrepreneur knows you need to build long-term growth.'

With various lessons learned, what was Rachel's best decision in the past few years, *'The best decision I made was the decision not to allow myself to be defeated.'*

'I think in the end, when it was taken away and we had to put it into administration, it was almost like a liberation. It felt like it had to happen and there was a grand purpose to it. I'd been doing it for 16 years and it was almost like someone telling me I had to move on. I think I had to clear out the Red Letter Days thing to let the new stuff flow in, and use the high profile for another purpose.'

Now Rachel is pursuing her first passion, the career path she wanted to take when she left school art. As CEO of EasyArt.com, Rachel's new project is to take that company through a more stable growth phase to AIM. But this time round, she knows exactly what NOT to do, and can put all that learning, both from making mistakes and creating a successful pioneering business, into good use.

Lessons: Put the right controls in place if you must step away from the business, don't allow yourself to be defeated if things do start to slide out of control and beware the vultures as you grow.

CASE STUDY

Julie Meyer famously took the dotcom world by storm when First Tuesday, a company she co-founded, became the largest global network of entrepreneurs, expanding from 17 cities in 1999 to 100-plus with half a million registered users, all via word of mouth. A boardroom coup saw First Tuesday sold off for $50 million when Julie was outvoted by the co-founders who'd been letting her run the business and put in all the effort.

'I knew that the deal is always done at the beginning intellectually, but probably didn't know that in practice. When First Tuesday moved from being a cocktail party to a business I tried to set it up such that the people putting the effort in to work on the business would be in the driver's seat. But when the other founders refused the proposed shareholding that I prepared to ensure you had the value accruing to the people who were building the value, I was at a loss.'

'The most difficult decision was not setting up First Tuesday in a way which would lead to value creation for the city leaders around the world who I brought in. They believed in me, trusted me and believed in my leadership, and I ultimately wasn't in a position to help them receive some of the value from the deal. So if you take relationships seriously like I do and people are disenfranchised and you are no longer in control, it's very tough.'

'Hundreds of people around the world just couldn't believe that I wasn't in control and were saying, "What do you mean you got outvoted at the boardroom?" They just couldn't understand, because they perceived me as the driving force, and thought I was in control of the whole thing. They didn't even know the names of the other founders. 'Nick Denton, Adam who?'

'Realising the only person I could blame was myself, because I'd known at the beginning that the company wasn't set up correctly, but not knowing how painful the results could be, of having to look people in the eye and saying "I'm really sorry I got outvoted and I can't help you."'

'*I should have just walked away and said, "you know what, I'm going to call this First Wednesday or Julie's Network Business", and I shouldn't have gone into business with people who were giving me the kind of red alert sign that they weren't my business partner, but rather wanted an unfair reward for not building the business, but just having been there at the time of the cocktail party.*'

'*The major value creation for First Tuesday was when I took it internationally and I did that on my own. So it was a case of learning the hard way that the deal is done at the beginning and once you set a deal with another person it's very difficult to correct it.*'

Since then, Julie has made great decisions, her best being to set up Ariadne Capital when she did. '*In many ways I could have just ridden on my First Tuesday credentials for quite some time, but I decided to **be** the change and I felt what I set out to achieve with First Tuesday I hadn't quite achieved, so I thought I'd build that platform again. It's been a tough four years, but I've never had a day where I felt it was the wrong thing to do, it's made me more engaged in the future, more optimistic, feeling as if I'm in control. So that was the best thing I did.*'

'*And now that the market is starting to take off again four years later, 2004 has been a great year for Ariadne. So setting up Ariadne and doing it when we did are the best decisions.*'

Lesson: The deal is done at the beginning. Trust your instinct always and act on it. Set your business up so those who bring value to it are able to make key decisions.

CASE STUDY

'*One good example of a mistake we've made is that we underestimated what people would do with our product in the supermarkets,*' explains Sally Preston of Babylicious. '*We simply hadn't anticipated that people would slide the sleeves off as many times as they did to look at the product,*' Sally explains.

'*The consequence was that it caused our tamper evidence tabs to be literally worn away. In hindsight we should have anticipated that a bit better, but as soon as we identified the problem, we found a solution instantly. The ramifications were big, and it was difficult to deal with because we had stock in all the wrong places, and ended up recalling bits of stock and resealing it, so it was very difficult to manage operationally.*'

But Sally says that accepting that you will make mistakes in business is half the battle. '*If you sit there and say "it's not fair" you won't go forward really, so you just have to get on with it.*'

Lessons: Create prototypes of products and packaging and test/get feedback on how they're handled in the marketplace.

CASE STUDY

The main issue for A Quarter Of came when the business outgrew its premises and was forced to move at its busiest time of year.

'*We were in a 1,000 sq ft office and on our record day before Christmas, we sent out one and a quarter tonnes of sweets. Literally we'd get deliveries coming in on pallets, but the unit we were in had normal size doors, so we were hand unloading while the four or five pallets arrived at the same time, and it was an absolute nightmare with space so tight.*'

As a result, A Quarter Of moved to an industrial unit with big roller shutter doors and more space, to cope with the numbers when necessary. 'We put a sign on the site telling people we'd be shutting for Christmas just to get everything out we'd had in. So we lost the busiest two weeks of the year because we couldn't cope with it and ran it very close, ten of us working seven days a week to get the stuff out.'

Corners had to be cut too, with the regular paper bags dispensed with to save time. '*We could get out an extra ten orders a day if we left them out.*'

'*You have to manage the growth because you don't want to expand too quickly as that can be a killer to companies,*' advises Michael. '*But as an internet company you're always dependent on the orders coming in, and if* The Sun *decide to write about you, you get a month's worth of orders in a day, so you need the flexibility to cope with that without overstretching things, because bigger premises mean bigger overheads.*'

Finding suppliers in the first place was another early headache for the business, as was cashflow. '*When we got the first lot of PR we had a sudden burst of business and, at the time, the processing company was holding on to the credit card payments for five weeks before we'd get it. So I was spending £5,000 a week on sweets and £2,000 a week on postage, with no credit, so I had five weeks of that before getting any money in, building up 35,000 of debt before getting the money back.*'

Lesson: Be flexible and prepared for growth and cashflow issues.

The Final Word

'*You cannot delegate entrepreneurship. If you are going to make mistakes make them yourself.*'
Stelios Haji-Ioannu, easyJet

And remember, regardless of success or failure it's better to give it a go!

'*I've never met a person who's said I wish I hadn't done that. But I've met a lot of people who didn't bother with their idea and have said, Gosh I wish I had done that.*' Simon Woodroffe

And it's never too late. Simon Woodroffe was 40 before he decided to set up his own business. Now he's a multi millionaire businessman.

'*You know the most important bit of advice?*' Dame Roddick asked me. '*Don't be bloody boring. Nobody wants to hear about your business, it's the most boring thing when you have people for dinner and they want to talk about their business. Talk about art, talk about anything, not your business. At least ban it for more than three minutes. That can be tedious. We must have been so boring in the early days.*' Of course there's no danger of Dame Roddick being boring as she fights to free the Angola Three (men locked up by the US in solitary confinement for longer than I've been alive for crimes they didn't commit) and pledges her support to help humanity.

'The Queen once said to me, 'You're always moving, you're always so busy,' and I said, 'I'd rather wear out than rust to death.' Dame Anita Roddick

Don't rust. Keep on going. Because you can do it!

Write three things you will do immediately to improve your chances of success.

1 _____

2 _____

3 _____

Grit your teeth and hang on tight – welcome to the entrepreneurial rollercoaster ride. A journey paved with pain, perspiration and pressure, littered with potential luxuries and luck, and ending in delight or disaster. Either way it's an experience you'll hold with you forever.

STEP 43: WE HAVE LIFT OFF!

Congratulations. Once you've completed all the exercises and ticked off tasks in the ultimate business start-up checklist (next chapter), you're ready to launch. One last thing to remember is to give other small businesses your custom. Feed the growth; water your shoots and theirs and watch the garden of small business bloom across Britain.

I wish you all the very best of luck in your new venture.

Enjoy, believe, smile

CHAPTER FOURTEEN

The Ultimate Business Start-Up Checklist

This chapter summarises the key questions and actions from the rest of the book with a checklist for you to complete.

Go through this **ultimate start-up checklist** and tick each box as you complete the exercises or as you continue preparing to launch the business.

By the end of this chapter, you should be…

… ready to start-up your very own business!

☐ Do you understand the implications of setting up your own business: do you have a clear idea of the advantages and disadvantages of going it alone and a plan to deal with the disadvantages?

☐ Have you written down and sketched out your long-term vision and your short-term goals? Do you have your 'map' and 'destination' figured out?

☐ Have you bought yourself an Ideas and Inspiration scrapbook, notebook and dictaphone to record your ideas?

☐ Have you begun to dump your data: ideas, opportunities, possibilities?

☐ Do you know where you will find daily inspiration: from what and whom you'll take your inspiration?

☐ Do you believe in your idea and your ability to bring it to fruition? Do you have enough passion in your idea?

☐ Have you got your fear factor in check and uncovered what's held you back in the past?

☐ Have you thoroughly assessed your skills, strengths, weakness, creative ideas, opportunities and threats, and completed your ACE analysis worksheet?

☐ Do you know where the gaps are and how you'll fill them? Have you considered future or current staffing requirements and profiles? Who are you really likely to need? Will you fill in the gaps by learning additional skills, or by taking on partners or staff or by having someone else manage the business from the outset?

☐ Have you polished your opportunity-spotting antennae?

☐ Are you online with an internet connection and computer at home? Whether or not you have a website, you really should harness the information age by getting yourself connected to the web, even if only as a research tool.

☐ Have you conducted sufficient market research on the market, the competition and customers? Can you describe what your three main competitors offer and how you will differ? Can you list their prices, locations, strengths and weaknesses?

☐ Have you assessed the strengths, weaknesses and viability of your business idea? Do you have a great product or service?

☐ Have you joined relevant business networks, discussion boards and associations and subscribed to relevant magazines? I can recommend Better Business Magazine (www.better-business.co.uk) and Real Business (www.realbusiness.co.uk)

☐ Have you a contingency plan in case of seasonal sales?

☐ Have you considered all the necessary items when pricing?

☐ Do you know how you'll generate repeat custom?

☐ Have you looked into licensing and franchising possibilities for your business?

☐ Have you identified your market share, and ascertained the level of demand?

☐ Have you segmented your audience into niche targets and profiled them? Have you uncovered common characteristics among your potential customer groups (demographically/psychographically)?

☐ Have you located where your customers go to find information such as yours and decided how you'll communicate with them; through what means?

☐ Have you had your market survey completed by potential customers and recorded results?

☐ Have you uncovered the core benefits of your product or service and the solutions it offers?

☐ Have you worked out your sales cycle and how long will take to break even?

☐ Have you collected and recorded evidence of your market growing, declining or remaining static?

☐ Do you have a business location in mind and a plan for how to assess and acquire it?

☐ Have you created a media and publications document full of contact details and web addresses of targeted magazines, newspapers and online publications and e-zines?

☐ Have you completed the market research worksheet?

☐ Have you selected your business name? Have you registered it as a domain name (web address) and have you looked into whether it fits the criteria for a successful trademark registration?

☐ Have you clearly defined and written down a description of your brand personality?

☐ Have you written down your point and purpose and how you'll capture the hearts and minds of your customers and team?

☐ Have you figured out your unique selling proposition (USP)? Do you have a strapline?

☐ Have you written your 'elevator pitch'?

☐ Have you had your logo designed, or sketched ideas to provide a designer with? Have you gathered print quotes for business cards, letterheads and other materials for launch?

☐ Have you listed potential partners (in-house or outsourced)?

☐ Do you know how your business will operate and with what status (ie sole trader, limited company, partnership.)?

☐ Have you notified the relevant authorities, registered with Companies House and notified the Inland Revenue?

☐ Have you applied for the relevant operating licences and sought all the correct permissions and registrations from the necessary statutory bodies? Do you know your health and safety requirements and do you have a health and safety certificate and fire certificate/authorisation?

☐ Have you checked your credit rating using Equifax?

☐ Do you know what insurance you will need and understand your liabilities? For example, by law you will need employer liability insurance if you intend to employ staff, and third party car insurance. Other insurance types include: public liability, property insurance, contents insurance, personal health insurance, fire, theft, business interruption, professional liability, trade credit insurance, engineering insurance. Do you need a licence to operate? Have you checked with local authorities?

☐ Have you written your business profile outline and business plan? Set initial goals and targets for the business? Produced forecasts, projections and estimates for the business?

◆ EXERCISE ◆

As a final exercise, complete this Business Profile

The business is a _____. It will provide _____
_____ for _____ . It is different from the competition because it _____.
The founder (me) has _____ years' experience in _____.
Other skills/qualifications the founder has include _____
plus contacts in the _____ industry. The skills and knowledge I am missing include _____. The gaps will be filled in by _____
_____. The idea will work because _____
_____
_____.
The initial aims of the business are _____. Possible obstacles and initial challenges include: _____ which I could get over by _____. The equipment I need includes _____. The long-term vision for the business is to be _____ in five years' time and _____ in ten years' time. Customers will choose _____ because _____. My reasons for starting my own business are _____.

☐ Have you created an action plan that is specific, measurable, achievable, relevant and time-restricted? Eg: do _____, by _____ in order to _____ because _____.

☐ Do you have a plan for growth? Are your intentions to grow organically or manically?

☐ Do you know how much money you'll need to start up? Have you tallied up your estimated start-up costs? Do you have a funding plan?

☐ Do you know how much money you'll need to bring in to the business to survive and pay staff for the first few months? Have you considered hidden costs, such as extra postage, stationery or distribution costs; minimum stock purchase levels, extra packaging or higher bills?

☐ Have you listed and identified quantities of all the materials you'll need to purchase, from a cash book and kettle to sales and payment record folders, stock and stationery? Have you identified storage facilities for materials? Do you have an asset acquisition timetable for when you'll need the money?

☐ Have you contacted, compared and chosen your supplier(s)?

☐ Have you found a potential accountant? Have you asked them what turnaround time and service guarantees they might offer? Have you found out if their prices are fixed and how long it takes them to prepare accounts?

☐ Do you have a basic understanding of cashflow, book-keeping and VAT? Have you made a decision on whether or not to register for VAT voluntarily?

☐ Do you have an exit plan to sell the business within five or ten years, to go public and sell shares in the business within seven years?

☐ Have you considered what you could barter or trade and how you might keep your costs down?

☐ Have you listed potential sources of finance and found out which grants or loan schemes are applicable and available to you?

☐ Have you contacted your local authorities for advice on sources on funding?

☐ Have you found and set up a good business bank account? Most banks offer free banking to start-up businesses for a year or more, which is a great way to avoid high bank charges and fees.

☐ Do you know which part of the marketing pie you are on; which marketing strategies you will therefore be using and what materials (collateral) you will use to get your message out there?

☐ Have you completed your marketing plan?

☐ Have you crafted your marketing messages and materials?

☐ Have you written a clear customer service policy and invested in customer database software or some way or recording customer contact information and results of contacts with them?

☐ Have you created a green and ethical policy? Have you considered ways you'll manage waste and recycle; buy from ethical suppliers and use resources sensibly?

☐ Have you listed ways your business might involve or help the local community and/or serve the global community?

☐ Have you planned your website and reasons for having one: web content, navigation and design?

☐ Have you sourced a web designer and developer and asked for references, examples and how they can prove they won't let you down?

☐ Have you done your online competitive intelligence and sourced a potential user focus group to collate feedback and research from?

☐ Do you know which online marketing strategies you will use to launch and promote your website?

☐ Do you have a mentor lined up to help guide you?

☐ Is everything tidy and organised?

☐ Have you considered how you'll protect and save your data/information: your paperwork, your clients' projects or contact information, invoices and other crucial business data? How will it be stored? How will you back up information and keep copies off site?

☐ Do you have a support network of friends and family, including contacts you meet online?

☐ Do you know what tasks you will delegate?

☐ Are you ready to embrace change?

☐ Are you feeling ready to learn and be open to that concept continually?

Remember, **luck is where preparedness meets opportunity**, so go out there and get lucky with your own business.

Good luck. Enjoy the journey.
Cheryl Denise Rickman x

CHAPTER FIFTEEN

Useful Resources for Small Business Start-Ups

This chapter collects contacts and website details into a directory of useful resources to help small businesses start up and succeed.

Local Enterprise Agencies (LEAs)
www.nfea.com
National Federation of Enterprise Agencies (NFEA). Lists every county's LEA and links to contact information for each. NFEA is a network of independent, but not for profit, Local Enterprise Agencies committed to responding to the needs of small and growing businesses by providing an appropriate range of services.

Small Business Advice and Resources
www.better-business.co.uk
Resources for microbusinesses, entrepreneurs and freelancers.

www.bsbi.co.uk
The Big Small Business Initiative. Backed by major companies, offering helplines, factsheets, discounts, advice and consultancy on all aspects of setting up and running a small business.

www.businessbureau-uk.co.uk
Useful advice and information on starting up and running a small business. Articles, guides and links.

www.tvc.org.uk
Chamber Business Enterprises. Offers business support, advice, membership, and other services including networking, trade, worldwide supplier sourcing and access to export and business information.

www.growingbusinessawards.co.uk
Growing Business Awards. An awards scheme for start-up small businesses in the UK (those with between one and 500 employees).

www.Tycoon.com

Accompanies Peter's Tycoon series on ITV with a Business Builder and various other useful tools and advice.

www.PeterJones.tv

For insight, inspiration and investment and a range of business tools

www.realbusiness.co.uk

The U.K's leading magazine for growing companies.

www.thelightbulbfactor.com

The Lightbulb Factor. New business ideas service for budding entrepreneurs seeking inspiration, with a new small business idea every month.

www.enterpriseforum.co.uk

Centre for Enterprise. Forum intended to provide a virtual discussion forum for contributing to current thinking in research, policy and practice related to management development and small business enterprise.

www.young-enterprise.org.uk
www.yes.org.uk

Encourages and develops enterprise skills in those aged 15-25 years.

www.bawe-uk.org

British Association of Women Entrepreneurs.

www.ukbi.co.uk

The UK Business Incubation (UKBI) website contains details of all UK incubation projects, sources of finance for incubators, best practice guidelines, news and events, and is generally a forum for the exchange of information to help potential and existing UK incubators, and small businesses generally.

www.chamberonline.co.uk

British Chambers of Commerce website.

www.bam.ac.uk

British Academy of Management. Describes the organisation and its objectives and gives information about activities, membership and fellowship, journal, conferences and constitution.

www.iod.co.uk

The Institute of Directors (IOD). UK organisation representing individual company directors.

www.ruralopportunities.org

The Prince's Trust Rose Project. Helps young people living in rural areas of Yorkshire and North Lincolnshire to set up businesses, providing them with advice and a free website.

www.t4w.co.uk
These4walls. London-based think tank and networking forum for professionals in the marketing and communications industries. Contains industry news, details of events, membership information and other resources.

www.bl4london.com
Business Link for London small and medium sized businesses.

www.ethnicbusiness.org
Ethnic minority business forum. Offers assistance and advice to ethnic minority businesses and entrepreneurs in the UK.

www.skillsforemployers.gov.uk
Skills for employers website.

www.2-small-business.com
Small Business Resource. Offers small business service to entrepreneurs. Includes services, resources and discussion forum.

www.startups.co.uk
Startups.co.uk. A comprehensive directory of information about starting up and running a business.

www.businesslink.gov.uk
Practical help/advice to businesses.

www.smallbusiness.co.uk
News, advice and directory of useful resources for small businesses.

www.mybusiness.co.uk
Free resource for small businesses. Advice, links and in-depth guides.

www.startupright.co.uk
Start up advice, resources and articles for small business.

www.starttalkingideas.org
Make Your Mark – Start Talking Ideas is an ambitious campaign to bring about a cultural change in the UK and inspire 14-25 year olds to 'turn their ideas into reality'.

www.sbrt.co.uk
Small Business Research Trust.

www.shell-livewire.org
Shell LiveWIRE – Business Startup Advice.

www.nesta.org.uk
NESTA – the National Endowment for Science, Technology and the Arts. Invests in talented people and innovative ideas.

www.prowess.org.uk
This UK network supports the growth of women's business ownership and has an extensive listing of helpful business bodies throughout Britain.

www.ideas21.co.uk
IDEAS 21 offer free sessions in London and Manchester to women who want to turn an idea into a business.

www.smallbusinesseurope.org
Organisation seeking to maximise the interests of UK small and medium sized enterprises.

www.london-se1.co.uk
Mentoring scheme for local small businesses.

www.minority4business.co.uk
Independent advisory body representing the interests of minority ethnic businesses.

www.homeworking.com
Resource for those working from home featuring classified ads, a forum and a library of information.

www.tradeport.org
Trade Port. Learn how to export things, find trade leads and company databases. Find international buyers, market research and more.

www.tradenetireland.com
TradeNet Ireland is an online business to business network facilitating all-Ireland trade and providing SMEs with a matching service for sourcing customers, suppliers and trading partners in Ireland.

www.scottish-enterprise.com
Scottish Enterprise website.

www.fpb.co.uk
Forum of Private Business. Aims to influence laws and policies affecting small to medium sized businesses. With membership information, research resources, documents for download and news.

www.fsb.org.uk
The Federation of Small Businesses. Lobbying group for SMEs.

www.nesprogramme.org
New Entrepreneurship Programme.

www.princes-trust.org.uk
The Princes Trust.

www.theworkfoundation.com
The Work Foundation is an independent, not-for-profit think tank and consultancy.

www.ipd.co.uk
Institute of Personnel and Development. Development and promotion of good practice in the field of the management and development of people.

www.iipuk.co.uk
Investors in People UK. Public body responsible for the promotion of the Investors in People standard, driving its progress forward through promotion and monitoring.

www.free-bee.co.uk
Free-Bee offer a range of 'free' services to UK businesses, including 0800 phone numbers.

www.vrg.co.uk
The Venue Resource Group. Providing service for hotel reservations, meetings, incentives and business travel.

http://my1stbusiness.com
Business start-up support service helping entrepreneurs. From £49 for an annual subscription.

www.sybmagazine.com
start your BUSINESS Magazine is a bimonthly publication that aims to help businesses start-up, grow and flourish in every aspect.

Company Formation

www.quickformations.co.uk
Online company formation to set up your limited company.

www.duport.co.uk
Set up your new limited company automatically.

Forums and Networks

www.ecademy.com
Online network connecting business people.

www.ukbusinessforums.com
UK Business Forums. Chat, discussion and networking for UK businesses.

www.taforum.org
Trade Association Forum.

www.busygirl.com
Aurora Women's Network. Europe's leading corporate and entrepreneurial women's network.

www.digitaleve.org
A unique women's organisation about community, technology and creativity.

www.ibf.com
International Business Forum. Links, business opportunities, resources, reports, forms and more.

www.womanowned.com
Networking opportunities and information for women interested in starting and growing a business.

www.beyondbricks.com
Beyondbricks.com – The Department of Trade and Industry's portal for entrepreneurs. Offers a community for networking with suppliers, customers and investors, guidance, resources and tools for business development.

www.businessconnection.org.uk
The Business Connection. A networking club for new business people in West London.

www.leadx.com
LeadX – The Business Lead Exchange. An online networking site for sales and marketing professionals to exchange valuable sales leads and contact information about prospects.

www.entrepreneurial-exchange.co.uk
Scotland's premier networking group.

Government Business Information Resource Sites

www.dti.gov.uk
Department of Trade and Industry.

www.hse.gov.uk
Health and Safety Executive website.

www.inlandrevenue.gov.uk
The Inland Revenue – for tax information and forms.

www.hmce.gov.uk
HM Customs and Excise – for VAT information.

www.companieshouse.gov.uk
Companies House for information about all registered companies and what you need to know and do as a limited company.

www.dataprotection.gov.uk
Data Protection Registrar.

www.patent.gov.uk
Trade Mark and Patent Registrar.

Your Goals

www.goalpro.com
Goal recording tool.

www.wish2getha.com
Store wish lists and find motivation.

Researching Resources

www.postcodeanywhere.co.uk
Postcode Anywhere. Web-based address and postcode finder for over 27 million UK addresses.

www.tracesmart.co.uk
UK Roll. Offers UK electoral roll searches and reports.

www.re5ult.com
RE5ULT searches the internet and other sources to supply its customers with must-have information. Send your question to RE5ULT via text message from your mobile, by e-mail or directly to the pool of experts online and receive an answer quickly using the same medium also provides 82ask.com service.

www.freshminds.co.uk
Fresh Minds is a research company providing companies with fast and accurate market research and analysis, carried out by their bank of Minds, a collection of graduates, MBAs and PhDs from Europe's top universities supported by a team of in-house project managers.

www.varinternational.com/measure_market.htm
Provides a full service market research facility.

www.zoomerang.com
Business Market Research. Online survey software allows users to create and send surveys.

www.irn-research.com
IRN provides market research and business information consultancy to large and small organisations across a broad range of industry sectors.

www.nop.co.uk
NOP Research Group is part of NOP World, one of the world's largest market research and business information companies, offering both custom and syndicated research.

www.freepint.com
FreePint is a network of 66,796 information researchers globally. Post your tricky research questions or sign up for newsletters.

www.marketresearch.com
MarketResearch.com is an aggregator of global business intelligence representing the most comprehensive collection of published market research available on demand.

www.snapdata.com

Market research toolbox. Specialises in top-line international market research overviews. All data is compiled in house by the Snapdata Research Department, an international team of research experts.

www.mrweb.com

Aiming to represent the UK market research industry online; resource for links to suppliers of market research, through a database of agencies and consultants as well as news, events and careers services.

www.2020research.co.uk

Full service agency with particular experience in finance, retail, media, training and IT.

www.act2.co.uk

Specialists in youth research of adults, children and teenagers. Concise site with outline of company philosophy and tasters of example research and commentary.

www.bmrb.co.uk

One of the largest UK agencies. Owners of the Target Group Index – TGI – portfolio of surveys. Expansive site which includes access to their free knowledge archive – reports, papers, newsletters, case studies.

www.researching.co.uk

Full service consultancy based in Glasgow.

www.keynote.co.uk

Specialist online publishers of market information reports, all of which are listed on the site along with details of additional services they offer.

www.mori.com

MORI – Market & Opinion Research International. One of the largest agencies in the UK and well known for their widely published polls. Expansive site detailing all of their operations. Also offer a free weekly e-mail: MORI Poll Digest.

www.virtualsurveys.com

Specialist online research agency focusing on utilising the internet. Details of the services offered and access to published papers and related news articles.

www.audienceprofiler.com

Internet market research firm providing customised quantitative research.

communitypoll.com/

Write/post surveys and questionnaires online. Bar graphs and deep analysis.

www.jup.com

Jupiter Communications. Market research and analysis on the consumer online industry.

www.clickz.com/stats

Nua Internet Surveys. Authoritative and widely cited source for internet statistics covering a wide range of topics with a strong global focus.

www.emarketer.com
Research on the e-marketplace.

www.nielsen-netratings.com
Information on website usage, internet access and advertising data.

www.statmarket.com
Updated daily and based on stats from over 65,000 sites. Everything from search engines and browsers to screen resolutions and ISPs.

Learning Resources to Fill In the Gaps

www.learndirect.co.uk
Distance learning plus hundreds of online courses and information on 2,000 learndirect centres and 700,000 courses.

www.beginners.co.uk
A database of IT training courses.

www.goclearthinking.co.uk
Clear Thinking Ltd. Authorised training centre for Autodesk, Discreet, Macromedia and Maxon, based in Romsey, Hampshire. One to one training available.

www.acquireit.co.uk
IT and internet training specifically for businesses and the over 50s within Surrey and Sussex. The site also contains daily news, reviews, content for the over-50s and businesses, features and discussions.

www.advance-training.co.uk
Training courses for Dreamweaver, Frontpage, JavaScript, Adobe Photoshop and HTML, presented on-site at your offices, within the UK. Also seminars and consultancy on search engine optimisation and successful web marketing techniques.

www.casetraining.co.uk
Case Consultants. Web applications development training on client sites.

www.corps.co.uk
Corps Business. New media training, recruitment and design studio services. Located in central London.

www.buildingyourbusiness.co.uk
Business advice, coaching and training courses for the owners of small businesses who are looking to take more control over their companies.

www.trainingfromscratch.co.uk
Courses on Dreamweaver, Fireworks, Flash, GoLive, Photoshop for anyone involved with web design. Based in Edinburgh and Glasgow.

Finances

www.j4b.co.uk
Searchable database for Government and European funding.

www.grantsnet.co.uk
Provides a searchable database of UK grants, loans and funding schemes.

www.insurance-brokers.net
A-Z of insurance broker websites.

www.financialmanagementdevelopment.com
Free resource on financial management development. Includes downloadable documents.

www.is4profit.com
Business information resource for SMEs.

www.bba.org.uk
The British Bankers Association. Contains news, views, reports, surveys and comparisons, plus links to bank websites.

www.moneyfacts.co.uk
Compare business bank accounts or personal accounts and find all you need to know about personal and business finance.

www.payontime.co.uk
The Better Payment Practice Group. Information on good payment practice for UK businesses, including guidance on the Late Payment legislation.

www.justclaim.co.uk
Just Claim is a software package that will help you get paid on time. It acts as your guide to the court procedures and enables you to fill in the official forms on your own computer. It also provides a comprehensive guide to the court procedures, and has a short guide to the new late payment legislation. Some information is provided free of charge.

www.uk-factoring-company.com
UK Factoring Company providing invoice discounting for small business from £50k turnover.

www.enterprise-centre.co.uk
Provides cashflow forecast resources and other business guidance.

www.factoringhelpline.co.uk
Factoring and cashflow solutions.

www.mmi-online.co.uk/Help/index.htm
Free online tax and accounts clinic

www.cranleys.co.uk
Accountancy services and fact sheets.

www.bepaidontime.co.uk
The DTI estimate that 10,000 businesses go bust every year because of poor debt collection and late payment of their invoices. This site helps businesses to be paid on time every time to avoid the same.

www.1stphasesolutions.co.uk
Specialists in business plan creation and circulation to business angels.

www.dti.gov.uk/sflg
Small Firms Loan Guarantee Scheme.

www.thecadmusorganisation.ltd.uk
Capital Partners Group. Business angel funding for entrepreneurs and established ventures.

www.entrust.co.uk
Entrust. A business angels network for companies established or setting up in the North East.

www.equitylink.co.uk
Service facilitating matches between investors and small businesses.

www.findyouridealbusinesspartner.com
Find Your Ideal Business Partner. Business partner online matchmaking service.

www.geif.co.uk
Great Eastern Investment Forum. GEIF links early stage companies seeking capital with business angels.

www.ariadnecapital.com
Ariadne Capital: Global investment and advisory firm.

www.solenthub.co.uk
Solent Investment Opportunity Network. A service to early stage companies and private investors in the Solent area.

www.southwestinvestmentgroup.co.uk
South West Investment Group. Help in the provision of investment finance and grants for businesses throughout the South West.

www.strategian.co.uk
Strategian Ltd. Strategy planning and action for potential businesses.

www.nwda.co.uk
TEChINVEST. One of the most successful business angel introduction services in the UK.

www.oion.co.uk
The Oxfordshire Investment Opportunity Network.

www.venturesite.co.uk
The Venture Site.

www.triodos.co.uk
Triodos Match Ltd. Links businesses which need capital with people who have capital.

www.prelude-ventures.com
Prelude Ventures. A leading early stage, technology focused venture capital company.

www.bvca.co.uk
British Venture Capital Association (BVCA). Official body representing the majority of venture capital and private equity in the UK.

www.firsttuesday.com
First Tuesday. Global e-commerce network.

www.venturateam.com
Helps with both taking start ups all the way through to success and building new ventures for multi-nationals.

www.alliance-leicestercommercialbank.co.uk
Alliance and Leicester.

www.aibgb.co.uk
Allied Irish Bank.

www.business.barclays.co.uk
Barclays Business Banking.

www.co-operativebank.co.uk
The Co-Operative Bank.

www.ukbusiness.hsbc.com
HSBC Business Banking.

www.lloydstsb.com
Lloyds TSB.

www.NatWest.com/smallbusiness
Natwest Bank.

www.rbs.co.uk/small_business
The Royal Bank Of Scotland.

Legal Resources

www.own-it.org
Free intellectual property resource centre. Own It provides free legal contract templates available for download, free legal advice and free seminars to enable creative

people to make the most of their ideas and protect them via trademarks, patent, copyright and licensing.

www.freelawyer.co.uk
Free legal guidance and help. Get online help from virtual lawyers.

www.weblaw.co.uk
UK internet law arm of US law firm Sprecher Grier Halberstam. Specialise in internet law, e-commerce law, e-commerce contracts, website design contracts, domain name law, trade marks and the legal aspects of computer law.

lawdocs.co.uk
Legal documents and free legal information for the UK.

www.intellectual-property.gov.uk
Information on intellectual property in the United Kingdom, from The UK Patent Office.

www.copyrightservice.co.uk
UK Copyright Service. Providing copyright registration services, information and advice for the United Kingdom.

www.online-law.co.uk
Search for lawyers on the web in the UK.

www.legaladvicefree.co.uk
Legal Advice Free offers free legal advice on UK Law. Has a solicitor search engine to find a solicitor near you.

Recommended Website Designers, Domain Name Registration and Hosting

www.bluebit.co.uk
Highly recommended web design and development company.

www.zebedeecreations.com
Recommended web design and development company.

www.vivid-image.co.uk
Recommended web design and development company.

www.pedalo.co.uk
A web design agency based in Chiswick, west London working across sectors developing attractive and user friendly sites.

www.rackspace.com
Managed, dedicated and scalable web hosting for businesses.

www.just-the-name.co.uk
Domain name registration.

buildit.sitesell.com/improveyoursite.html
Site Build It. All in one site-building site-hosting and promotion package if you want to do it yourself.

www.web-source.net
Guide to professional website design and development.

www.rnib.org.uk/digital/
Good website design initiative for accessible websites.

www.w3.org/WAI/
Web accessibility initiative.

Recommended Logo and Graphic Designers

www.meltingpot.co.uk
Melting Pot is a different kind of graphic design agency, providing creative solutions to print, marketing and web problems. Based near Chichester, West Sussex.

www.aricotvert.co.uk
Aricot Vert has built up a reputation over nearly 15 years for providing innovative and exciting design solutions for identity, literature, environments and digital design. Designing visual communications solutions that support your business strategy.

inkdotdesign@hotmail.com
Ink Dot Design.

www.logodesign.co.uk
Logos, print, exhibition, advertising and website design.

www.printbuyers.co.uk
Printbuyers. A free service providing several printing quotes, from different printing companies, for you to compare.

Managing and Making The Most of Your Website

www.webdesignclinic.com
This site offers information on colour theory and how to get your website design right.

www.webtrends.com
This site offers one of the most popular analysis products available. Provides info on site visitor numbers, how they find you, where they go and where they exit. This allows you to get a better idea of your target audience and tweak your site and content accordingly.

www.siteconfidence.co.uk
Site Confidence offers a free trial of the website monitoring package. This reports any site downtime, and is a great way to monitor when your site goes down – it may happen more often than you are aware of.

www.useit.com
Usability information resource from usability guru Jakob Nielsen.

myws.sitesell.com/improveyoursite.html
Make Your Words Sell handbook to ensure your words grab your visitors' attention and persuade them to take the action you want them to take.

myss.sitesell.com/improveyoursite.html
Make Your Site Sell handbook to help you make the most of your website and profit online.

myps.sitesell.com/improveyoursite.html
Make Your Price Sell handbook to ensure you price right online.

www.grokdotcom.com
Online conversion rate newsletter to help you maximise your online conversion rates from visitors to customers.

www.futurenowinc.com/ccrcalculator.htm
Free conversion rate calculator. Work out your website conversion rate for free.

www.electronic-payments.co.uk
Online payment solution comparison tool.

www.webcopywriter.co.uk
Web copywriting expert – yes it's me again.

www.tipsbooklets.com
Tips Products Int. Transform your knowledge into electronic and hard copy tips booklets to use for marketing, motivating and making more money.

egoods.sitesell.com/improveyoursite.html
The whole 'digital goods for sale' space is soaring. Anything can be digitised – sell it.

www.magicwordsthatmakeyourich.com/g.o/improve
Magic Words That Bring You Riches. This e-book is written by Ted Nicholas, widely recognised as one of the greatest direct marketing wizards of all time. In 'Magic Words' Ted reveals 17 magic words.

www.hypnoticwriting.com/g.o/improve
Hypnotic Writing. The latest in a growing line of marketing courses. A must for anyone who wants to write persuasively.

www.southphotography.co.uk
For pictures that jump off the page. Specialists in set price product photography, with prices from £24, a free email approval service and guaranteed fast turnarounds.

Marketing and Web Promotion

www.abundantreferrals.com
Articles and information about generating referrals.

www.Doyourownpr.com
Paula Gardner shows you how to do PR for your business without breaking the bank.

www.Leanmarketing.co.uk
Another useful site for consultants and coaches from Debbie Jenkins.

www.new2marketing.com
Provider of affordable marketing services to start-ups and small businesses. Select ingredients you need to make a marketing campaign a success.

www.iwks.com
Internet Works magazine. Gives practical advice on web design, promotion, usability, e-mail, marketing, networking and link development.

www.cim.co.uk
Chartered Institute of Marketing.

www.prweb.com
Announce your news using this press release distribution site.

www.pressbox.co.uk
Free press release distribution service, can also write press releases for you.

responsesource.com/releases/rel_submit.php
Submit press releases for a small fee.

www.webpromotion.co.uk
A portal with links to useful sites that help promote your website.

www.mediauk.com
Marketing Resources Ltd. B2B marketing solutions, tips and a newsletter.

www.workz.com
Useful articles for webmasters.

www.clickz.com
A range of articles to help you profit online.

www.affiliatewindow.com
Affiliate Window. UK affiliate marketing company with an emphasis on providing cutting edge technology and tools.

www.affiliatemarketing.co.uk
The resource guide for affiliate program managers.

www.academyinternet.com
Internet training courses for business.

www.wilsonweb.com
One of the most substantial online marketing and promotion resources on the web, includes a detailed knowledge base of articles, reviews, expert tips and more.

www.chinwag.com
Chinwag.com is a community for website owners, with discussion lists of web usability, marketing and more.

www.searchenginewatch.com
The famously up-to-date search engine resource which contains everything you need to know about search engine optimisation, and how each engine ranks pages.

www.searchfactor.com
Guidelines, knowledge and tips to help webmasters achieve better ranking on search engines.

www.searchengineforums.com
Chat online to others and ask search engine questions.

www.wordtracker.com
Find out what the most popular keywords and search terms are on the web.

www.ideamarketers.com
Free articles, content and e-zine builder.

www.howIpromotemywebsite.com
Basic and practical website promotion guide.

www.link-popularity.com
Check your inbound link popularity here.

www.linkstoyou.com
Enables you to check links in to sites and swap links with others.

www.alexa.com
Uncover details about other sites, including their traffic ranking.

www.womenspeakers.co.uk
The UK and Europe's Only Dedicated Source for Outstanding Women Speakers and Facilitators. So, if you need an inspirational speaker for your own launch event or are a female expert or motivational coach yourself looking to raise your profile, you know where to go.

Outsourcing for Skills You Need/Posting Projects for Freelancers

www.GetAFreelancer.com
Get custom work done for your site. Marketplace for buyers and sellers.

www.brainbid.com
BrainBid.com. Employers post projects. Free agents bid on the projects.

www.CityITjobs.com

IT contractor marketplace, where employers and freelancers contract with each other using an auction format.

www.FreelanceAuction.com

Online auction marketplace for outsourcing custom programming work, website design and graphic design services, where freelancers bid on job requests.

www.freelancewebprogramming.com

Marketplace to find freelance web programmers, script programmers and graphic designers.

www.freelancewebprojects.com

Online auction for custom programming outsourcing, web design and graphic design. Connects webmasters with freelance programmers and web designers.

www.freelancersdirect.com

Offers project managers the ability to post projects online and service providers the ability to bid on them.

www.freelancespot.com

A marketplace for services. Project managers post a project for bidding. Freelancers bid on current open projects.

www.elance.com

The first worldwide professional services marketplace.

www.selectadesigner.com

Online auction marketplace where project providers and professional graphic designers connect.

www.freelancers.com

Directory of freelancers and jobs for freelance writers, designers, web design and developers, illustrators, photographers, creatives of all types.

www.expertsontheweb.com

Directory of freelance translators. Post resumés and search for jobs.

www.german-translator.com

Directory of freelance translators working in German.

www.ework.com

A market-based online exchange where project managers and e-working web professionals connect, engage and work together to complete projects online.

Work-Life Balance

www.dti.gov.uk/work-lifebalance

The Work-Life Balance campaign. The Government introduced the Work-Life Balance campaign in 2000. The campaign was to help employers to recognise the benefits of adopting policies and procedures to enable employees to adopt flexible working patterns.

www.workingbalance.co.uk
Major public sector conferences: Manchester, Belfast and more UK venues.

www.cushiontheimpact.co.uk
Lifestyle management and concierge services. Practical help with your busy life. No membership fees.

www.parentsatwork.org.uk
Organisation providing information for working parents and their employers on employment rights, childcare and flexible working. Run Employer of the Year and Britain's Best Boss annual awards and have published two recent pieces of research: Working and Caring in London 2002 and Quality of Life in the City (of London).

www.tca.org.uk
Europe's largest organisation dedicated to teleworking with a membership of over 2,000 individuals and organisations.

www.nomoreclutter.co.uk
No more clutter is a professional decluttering and organising service for home or office.

www.mindtools.com/page5.html
How to get the most from your time.

www.employersforwork-lifebalance.org.uk
EFWLB aims to help all UK organisations implement and continuously improve sustainable work-life strategies which meet customer needs, corporate goals and enhance the quality of life for individuals.

www.flametree.co.uk
Flametree is a specialist consultancy working with organisations to respond to the work-life balance challenge.

www.flexecutive.co.uk
Flexecutive from the Resource Connection is a leading specialist in flexible work and work-life balance, including consultancy, recruitment and IT solutions divisions, all built on a foundation of extensive research.

greatplacetowork-europe.com
100 workplaces that have created especially great workplace environments.

www.workfamily.com
A global clearing house for work-life professionals. Produces monthly work-life news and trend digests.

www.workingwoman.com
Formerly Working Mother Magazine. The results of their annual Employer of the Year Award are published online.

www.ivillage.co.uk/workcareer/worklife/
Useful articles on juggling work and life.

www.w-lb.org.uk
Work Life Balance Trust. UK site dedicated to initiating, organising and stimulating debate and action on work-life balance via conferences and seminars, research, and publishing reports and surveys on the subject, plus advising Government departments on relevant issues.

www.flexibility.co.uk
Resources for flexible work including work-life balance resources and Working Life in Balance events.

www.number-10.gov.uk/output/Page1440.asp
Work-life balance factsheet from the Government, reviewing the benefits and options for work-life balance.

For more work-life balance articles and case studies visit:
www.better-business.co.uk/07articles/sc_work_life_balance.shtm
www.better-business.co.uk/07resource/r_work_life.shtm

Importing and Exporting

www.uktradeinvest.gov.uk
The UK Government website with free information to help you do business internationally.

www.export.co.uk
UK Centre of Exporting Excellence. British exporters' website with free and direct access to UK companies with helplines if you need assistance.

www.walestrade.com
Helping Welsh companies establish themselves in overseas markets and forge business alliances with counterparts worldwide.

www.scottishdevelopmentinternational.com
Provides practical information on market research, missions and finance, helping Scottish companies to exploit international opportunities.

www.fco.gov.uk
Providing a central resource for any matters concerning overseas relations and foreign affairs.

www.ecgd.gov.uk
Export Credits Guarantee Department. Site of the official export credit agency, provided to help UK companies trading overseas. Includes rates, press releases and contacts.

www.britishchambers.org.uk/exportzone/
Advice, information and useful links helping you to turn your export potential into export success.

www.taforum.org
The Gateway to UK Trade Associations and Business Sectors. The website also aims to assist buyers, Government departments, researchers, the public and other enquirers wishing to access information about UK trade associations and business sectors.

www.cbi.org.uk
This website has been designed to provide access to practical information about how the CBI (Confederation of British Industry) serves its members.

Customer Services and Relationship Management

www.proedgeskills.com/customer_service_articles.htm
Free customer service articles.

www.performanceinpeople.co.uk
Performance in People. Complete solutions for clients looking to improve customer service.

www.skill4.com
Caring for customers. Build relationships with customers. Keep them and their business.

www.activia.co.uk
Customer care training. Bespoke training on your premises or at offices in Slough (Berks).

www.managementtraining.uk.com
Customer service: do you want to improve? Visit the experts.

www.atsmedia.com
Customer service videos. Free preview of training videos.

www.adelphi-associates.co.uk
Customer care training. Approved by The Institute of Leadership and Management.

www.ptp.co.uk
Customer care training. Available in 50 UK cities from PTP. Public or bespoke in-house training.

www.custominsight.com
CustomInsight internet surveys. Create and administer internet-based surveys for any purpose. Ideal for customer satisfaction surveys, employee satisfaction surveys, 360° feedback, market research.

www.destinationcrm.com
destinationCRM.com. Assist in the development of customer-centric e-business initiatives and ventures in technology, communications, finance, retail, advertising and healthcare industries.

www.ecrmguide.com
eCRMGuide. Customer relationship management in the e-business world.

www.theacagroup.com/customerservice.htm
How to improve customer service. An informative article on how companies can immediately begin to improve customer service.

www.dmsupport.com
Online customer service. Provides 24-hour online customer service for online businesses which lack in-house resources.

www.customer-service.com
Service Quality Institute. Description of services and seminars offered, online store, discussion forums, articles and tips, news and press releases and free newsletter.

www.yourlearningcurve.co.uk
Learning Curve. Tailored training courses in customer service and customer care for UK companies. Also includes a growing collection of 'how to' articles.

www.act.com
ACT! Contact management software including contacts, calendars, and to-do lists for small and medium size organisations.

www.salesforce.com
Sales Force. Online customer relationship management (CRM) service delivering customer support, help desk, marketing reporting and analysis, best-of-breed sales force automation and leads management.

www.crmuk.co.uk
CRM (UK) Ltd. Customer relationship specialist. Profile, services, clients, forum and downloadable information sheets.

www.eccs.uk.com
The European Centre for Customer Strategies. More than just an information portal, ECCS is a total business support system and a reference site for everybody involved in gaining, keeping and growing customers. Membership to ECCS is free.

www.maximiser.com
Multiactive Software. Customer relationship management and contact management software with sales force automation, marketing automation, customer service, and e-commerce tools for small and medium businesses.

Ethical Business and Social Responsibility

www.ethicalmoneyonline.com
Ethical Money provides ethical investment management and advisory services.

www.ethicalperformance.com
Newsletter for socially responsible business.

www.actionaidrecycling.org.uk
ActionAid Recycling reduces waste by collecting empty printer, photocopier and fax cartridges, and unwanted mobile phones; and reduces poverty by giving 80 per cent minimum of their profits to the charity ActionAid which works with over nine million of the world's poorest people.

www.computeraid.org
Every year in the UK approximately 2.5 million computers are dumped in landfill sites. This site helps reduce that figure.

www.ecotopia.ukf.net
The gathering place for cultural creatives, greens and smiley happy people.

www.itforcharities.co.uk
The IT resource guide for UK Charities and Non-Profit Organisations.

www.thecarbontrust.co.uk
The Carbon Trust provides free, practical advice to business and public sector organisations to help you reduce energy use. Saving energy saves you money – and helps combat climate change by cutting carbon emissions.

www.bitc.org.uk
Business in the Community.

www.bitc.org.uk/skillsforlife
More than one in five British employees have poor literacy and numeracy skills. Free training is available for all employees through the Government's Skills For Life Campaign.

www.csv.org.uk
The UK's largest volunteering and training organisation.

www.envirowise.gov.uk
Envirowise offers UK businesses free, independent, confidential advice and support on practical ways to increase profits, minimise waste and reduce environmental impact.

www.eca.gov.uk
Enhanced Capital Allowances (ECAs) enable a business to claim 100 per cent first-year capital allowances on their spending on qualifying plant and machinery.

www.article13.com
Article 13 are specialist advisers on issues of corporate governance and responsibility.

www.wrap.org.uk
WRAP's mission is to accelerate resource efficiency by creating efficient markets for recycled materials and products, while removing barriers to waste minimisation, re-use and recycling.

www.green-business.com
Environmental accreditation body of tourism related businesses in Europe.

www.egeneration.co.uk
Building sustainable business.

www.wastewatch.org.uk/business/wwbn_home.aspx
Waste Watch Business Network.

www.environment-agency.gov.uk/business
The Environment Agency business pages.

www.environment-agency.gov.uk/netregs
NetRegs. Designed to help small businesses navigate through the maze of environmental legislation.

www.new-academy.ac.uk
New Academy of Business. Founded in 1995 by Anita Roddick to provide entrepreneurs, managers and organisational leaders with the insights and capacities necessary to respond progressively to the emerging challenges of sustainability and organisational responsibility.

www.unv.org
United Nations Volunteers.

www.dfid.gov.uk
UK Department for International Development.

www.teriin.org
TERI-Europe. The Energy and Resources Group.

www.anitaroddick.com
Get informed, get outraged, get active. Anita Roddick's weblog on human rights, social responsibility and making a difference.

www.takeitpersonally.org.uk
Practical ways to make a difference today. An activism portal where users can take direct action from their desk.

Websites of Case Studies in this Book

www.ilikemusic.com
www.uk.thebodyshop.com
www.wildwestjerky.co.uk
www.lastminute.com
www.sharpcards.com
www.coffee-nation.com
www.yosushi.co.uk
www.aquarterof.co.uk
www.feelgooddrinks.com
www.babylicious.co.uk

www.iwantoneofthose.com

www.figleaves.com

www.period-property.co.uk

www.garden.co.uk

www.teambuilding.co.uk

www.thecakestore.com

www.anythingleft-handed.co.uk

www.benjerry.com

www.chocaid.com

www.hug.co.uk

www.co-operativebank.co.uk

www.patagonia.com

www.levistrauss.com

www.vodafone.co.uk

www.bestbear.co.uk

www.aricotvert.co.uk

Recommended Reading

Anyone Can Do It: Building Coffee Republic from Our Kitchen Table: 57 Real-life laws on entrepreneurship Sahar Hashemi, Bobby Hashemi.

Business As Unusual: The Triumph of Anita Roddick. Dame Anita Roddick.

Start Up!: How to Start a Successful Business from Absolutely Nothing, What to Do and How It Feels. Liz Jackson, Michael Spain

How to Become a Rainmaker: The Rules for Getting and Keeping Customers and Clients. Jeffrey J. Fox.

Getting Clients, Keeping Clients (Wiley Financial Advisor series). Dan Richards.

Who Moved My Cheese?: An Amazing Way to Deal with Change in Your Work and in Your Life. Spencer Johnson.

The One Minute Manager (One Minute Manager series). Kenneth Blanchard, Spencer Johnson.

The Beermat Entrepreneur: What You Really Need to Know to Turn a Good Idea into a Great Business. Mike Southon, Chris West.

The Book of Yo! (Instant Knowledge). Simon Woodroffe.

Body and Soul: Profits with Principles — The Amazing Success Story of Anita Roddick and The Body Shop.

Take It Personally: How to Make Conscious Choices to Change the World. Anita Roddick.

A Revolution in Kindness (2003). Edited by Anita Roddick.

Fish!: A Remarkable Way to Boost Morale and Improve Results. Harry Paul, John Christensen, Stephen C. Lundin.

Be A Successful Consultant. Susan Nash.

E-business Essentials: Ten Key Steps to E-volutionise Your Business. Bruce Durie.

Raising Start-up Finance: Get the Right Funding to Start Your Business. Phil Stone.

Tycoon. Peter Jones (with help from yours truly).

The Real Deal. James Caan.

Setting Up and Running a Limited Company: A Comprehensive Guide to Forming and Operating a Company as a Director and Shareholder. Robert Browning.

Understanding Business Accounting for Dummies (UK edition). Colin Barrow, John A. Tracy.

Book-keeping and Accounting for the Small Business. How to Keep the Books and Maintain Financial Control Over Your Business. Peter Taylor.

Understanding Small Business Accounting. Learn the Essentials of Financial Accounting and Stay in Control of Your Business. Phil Stone.

Get Noticed, a 30 day workbook to raise your small business profile in 30 days, or less. Paul Gardner.

Index